Library of
Davidson College

William Carlos Williams
A Poet in the American Theatre

Studies in Modern Literature, No. 7

A. Walton Litz, General Series Editor
Professor of English
Princeton University

Paul Mariani
Consulting Editor for Titles on William Carlos Williams
Professor of English
University of Massachusetts/Amherst

Other Titles in This Series

No. 1	*Faulkner's Uses of the Classics*	Joan M. Serafin
No. 2	*A Touch of Rhetoric: Ezra Pound's Malatesta Cantos*	Peter D'Epiro
No. 3	*Wallace Stevens and Company: The Harmonium Years, 1913-1923*	Glen G. MacLeod
No. 4	*The Latin Masks of Ezra Pound*	Ron Thomas
No. 5	*Studies in Joyce*	Nathan Halper
No. 6	*The Last Courtly Lover: Yeats and the Idea of Woman*	Gloria C. Kline
No. 8	*The Presence of the Past: T.S. Eliot's Victorian Inheritance*	David Ned Tobin
No. 9	*A Thought to be Rehearsed: Aphorism in Wallace Stevens's Poetry*	Beverly Coyle
No. 10	*Inverted Volumes Improperly Arranged: James Joyce and His Trieste Library*	Michael Patrick Gillespie

William Carlos Williams
A Poet in the American Theatre

by
David A. Fedo

UMI RESEARCH PRESS
Ann Arbor, Michigan

Copyright © 1983, 1972
David A. Fedo
All rights reserved

Produced and distributed by
UMI Research Press
an imprint of
University Microfilms International
Ann Arbor, Michigan 48106

Library of Congress Cataloging in Publication Data

Fedo, David A.
  William Carlos Williams : a poet in the American theatre.

    (Studies in modern literature ; no. 7)
    "A revision of the author's thesis, Boston University Graduate School, 1972"–T.p. verso.
    Bibliography: p.
    Includes index.
    1. Williams, William Carlos, 1883-1963–Dramatic works.
I. Title. II. Series.
PS3545.I544Z5877 1983   812'.52   83-1132
ISBN 0-8357-1410-1

15 Years Later

on seeing my own play
Many Loves
on the stage for the first time

I recall
many a passage
of the original con-

versations with my
patients, especially the
women, myself

the interlocutor
laying myself bare for them
all there

in the play but who will
take the trouble
to evaluate

the serious aspects of
the case? One
of the actors by

dint of learning the lines
by heart
has come to me

his face aglow openmouthed
a light in his eyes
Nothing more

William Carlos Williams
Pictures from Brueghel (1962)

Contents

Preface   *ix*

1 The Shorter Plays   *1*
    First Efforts at Drama
    Sauerkraut to the Cultured
    The Year Abroad
    A Hair's Breadth from Production
    In Print: *Elia Brobitza*
    Two More Washington Plays
    Fragments "In the Works"
    The Productive '40's and '50's

2 *The First President*   35
    Preparing the Libretto
    The Nature of the Opera
    The Character of Washington
    The First President as Art
    The American Inheritance

3 *Many Loves*   67
    Genesis of the Play
    Changes from *Trial Horse*
    Accuracies
    Language for a New Theatre
    Tempo and Direction

4 *A Dream of Love*   *101*
    "Masterpiece" in the Making
    A Phantom Rules
    Dotty Randall
    Dr. Thurber
    Much to Say of Suffering

viii   Contents

5 *Tituba's Children*   127
   Witch Hunts Old and New
   Uncertain Focus
   Striving Toward Currency
   Too Many Directions

6 *The Cure*   149
   Shaking Himself Free
   Leanest and Toughest
   Familiar Limitations

Appendix A The Living Theatre's *Many Loves*   *163*

Appendix B Productions of *A Dream of Love*   *171*

Notes   *179*

Bibliography   *193*

Index   *199*

Preface

The purpose of this book is twofold: to describe the nature of William Carlos Williams' lifelong interest and participation in the American theatre and to study his achievement as a dramatist. Dr. Williams has been and will continue to be chiefly known as a poet (rather than as a playwright or novelist), but his plays are important both because they help readers better understand his other works and because they stand as special contributions to our native drama. For all of their imperfections, the plays deserve a wider audience.

For help in this study I am indebted to the following persons: Mrs. Florence Williams, James Laughlin, K. C. Gay, Donald Gallup, Mary M. Hirth, John C. Thirlwall, Clinton J. Atkinson, Julian Beck, B. J. Whiting, and Susan Fedo. Helen Vendler and John Malcolm Brinnin, my professors at Boston University, were of special assistance, and I thank them for their many kindnesses.

Permission to quote from unpublished materials in collections at SUNY at Buffalo, Yale University, and the University of Texas was kindly granted by these institutions and by Mrs. Williams and James Laughlin at New Directions.

Portions of this book appeared in somewhat different form in *Contemporary Literature* and *William Carlos Williams Review.*

Quotations from the works of William Carlos Williams are reprinted by permission of New Directions Publishing Corporation, copyright as follows:

The Autobiography of William Carlos Williams. Copyright 1951 by William Carlos Williams.

The Build-Up. Copyright 1946, 1952 by William Carlos Williams.

Collected Earlier Poems. Copyright 1938 by William Carlos Williams.

Collected Later Poems. Copyright 1944, 1948, 1949, 1950 by William Carlos Williams.

Interviews with William Carlos Williams: "Speaking Straight Ahead." Copyright © 1976 by the Estate of William Carlos Williams.

In the American Grain. Copyright 1925 by James Laughlin.

I Wanted to Write a Poem. Copyright © 1958 by William Carlos Williams.

Many Loves & Other Plays. Copyright 1936, 1942, 1948 by William Carlos Williams.

Selected Essays. Copyright 1954 by William Carlos Williams.

Selected Letters. Copyright © 1957 by William Carlos Williams.

The William Carlos Williams Reader. Copyright © 1962 by William Carlos Williams.

Copyright © 1972 by Florence H. Williams for material first published in dissertation by David A. Fedo, "William Carlos Williams: a Poet in the American Theatre."

David A. Fedo
Bentley College
Waltham, Massachusetts
December, 1982

1
The Shorter Plays

In his introduction to *The William Carlos Williams Reader,* M. L. Rosenthal writes:

> Prolific as he was in various genres, Dr. Williams was clearly a poet first of all, as the whole emphasis of his career and of his development as a craftsman proves. The rest of his work, therefore, is from a critical standpoint important primarily for its relationship to his poetry. Yet it is misleading to put the matter so, for much of that work is absorbing in its own right even if the reader has no interest in poetry.[1]

The assessment is fair and undogmatic, with exactly the right qualification. For before everything else Williams *was* a poet. "He thought of himself primarily that way," Mrs. Florence Williams has observed,[2] and it is clear to anyone familiar with the man's work that his poems—the hundreds of short lyrics and finally the epic *Paterson*—claimed the great share of his attention throughout a long and productive life. (His career as a suburban doctor is something else again.) But it is well to remember with Rosenthal that Williams' other writings constitute a considerable achievement as well, and are often filled with much the same vitality and vision that one finds in the verse. There are, for example, at least 52 short stories and four novels included in the body of his work; there is also his impressionistic history of the American experience (*In the American Grain*), along with the autobiography, essays, articles, reviews, letters, and translations.

Added to these are his plays—a number of unpublished works in special collections at Yale University and the State University of New York at Buffalo, and five full-length dramas collected under the title *Many Loves and Other Plays* and published by New Directions in 1961. These plays share many of the concerns and themes that one finds elsewhere in Williams: the poet's quest for a redeeming language, the ambiguities of sex and love, the tensions of the urban contemporary world, liberalism (social, political, artistic), the lessons of American history, the idea of the heroic, the imagination versus the real, the journey toward the Beautiful Thing, and the artist in search of himself (the question of autobiography). There might well be others included in such a list. The point is that the major plays, like the fiction, give a fuller and therefore more accurate sense of Williams; and they are also important in their own right as special contributions to the American theatre.

John C. Thirlwall's brief notes to the plays in *Many Loves and Other Plays* suggest how Williams maintained an active and continued involvement in the theatre over many years, even while he was making his important reputation in verse. (One is reminded of Henry James, or even of Robert Browning.) Thirlwall dates Williams' involvement in theatre from 1903, when he took the part of Polonius in a University of Pennsylvania Mask and Wig amateur production called *Mr. Hamlet of Denmark*.[3] Actually, Williams' introduction to drama and the theatre occurred considerably earlier. His father, William George Williams, "an Englishman who never got over being an Englishman"[4] (he was born in Birmingham but raised in the West Indies), read Shakespeare aloud, over and over, to the delight of his Rutherford family and friends. "Those were the marvelous days!" Williams recalls in his *Autobiography*,[5] and elsewhere he records the experience in more detail: "My father's greatest love was for Shakespeare which he read extremely well and without affectation. I heard all the principal plays with few exceptions during the long winter evenings when he would read to the family, for I must say that he did not read particularly to me, but to Mother as much as anyone else."[6] In response to a question in an interview for *The Paris Review* less than a year before his death, Williams again touched on the experience:

> My father was a business man, interested in South America. But he always loved books. He used to read poetry to me. Shakespeare. He had a group who used to come to our house, a Shakespeare Club. They did dramatic readings. So I was always interested in Shakespeare, and Grandmother was interested in the stage—my father's mother.[7]

The Shakespeare group was composed of certain of the family's neighbors who met intermittently during Williams' childhood, and it reflected in part the father's love for the theatre. (Mrs. Florence Williams remembered that her father-in-law also served occasionally as stage manager for amateur theatricals.[8]) The grandmother mentioned was Emily Dickenson, born in Chichester, England, orphaned early, and who, after giving birth to William George Williams (the father was either the son of an Episcopalian minister or an iron worker, according to grandson William Carlos Williams), came with her small child to America. "Grandmother had wanted to be an actress; that was her objective in coming here," Williams wrote in his *Autobiography* (p. 168). But she met and married in Brooklyn a Mr. Wellcome from St. Thomas and went to live in the West Indies.

Since the *Autobiography* is often so fragmentary, ignoring both important stretches of time and many of the ordinary details of his life, it is difficult to know how much live theatre Williams did see as a boy, or what it meant to him.[9] Did his father ever take him to plays in New York, just six miles from Rutherford? There is no record of it, nor is there any indication that Williams early discovered the work of dramatists other than Shakespeare. As a matter of fact, it was not really until Williams was enrolled at Horace Mann High School in Manhattan that he demonstrated a creative interest in literature at all. "My first poem was born like a bolt out of the blue," he notes in the *Autobiography* (p. 47). Williams was 18 years old at the time. Following graduation he enrolled in medical school at the University of Pennsylvania.

Transcripts of Williams' grades at Pennsylvania show that he performed well academically, and yet Williams recalls in the *Autobiography* (p. 50): "I enjoyed the study of medicine, but found it impossible to confine myself to it. No sooner did I begin my studies than I wanted to quit them and devote myself to writing." He turned for the moment to the theatre with characteristic energy and purpose:

> I had been accepted by the Mask and Wig Club at Penn and began to act in their plays. The theatre perhaps offered me my chance? I thought I'd quit medical school and get a job as a scene shifter! Such was my humility. I remember seeing Kyrle Bellow playing to Janet Beecher in *Romeo and Juliet*. I wrote Miss Beecher a letter which she never answered. I always answer letters, but others seldom answered those I sent out in my desperation. D. H. Lawrence never answered me, either, when once later I wrote to him.
>
> It cost only twenty-five cents to sit in the top balcony and see a good play in those days. I wanted to write plays—plays in verse! I saw the great Ben Greet Players outdoors in the Botanical Gardens with Edith Wynne Matthison as Rosalind in *As You Like It*. I climbed a ten-foot spike fence around the nearby cemetery to get in to that one. I had no money.
>
> (*Autobiography*, p. 51)

The Mask and Wig Club was to the University of Pennsylvania as the Hasty Pudding Club was to Harvard, only on a less lavish scale. Productions were inevitably satiric, topical, racy, larded with puns, music, and slapstick. Williams remembers in the *Autobiography* his success in his first production:

> It was in my second year [1903] that I went out for and "made" the Mask and Wig Club by singing "Tit Willow" from *The Mikado* for them. I had a round, smooth face, as shown by the half-tone in the Philadelphia Bulletin. Had my legs been equal to it, I should have got the part of a handsome girl in the varsity production which followed. As it was, they cast me finally as Polonius in *Mr. Hamlet of Denmark,* which ran at Atlantic City, Philadelphia (for a week), Wilmington, Baltimore and Washington.

> There, for the first time, I had the sensation of feeling an audience all my own for one delicious moment: I had interpolated a line kidding Teddy Roosevelt for his absence just then on a bear hunt in the Ozarks. I brought the house down. Even the cast broke into a roar. I was a hero.
>
> (p. 52)

A photograph of "Billy" Williams as Polonius, with a full white beard, appears in a medical school yearbook of the time.[10]

Williams interned for three years after graduation in the Old French Hospital and at the Nursery and Child's Hospital, both in New York. The experience at each institution turned out to be valuable, providing material later incorporated into his writings (including the idea for one of the main characters in the play *Many Loves*). In 1909 he returned home to Rutherford at 131 West Passaic Avenue and promptly brought out, at his own expense, his first book. It was called *Poems,* and the 26 representative selections were, as he recalls in *I Wanted to Write a Poem* (p. 10),

> obviously young, obviously bad. I took the only form I knew, rhymed couplets, learned from Milton. The poems should be classified as sonnets, not the Shakespearian [sic] sonnet, but the sonnet of Keats and other romantic poets. There is a definite Elizabethan influence; I loved the songs in *As You Like It* and I can see plenty of echoes of them in these early poems.

First Efforts at Drama

About the same time, meanwhile, Williams had written at least two of his shorter plays, *A September Afternoon* and *Betty Putnam*[11] (probably in that order). The flurry of activity only makes it evident that he was not at all clear as to the sort of writer he wanted to become, just as some years before he was not wholly clear at first on the kind of art form he would choose.[12] As Vivienne Koch observes,

> Williams' earliest literary impulses moved ambivalently between play-writing and poetry. While the poet appeared to conquer the playwright, Williams' need to *objectify* relationships (a primary source of drama) reasserted itself on and off with increasing intensity.

Koch adds:

> Williams' juvenilia in the drama are instructive. Like all beginnings, they tell much about his preoccupations and his shortcomings. In a rough way they are prophetic not only of his development as a playwright but also as a poet, for the writer is a total personality of which playwright, poet, novelist, critic are, after all, only separate facets.[13]

According to Koch, *A September Afternoon,* probably Williams' first effort at drama, was written near the end of his internship at the Nursery and Child's Hospital.[14] As we have seen, Williams was interested in putting verse on the stage, but here, as in most of his later plays, he eventually would settle for prose. *A September Afternoon* is a one-act play set during the Revolutionary War, a period to which Williams would return again and again in the shorter plays, in such works as *In the American Grain,* and finally in *The First President.* The scene is rolling farm country near Fishkill-on-the-Hudson in September of 1776, and the conflict that develops is between soldiers and the motley American rustics, the latter foolishly itching for a fight. Only two characters appear onstage in the play: Barney, an impulsive 17-year-old patriot who views the approaching battle as a chance to serve George Washington and his country, and his sister Marjory, who sees very little about either General Washington or war that is heroic. The play really turns into a kind of anti-war tract, for the rhetoric of Barney is the language of an over-zealous jingo:

> Marjy! Marjy! think of it! A real battle, with guns, *here*. Here Marjy! And I'm going to be in it — that is if the luck holds and they don't turn back.
> (p. 4)

> Every man must strike a blow this day for his country and for George Washington across the river.
> (p. 4)

> It's the country calling me. It's the call of liberty in my blood Marjy and when they charge out of the wood's edge there you'll see me tearing down the hill as I told you — in the face of their great fire — to be fighting with the men of the town and of this independent state and this free and great country — for the love of God and for the people that will come after —
> (p. 5)

> It's such men as me will be the great heroes in the cities in time to come.
> (p. 5)

For her part, Marjy sees the build-up of British troops and the gathering of her neighbors for battle as utter madness, a futile and dangerous game. "You're a lot of fools fighting over a cow and that's all" (p. 4). Washington is castigated as "the great hero that leads boys to be killed" (p. 7), a line which in a way portends the melodramatic conclusion. But Barney, inevitably, disobeys his father and rushes offstage to join the fierce skirmish on the hill, leaving Marjy alone to comment on the action. Soon he returns, victorious ("Oh, but won't George Washington be pleased when he hears of it!", p. 9) but wounded. It is not until the play's final moment, however, that we learn with a chill that the injury is in fact fatal: Barney suddenly topples to the ground at the curtain.

Koch correctly notes that the focus of *A September Afternoon* rests on "the moral conflict between Barney and his sister, each standing for a segment of colonial opinion, and each illustrating the perennial recurrence of two kinds of 'resistance' to circumstance."¹⁵ The assembling of men and the fighting in the wings are important only as a backdrop for this more private polarization. Barney is headstrong and unreasonable, disobedient and spiteful, a product of incendiary talk and rampaging war fever; when his more temperate father refuses to allow him to enter the fight, Barney cries aloud, "I hope you're shot! I hope to God you're killed outright!" (p. 1). Marjy is no pacifist or loyalist but rather a realist, who sees in rebellion only chaos and death. Moreover, she argues, Americans have no corner on virtue:

> They're fighting each other like a pack of lean dogs: I've heard father say it. And if you say it's any different in Philadelphia where the Congress of all the states is—the head of it all—I'll tell you they're worse than the rest: lying and backbiting and grabbing for the most they can lay hand to and fearing each other more than England or the Devil himself even. It's true and you know it and that's what you're fighting for!
>
> (p. 6)

The writing here is pedestrian (Koch says the dialogue seems to imitate Synge and other Irish folk writers¹⁶), but Williams nevertheless manages to maintain a kind of tension in the debate, and later the battle itself lends to the denouement a certain suspense even though it takes place, in the manner of the Greeks, out of the audience's range. But what is most interesting is the emergence of George Washington, even so early as this play, as a crucial point of interest and importance to Williams. There are intimations here of a concern that Williams will treat at length elsewhere, especially (but not exclusively) in *The First President*. What are the appropriate qualities of a leader? What is the nature of the heroic? Certainly Williams disqualifies Barney, the surly idealist, from such consideration (indeed, the very possibility is open to satire), but even in this slight play Washington, who is never onstage, looms behind the action as an ambiguous, distant force, a kind of raw energy, present only in the minds of the colonials, both hated and loved.

A September Afternoon presumably was written for outdoor performance at the Rutherford Town Tennis Club on Montross Avenue, but there is no available record (or recollection) of private or public presentation. *Betty Putnam,* however, was performed "on the embankment" next to the Club in the spring of 1909 (*Autobiography,* p. 106). The Tennis Club owned a small wooden building with only a few courts, but Williams played tennis and enjoyed the company. "There was a very active young group connected with it," Mrs. Williams recalled.¹⁷ *Betty Putnam* was subtitled in manuscript "A Short Play in Three Continuous Scenes." It is in fact the first of two dramatic treatments by Williams of the Salem witch trials, the more important of which would be *Tituba's Children* (completed in 1950).

Williams himself acted in *Betty Putnam* and assumed the directing; his brother Edgar also took one of the parts.[18] The play is of some length, running to 31 typewritten pages; of all the unpublished plays only *Sauerkraut to the Cultured* is longer. *Betty Putnam* has actually little to do with the specific social or political consequences of the witchcraft trials in Salem in the 1680's and 1690's. It does not, for example, deal with any of the major historical figures or events (as Arthur Miller was to do in *The Crucible* or as Williams himself does in *Tituba's Children*). As war provides a background to *A September Afternoon,* so does the witchcraft frenzy serve this play. But there are no trials or hangings, and no exorcisms or confessions. It is scarcely even "a Puritan play," as Mrs. Williams called it in 1963,[19] since theology is not at the center or even at the side of the action. Rather, the play is a study, and finally a comedy, of greed, and of the efforts of a young man and young woman (who grow toward a kind of mutual love) to escape a fate resulting from another's deceit.

The plot is melodramatic. Able Putnam has recalled his fair daughter Betty back to Salem from Boston where she has been attending school for some years; she is now 18, hard-headed, not a believer in witches (her father is shocked), and consequently she thinks that "Salem's full of blockheads" (p. 7). In the meantime, Able has arranged to have Betty married to the lackluster Sam Noyes, nephew of the Reverend Nicholas Noyes. We find out quickly that it is a marriage of convenience—that Able will have connected his daughter with a respectable family, and that the Noyes family, for its part, will gain an important piece of Putnam land. The property happens to be in Betty's name, however, and Betty, indifferent to young Noyes, balks at signing it over. Her father insists:

> For whose land is it then? It is your husband's land, which as all his is yours and all yours is his the land is just as much your land as ever it was before.
>
> (p. 12)

That is not quite the truth, because Nicholas Noyes, who assumes the role of villain (as he does in *Tituba's Children*), is Sam's creditor—a usurious one at that—and would himself take ownership of the land as payment for his debtor's obligations. Thus the moral crisis, as Williams renders it, becomes Sam's: he has grown to love Betty, but can he marry her knowing that he will assuredly deprive his wife of what is rightfully hers? He cannot, and decides rather to run away to sea. Meantime, Betty, who has little or no discretion, has written a dangerous little jingle, and we are reminded once again that superstition is alive in Salem:

> The devil cried Nick Noyes, Nick Noyes
> Where is my namesake? Ho!

> When answered him Beelzebub
> In Salem you must know.
>
> (p. 18)

It is of course overheard by the Reverend Mr. Noyes, who accuses Betty of being a witch, and when she in turn strikes him in the face—an action not unlike Billy Budd's hitting Mr. Claggart, although Noyes is not really hurt—she is in real peril. And so is Sam, who has not gone to sea and is now seen as an accomplice.

Williams makes it clear, however, that the minister is using the threat of exposure principally as bargaining persuasion to acquire the land, not because he really wants Sam and Betty dead. "Both are evil, both must burn" (p. 26), he says of Betty and his nephew, but he is avaricious, not bloodthirsty, and would rather be rewarded in a different way. He tells Sam:

> All I say is: win her for your wife by five o'clock and make her sign her land to you or remember! Fire! Burning! Tell her of that. And I warn you, for you shall go as well as she, so look to it—you as well as she—both of you!
>
> (p. 25)

The ultimatum alarms everyone but Betty, who has fallen into a kind of giddy resignation, perfectly content to die, and temporarily given over to silly philosophizing:

> Sam, think of this seriously—that for all our diligence and superstition the world will end when it will end, in merely merriment, come what may, and mark my word for it, I have read it in a book, it is true. Why Sam, is it not ridiculous to kill a little girl and Sam, a pretty girl for truly she hath put her thumb in her preacher's eye!
>
> (p. 23)

Of course, neither Betty nor Sam is executed, nor must Betty sign over her property. A last-minute stratagem devised by Sam, who has allegedly matured in the final two scenes, prevents his uncle from claiming the land or indicting Betty on a charge of witchery; the play ends happily, with intimations that the young couple may have a future together as one.

Betty Putnam is, in certain ways, a well-made play, with the joke at the conclusion neatly coming at the expense of the elder Noyes, who stalks off chagrined, vaguely threatening some future revenge. As in most farce, the villain is caught but not really punished, and everyone else goes his way. It is not really to be taken very seriously for, as Putnam says at the outset in a little speech (in limp verse) to the audience:

> If sometimes we grow serious and abuse
> Each other, take it not for ill,

> Remembering still
> We come to amuse.
>
> (p. 3)

And yet the comedy is really quite sluggish, almost simplistic, and what emerges instead is a patchwork of aphorisms, half-developed themes, aborted pieces of stage business, and characters who (save Betty) are only occasionally interesting. A case in point is Able Putnam, who appears at the beginning to intone the prologue, but who then serves merely to act the fool, and a poor one at that—he misplaces things, is derided by Betty, badgered and interrupted by Nicholas Noyes, and is finally even overruled by Sam. At the end he strikes one as an ineffectual simpleton, and Williams seems almost to discard him from the plot. Able's behavior is a mystery through and through: what motivates him to act the way he does toward Betty, for example, and why does he tremble so abjectly before Nicholas Noyes?

The trial of Sarah Cloyes as a witch, which superficially frames the action of *Betty Putnam,* might be one clue to Putnam's agitation, but Williams never makes the witch case clear or threatening. This is why one never feels that Betty herself is really in danger, and why the elder Noyes is never really frightening (or convincing). But Betty *does* at least distract us and is sometimes amusing. There is about her a hoydenish quality which is attractive—the little games she plays with her father and Sam (at first), her common sense, and her fierce independence ("I may not sing," she complains to her father, "lest someone cry, 'The Devil's in her!' ", p. 13). In the middle of the play, when Betty becomes half-mad like Ophelia and half-martyr like Saint Joan, Williams has obviously let the play get away from him, but at the end there is a fairly satisfying reworking of her character. Betty grows into a woman at last, and if not fulfilled she is at least content.

Sauerkraut to the Cultured

That Williams was still an inexperienced dramatist, lacking a real sense of form and without an appropriate prose style, is clear enough from the two plays just considered, but a look at another major short play of about the same period, *Sauerkraut to the Cultured,*[20] makes these deficiencies even more obvious. In a letter written to Julian and Judith Beck of the Living Theatre[21] in 1948, Williams remembers it as "a very old costume piece about Niew [sic] Amsterdam that I wrote in 1909." The play may actually have been written somewhat later than that for a civic occasion in Rutherford,[22] but in any event the manuscript bears Williams' old address of 131 West Passaic Avenue, so it must have been written before 1913 when he moved with his new wife to 9 Ridge Road. "This odd little play," writes

Vivienne Koch cautiously, "while lacking plot, movement or suspense, is charming and warm."[23] There is, as we shall see, some truth to this, but in his letter to the Becks about a possible production Williams himself tempers that judgment:

> Vivienne Koch who has been doing a piece on me for New Directions seems to think it's a good comedy—but very, very simple, almost in the class with the nursery rhyme. The language would need touching up too. But I warn you it's very elementary stuff—with a difference however, I hope.

The Becks did not pursue the possibility of its production further, and soon turned, as shall be seen, to *Many Loves.*

The play is subtitled "A Nieu Amsterdam Comedy," and deals with New York "after the Dutch have lost the town" to the English. The characters are Johan Friedrich Bach, a stodgy "not too jovial Dutchman" (though with a German background) who claims kinship to the musician Sebastian Bach of Leipzig; his daughter Lena Bach; and two young suitors, Karl Minnewit, an honest but phlegmatic Dutchman, and Fred Pickel, an English gallant. The plot of the play is rather predictable, and draws from traditions as old as the Roman comedies: Lena must choose whom she will love, and of course it turns out to be the dull but steady Karl rather than the more likely and assertive Fred. Old Bach, who abhors anything different or new, is satisfied with her decision; Fred poses a threat to the order of things, but he will not have to adjust his ways for Karl:

> Now let our old life begin again, and let it hence be known I am no gentleman and wish to be none. We'll have nothing but a plain post before the house and wear nothing but plain flowers.
>
> (p. 36)

A note on the final page of the manuscript—it is not in Williams' hand—suggests that *Sauerkraut to the Cultured* is "a humours play with a touch of the drawing room comedy" (p. 36). The description is a good one, but such a strategy does not make for rounded characterizations. Every person in the play speaks not as a real human being but as the embodiment of an idea or estate. Thus Bach is forever and always a true provincial, the New York Dutchman standing on his *commonness* and the credentials of the Old Age. He likes bread that suits "common strong tastes"; he laughs at a "good simple joke." He distrusts what is pretty (for example, a rose). When Fred tries to teach him chess, Bach throws it off as too complicated, and there follows this exchange:

> *Bach:* Keep away chess! You call that a game? It's labor to split the head. Why, what short of a game is it when it tires the head? Give me an easy restful game so that

> I can play without a thought and leave my mind free to wander pleasantly around into all odd corners.
>
> *Fred:* That shows you are a philosopher.
>
> *Bach:* I am nothing but myself. I pretend to nothing.
>
> (pp. 11–12)

Without pretense or the slightest ambition, Bach is consistent in his ordinariness, finding comfort and virtue in the simple life at every turn, extolling the pleasures of the dull and the unexciting—proud, in other words, of his "lowness" and tastes, even in music:

> Now for music! Music will bring back my content. All the Bachs were musicians and so am I. Some were organists, some were trumpeters, some played the fiddle but the genius of our family has left me only these three bells. Will I be sad? No. My genius lies in bells then. (Strikes one of the bells.) There's a tone for you! I never heard a better bell of that tone. Now you. (Strikes a second bell.) Music stirs me to the soul! Such a bell! When there is genius in a family nothing in the world can satisfy but the angel herself. Now singly. (Bing) Now together. (Bing, bing, bing.) I think my cousin Sebastian feels no happier in Leipzig when his choir sings. But my pleasure is simpler. (Bing, bing.) I think there is no better bell player in the world than I.
>
> (pp. 17–18)

Such insistence on the rewards of both being simple and dealing with simple things led Koch to write: "The play is an immature allegorical foreshadowing of the position Williams was later to develop in his aesthetic—his championing of the local, the indigenous, the 'common.' It underlies the kind of question which the young writer felt compelled to ask about."[24] But Koch overstates the case, rather like saying that because Virgil wrote about country people and the pastoral life he in fact championed the *simple*. This is obviously not true in Virgil's life and art, and not accurate with regard to Williams. Although later in the poetry and fiction Williams does indeed show great sympathy for the ordinary, in *Sauerkraut to the Cultured* he is more interested in playing jokes on his characters, and in having fun. For this is not a play about the pastoral ideal. (Furthermore, Williams never advocated, as did Thoreau, simplicity for simplicity's sake in life or art.) Bach is a kind of steadfast hero, but he is also, like some of the humours characters, a one-dimensional fool, incapable of change and inflexible even beyond sense. It is thus Bach himself who becomes the butt of mild satire throughout the play. His life is in fact a tiresome string of self-denials, finicky abstinences, and self-righteous proclamations ("Let no man call me a gentleman, I can still pretend to some honesty if they cannot," p. 18). Williams takes special pleasure in reducing Bach's pieties to absurdities, in, for example, the "flower" scene. Fred, out to woo Lina, offers her a rose as a gift for Bach. But Bach, accustomed to geraniums (the local flower), cannot accept the rose, which he sees as a symbol of affection and corrupt power. "I am vulgar," he cries. "Roses are not for me, I am no hypocrite. I will live honestly." (p. 9). In Bach's petty renunciation—one wonders how a rose is less honest than a geranium—Williams shows that self-denial at its worst is really only vanity, the pride of a puffed-up prude, and in Bach's case it is wholly absurd. "I am common" (p. 8) he insists. "I am low, very humble" (p. 19). It is the familiar Jonsonian trick, really older than Ben Jonson, of making a character sound more than he is, and letting the audience in on the truth slowly and with comic effect. Yet Williams never deflates his character or chronicles the decline with malice. At the end, Bach is simply displaced from the center of the stage, like Able Putnam in *Betty Putnam,* and attention is focused on the young lovers.

Sauerkraut to the Cultured ends with a kind of "competition for the girl," a fight to see who will eventually have the right to claim Lina's hand. But this is no tournament or duel. Instead Williams has Fred suggest that the rivals compete by deciding how to place a lantern, now required by law every night before all dwellings in the city, in front of the Bach house. The challenge is accepted, and of course Fred's plan is far superior to Karl's: the former proposes "a post of hickory, turned as I shall design, into elegant curves and on top a bronze lantern" (p. 24); the latter simply suggests that the lantern be set on a nail by the outside door. Karl eventually wins the competition, but not through his own ingenuity. It is Lina who deceives Fred and claims victory for the other, whom she has always, for scarcely a discernible reason, loved. But in all of this the most interesting character is still the loser, Fred, who catches one's interest from the beginning with a prologue in a sort of strained blank verse. Next to old Bach, he is the source of most of what is amusing in the play, and he is clearly the liveliest character of the four. With great energy he sets about to accomplish two things, educating old Bach and winning Lina. His design for the lantern shows characteristic ingenuity:

> It is all philosophically correct this time. First comes my new lantern, then we'll change the front of the house to fit that, then the inside to fit the outside, then the furniture to match the walls, then will come clothes to match the furniture and so on until all is raised to one level, that of my lantern.
>
> (p. 25)

But Fred, likeable and witty as he is, is as proud in his way, and as unchanging in his pride, as Bach is in his. He loses out in the end, presumably paving the way for the marriage of Lina and Karl.

Sauerkraut to the Cultured drags in the reading and must have moved very slowly in performance. It is interesting to see how Williams, who in his fiction and much of his poetry shied away from pointed climaxes, here tries for just such a narrative effect. But the crucial contest is really a letdown; it is trivial and lacks suspense, and for that reason *Betty Putnam* retains its interest much better at the end. The final scene in *Sauerkraut to the Cultured* is, in fact, turgid and without dramatic focus, and we will see in such later plays as *Many Loves* and *A Dream of Love* how much difficulty Williams had in concluding a play. The problems of form in Williams are reflected here in the style as well. The prose seems to be a step backward, heavy, stilted, artificial, and clumsy. The dialogue makes it impossible for the actors to pick up cues sharply, as in this prolonged discussion about hanging the lantern:

> *Fred:* And each man will have a lantern according to his condition. (To Bach.) How will you place yours sir?
>
> *Bach:* I? How? Why I will place a lantern.
>
> *Fred:* But how? How? Being in the very front of your house it will be seen what kind of a man you are by the lantern you hang.
>
> *Bach:* (Meditating.) There is a true problem that I had not forseen [sic]. That will require thought.
>
> *Fred:* You are right and so I bring my plan to you, thus you will understand it. It is that both Karl and myself shall propose to you how the light is to be placed and the one proposing best wins Lina.
>
> *Bach:* Hold, wait a minute, not so fast. In that case what have I to say, I have nothing to say.
>
> *Fred:* You can help Lina and me to decide which plan is best.
>
> *Lina:* Mr. Fred, when one of you has the best thought must I marry him?
>
> *Fred:* No Lina, how can we force you, but the one who wins will be a favorite for your choice, we expect.
>
> *Lina:* Yes, that is quite fair.
>
> *Bach:* I did not say so.
>
> (pp. 23-24)

And the exchange goes on and on over the same ground, tiresome and repetitious, and interminable. Such dialogue characteristically consists of back-and-forth questions and answers, and inevitable disagreements; no one except Fred ever takes the lead. *Sauerkraut to the Cultured* is thus even inferior to *Betty Putnam* in precisely that area—control of language— where Williams would later show extraordinary skill.

The Year Abroad

In the fall of 1909, meanwhile, Williams was in Leipzig, ostensibly to study pediatrics. He had just proposed to Florence Herman "and was," as he wrote in the *Autobiography* (p. 109), "conditionally accepted, penniless as I was." But his father provided the means for the trip, and Williams gladly sailed in mid-July. The year abroad was important for many reasons, but only one need be of concern here: it exposed him to both the best of European drama and to a wide range of music, especially the opera. Again in the *Autobiography* (p. 110), and additionally in the novel *The Build-Up*,[25] he gives almost identical accounts of seeing such plays as Ibsen's *A Doll's House* and *The Wild Duck* at the Altes Theatre; he also "attended the whole of Schiller's dramatic works from *Die Räuber* on," read some of Hermann Sudermann, and enrolled in a course at the University in modern British drama (*Autobiography*, p. 111).

Typically, Williams maintained an ambivalence towards many of these dramatists, especially Ibsen and Shaw, speaking of them sometimes with great respect, at other times with scorn. He seems to have approved of Ibsen in performance at Leipzig; he attended a performance of *Ghosts* in London in 1910 with Ezra Pound (*Autobiography*, p. 116), and quotes Ibsen approvingly in an important essay called "Against the Weather," first published in 1939.[26] An even more revealing "appreciation" of Ibsen appears in his little-known essay "Prose About Love," which Williams wrote in 1918;[27] the references to Ibsen show a fairly wide familiarity with his work, and display the mixed feelings of one who is regarding a grand and respected failure. Writing about the traditional prose writer's treatment of love, Williams says in part:

> Ibsen is a swelter [sic] of ignorance on this point, the most illuminating example of the perverse possibilities for inverted power in the phase "I love you!" that can be found, and for the reason that Ibsen truly knew love, — felt its power, but succumbed to its difficulties. God rest the ashes of a king!
> ...Only in the morose and abnormal mind of a Hedda Gabbler [sic] can Ibsen safely spread his wings — and then he must kill the lady to escape his audience and keep his play upon the boards.
> The silly "modern" plays about illicit love affairs after marriage end either happily in a burst of laughter or sordidly with the discharge of a pistol. The explosions of the gunpowder or laughter I suppose are to cover the fact that the plays are without intellectual climax whatever. They end and the audience has been insulted and likes it.
>
> (p. 6)

There is also a suggestion of Shaw in the final paragraph of the above discussion. From the *Autobiography* (p. 133), we know that Williams had written, sometime between 1914 and 1922, a play called *Frances for Freedom* which "pretty closely followed the pattern of Shaw's *Fanny's First Play*."[28] Now Shaw was never as important to Williams as another Irishman, James Joyce, but Williams knew Shaw's work rather well, and maintained contradictory feelings about it. (His friend Ezra Pound would be typically more severe on Shaw the dramatist, who was, according to Pound, "the intellectual cheese-mite, constantly enraptured at his own cleverness in being able to duck down through one hole in the cheese and come up through another.")²⁹ In "Prose About Love" Williams speaks, for example, of *Candida:*

> Shaw's *Candida* goes along rather amusingly in the spirit of a childish (though false, as it turns out later) democracy of thought, aping the puzzled romanticism of Ibsen. We are given a few nice Dickensesque caricatures of English middle class life, but in addition the feeling is of an actual love tussel [sic] going on under this inconsequential surface. But then, having got his situation rather well in hand—love on the high road to satisfaction—the author shies at the last barrier and conceeds [sic] to his audience that he has been after all merely manipulating his effigies for a melodramatic concession to "the play" by which a false logic is forced into Candida's mouth, making a conventional finis. What really has happened is that Shaw looses [sic] his nerve.
>
> *Candida* is the beginning and the end of all attempt made by Shavian thought to cope with this difficult phrase, I love you! After this first play there is never again an attempt to meet the situation face to face but there goes on a cheap tomfoolery,—always stopping short of the denouement which might have ended *Candida* brilliantly—but distastefully to the thought of the day.
>
> (pp. 6-7)

Williams does not seem to give Shaw a fair reading, at least in *Candida*. But in other ways he was, as we shall see, in debt to Shaw, and to those others like Noel Coward who followed somewhat in Shaw's wake.

Williams' interest in opera had its clearest expression in his own libretti for *The First President* and *Tituba's Children,* both of which will be considered later at length. That opera would be important to his writing was clear as early as his years at the University of Pennsylvania, when Williams, working on a long romantic narrative poem, repeatedly found himself thinking of Wagner—*Parsifal* and *Tristan,* especially (*Autobiography*, pp. 59-60). In Leipzig, meanwhile, his participation was as observer, and he saw such works as Wagner's *Götterdämmerung* and Strauss' *Electra*. Williams' tastes were various, from Verdi to Gilbert and Sullivan. Mrs. Williams noted that Dr. Williams saw the entire *Ring* through several times in New York and Vienna.³⁰ At the same time Williams had keyed himself to other musical forms as well, and his writings are dotted with references to Bach and Beethoven. (Music had always been in the home. His mother was a pianist, and something of a singer.) He would in the years ahead come to know as friends such composers as George Antheil and Virgil Thomson. Finally, the trip also brought him into apparent contact with the work of the dramatist Maurice Maeterlinck—he is mentioned in "Prologue to *Kora in Hell*"³¹—and in Paris Williams went to the Comédie Française, where he saw Edouard Pailleron's *Le Monde où l'on s'ennuie,* "which had," he noted in the *Autobiography* (p. 119), "a chilling effect on me: remote, stilted, completely artificial." The rejection is typical: Williams knew what he did not like. What he *liked* in theatre, as we shall see, was a more complex matter.

A Hair's Breadth from Production

Returning to Rutherford, Williams became associated with the poet and playwright Alfred Kreymborg, among others, and in 1915 became involved in the joint publication of a small magazine called *Others*. Williams was the associate editor. He was now married (1912) and established in a busy practice at 9 Ridge Road, the roomy frame house at the corner of Park Avenue, but he was living a literary life as well, making friendships with Marianne Moore, Kenneth Burke, Malcolm Cowley, and Man Ray— members and nonmembers of the "Grantwood group." It was through the entrepreneurial Kreymborg that Williams was drawn into another such group (though much more formal and ambitious), the Provincetown Players. Kreymborg's short verse plays, some written for a group call Poet Mines, had attracted modest attention, and the Provincetown troupe in 1916 had offered to produce at its renovated Greenwich Village stable a work called *Lima Beans*.[32] Kreymborg had subtitled it, rather pretentiously, "A Scherzo Play in One Act." Its verse was swift-paced, almost Skeltonic, with consecutive contorted rhymes. Of the play Williams writes in the *Autobiography* (p. 138): "It had three parts: the soubrette, to be played by Mina Loy; the huckster, to be undertaken by the promising young sculptor Bill Zorach; and I was to play the lover." The plot was simple and aborted, revolving around a dinner menu: the woman has decided to serve string beans instead of lima beans, and there is a row.

Williams and Loy, the young poetess, had been asked to perform because Kreymborg knew they "had some experience in amateur theatricals."[33] Actually, most of the Provincetown members had come from fields not directly related to the professional stage; one thinks, for example, of Edna St. Vincent Millay. In their account of the development of the Provincetown Playhouse Helen Deutsch and Stella Hanau discuss the personnel:

> They were not, for one thing, people of the threatre; they were not professional actors or professional playwrights; they had no attitudes or dogmas gathered from the stage. Nor did they belong to that leisured class of uncreative dabblers so familiar in the little theatre movement. They were novelists, journalists, painters, sculptors, teachers and architects, destined most of them to be successful in their own fields.[34]

With MacDougal Street a half-hour away from Rutherford by train, Williams, treating children all day (and writing poems whenever he could squeeze in the time), went ahead with the production. *Lima Beans* was to be performed second on a bill that included young Eugene O'Neill's short sketch *Before Breakfast* (the opening playlet) and Neith Boyce's *Two Sons*. Williams recalls in the *Autobiography:*

> It was tough, but I somehow got in to rehearsals from Rutherford three nights a week after office hours. It fascinated me. I had had some minor experience on the stage at college and, who could tell? there, perhaps, lay the future.
> Anyhow we set to work. Often we had to wait in that narrow, cold hall while one of O'Neill's plays was being drilled. I can remember the one playlet *Fog*. I've never forgotten it — a small boat offshore half seen before a fog improvised with a voile curtain of some sort, and men calling to each other in a dangerous situation. Out in the hall stood old man O'Neill, he of Monte Cristo fame, yelling out directions and suggestions to his son and the actors. Very moving.
> Then would come our turn to run through our lines. Bill Zorach, looking like Harpo Marx, would call out his wares and I'd do my best — but it was a fragile bit. I had to take Mina in my arms at one point and kiss her. I couldn't see it as a passionate gesture but rather as a glancing sort of china-doll kiss. I went through it but someone in the dark of the hall yelled up at me, "For God's sake, kiss her!"
> It wasn't my idea of the part. As a result no one was satisfied. We played it three nights. A qualified success.
>
> (pp. 138-39)

The experience was valuable to Williams in two ways. It gave him some practical experience in the professional theatre, and it brought him into contact with some of the liveliest minds working in that art. The Provincetown group was innovative, alert, open to new ideas, and interested in scripts that had a literary quality as well as production promise. (One remembers, for example, that it was here that Wallace Stevens' short play, *Three Travelers Watch A Sunrise,* was produced in 1920, and in 1928 E. E. Cummings' rambling work *Him* was staged. Both failed in the theatre, but remain important despite that failure.) Williams' introduction to the work of Eugene O'Neill was, as he suggests above, of real significance, even though Williams and O'Neill (who was even then a loner) never struck up a friendship, in fact never even talked. "In all the times the playwright and the poet saw one another around the theatre," writes Louis Sheaffer, "they never exchanged a word."[35] Yet O'Neill left his impression, and Williams showed, according to his wife, a lifelong interest in and appreciation for O'Neill's work.[36] O'Neill was scarcely the typical American dramatist of the time, nor was the Provincetown Playhouse similar to any other theatre movement in the country. Such freshness interested Williams, appealed to his instincts in his search for a new (and more honest) American idiom. "He liked anything that had a twist of the bizarre and unusual," wrote his friend Kathleen Hoagland.[37] It is fair to say that Julian and Judith Beck's Living Theatre held some of that appeal some 35 years later. (It is also interesting to note the implicit similarities between the Provincetown Playhouse and the Living Theatre, not only in the revolt against what was considered bourgeois and traditional drama but in actual experimental techniques. Some of these aspects will be considered later.)

Williams' participation in Kreymborg's play seemed to reestablish in his own mind once and for all the desire and energy to write plays. From 1916 to 1921 was for Williams a period of great creative activity: in 1917 he published *Al Que Quire!*; in 1920, *Kora in Hell*; followed a year later by *Sour Grapes*; and two years later by *Spring and All* and *The Great American Novel*. His best work in all areas was yet to come, but what was important about these years is that Williams was not yet closing off avenues of expression, not limiting himself to one mode. It is astonishing to discover the number of plays Williams actually was working on during the period; most of them, unfortunately, do not survive. One of these, as he tells us in the *Autobiography* (p. 133), was a play with a theme similar to that of *Golden Boy,* Clifford Odets' melodrama produced by the Group Theatre in 1937. "It was," Williams writes, "about a tough guy breaking up from under into local society." As in *Golden Boy* there was a fight, though in Williams' play it was conducted with gloves in a kitchen. Williams paid to have this play and *Frances for Freedom* typed by a professional in New York; then he burned both, apparently unwilling to let them stand. For the Provincetown Players he wrote another play,

> calling for an improvised curtain made of newspaper with a flagpole sticking through the center of it over the first seats of the audience. At the start of the play the paper screen was ripped down by the actors and the play was on. A lascivious sort of action of some sort with players designated as Bright Young Men, etc., which Mattie Josephson said reminded him of Dekker or whoever it might be. The whole piece disappeared.
> (*Autobiography,* p. 139)

In the meantime Williams, who took all of this effort very seriously, had begun "to make myself an outdoor stage for the plays I was writing" (*Autobiography,* 153). Construction was begun in Williams' own yard. Land was leveled and screened. But no plays were ever produced there, although the area was used once for a sort of neighborhood entertainment.

Williams' association with Kreymborg led him to write *The Old Apple Tree,* another short one-act play, but this time in verse. Williams ranked it as the best of his short plays, but it never was to be produced by the Provincetown Players (for whom it was intended), or by anyone. Kreymborg lost the only copy. "This was a good play," Mrs. Williams said. "It was the sorrow of his life."[38] Williams recalls in *I Wanted to Write a Poem:*

> Right at this time (1920 and '21) we were all writing plays hoping for production in one of the little theatres. I wrote a little play in verse called "The Apple Tree" [sic]. I was quite proud of it and sent it to Alfred. He was enthusiastic and told me that it was to be produced with a play of his in a little theatre in New York. But what happened—well, I

found out that Alfred was going to have his play produced with Edna St. Vincent Millay's first play, *Aria da capo*. I went to Alfred who said something like this: "Oh well, Bill, we all have to work for ourselves." I said I didn't blame him and that I probably would have done the same thing myself. But I wouldn't have. I asked him to give me back the play. He had lost it. There was only one copy. I remember only two lines from it. Two characters are discussing the sap of the tree. He tastes the sap and says: "It's bitter." She says: "Have some more." It was a sort of dance play, with pantomime between the lines. The apple tree was the mother; the blossoms and fruit were her children. It's all past now but gee it hit me hard. I was so anxious to succeed in the theatre. My first interest was the theatre. I was at home on the stage. I loved to act in college plays. I even contemplated giving up medicine to be a scene shifter. It was never quite the same with Alfred and me afterwards.

(pp. 29-30)

In his *Autobiography* (p. 140) there is an alternate ending to the story. Williams had given Kreymborg a second play—apparently not *The Old Apple Tree*—to be produced at something called the Bramhall Theatre. He elaborates:

But nothing happened. I was busy with my work and thought there'd been a delay of some sort or another until one day in the city I asked Kreymborg what had happened.

He was embarrassed and said he was broke and a man had to try to make a dollar here and there as he could and that in fact he was putting on a bill with Edna St. Vincent Millay, a play called *Da Capo* and did I mind?

Did I mind? Well, it knocked me cold. I saw the bill and really enjoyed it, but from that time on Kreymborg and I didn't get on so well.

Williams' only direct reproach regarding the loss of this play or *The Old Apple Tree,* as reported by Kay Boyle, was to say that he was "sick over it." Boyle adds, in explanation: "There was no venom, no imbalance in the man."[39] And yet almost 40 years later Williams could write, remembering with a certain bitterness: "I have always wanted to write for the stage but it has always proved a will-o-the wisp for me, production has always escaped me by a hair's breadth."[40]

In Print: *Elia Brobitza*

If actual stage production eluded Williams, he had been able about this time to see another one of his plays at least find its way into print. This short work was called *The Comic Life of Elia Brobitza,*[41] and ran as the lead piece in the journal *Others* in 1919. Williams had been at one time the magazine's associate editor, but he had lost interest and finally resigned, calling the publication "a rat in the garbage heap of New York."[42] But for a good period of time Kreymborg remained its editor, and since the two were still on relatively good terms, and Kreymborg was inevitably attracted to verse drama—a lifelong hobbyhorse—this peculiar play was published.

It remains uncollected, and sadly so, for despite certain inelegancies it is by far the best of the earliest plays we have extant. As James Guimond points out,[43] the play is an elaboration on the character and theme of Williams' poem, "Portrait of a Woman in Bed,"[44] first published in *Al Que Quiere!* in 1917. The central figure is Elia Brobitza, a very old woman (in the poem her name is Robitza), vaguely modeled on Williams' grandmother, Emily Dickenson Wellcome, who lived to be 82 and became, as Williams once wrote, "the wolf of the family."[45] There are notes extant in the Williams collection at Yale (dated November 20, 1948) which seem to map out a play on the same person, who is this time called simply "The Old Woman."[46] What emerges in the play *Elia Brobitza* is a more rounded person than the poem presents, a realized character and a dreamer who has been broken and abused; the portrait in the drama is thus a much more sympathetic one than in the poem, where Robitza's dramatic monologue gives one the impression of a whining complainer—a hag.

It is this monologue, which runs 55 lines in the poem, that serves as the core of the play. In "Portrait of a Woman in Bed," Robitza is complaining to unnamed visitors about her situation: she is penniless, friendless, neglected by her sons, and without a future:

> Try to help me
> if you want trouble
> or leave me alone—
> that ends trouble.
>
> The county physician
> is a damned fool
> and you
> can go to hell.
>
> You could have closed the door
> when you came in;
> do it when you go out.
> I'm tired.
>
> (p. 151)

Such unrelieved cynicism in the poem is softened and even made humorous in the play by what precedes and follows the monologue, which is incorporated complete, but with some interpolations and stylistic changes, into the dialogue. The play is staged as a kind of dream vision, with flashbacks and almost cinematic projections into the future. Elia is first observed as a lonely young girl walking outside a hotel in the winter and in the wind, while inside at a lighted window a couple is enjoying dinner. Elia's sense of isolation is increased with each new action. Jim, apparently a former lover (husband?), enters, and when Elia attempts a desperate reconciliation, she is cruelly rebuffed (as the stage directions make explicit):

> He shakes her loose and strikes her. She falls limply without a sound as he pulls his hat down and runs out. The shabby witness slouches past her and slinks away into the night.
>
> The couple inside smoke and drink as before.
>
> (p. 3)

Elia is already, as Guimond suggests, a victim of betrayal and indifference,[47] but this fact becomes even more clear after a sudden transformation; she is now the old woman of "Portrait of a Woman in Bed," haranguing two men who appear to be waiting upon her, but who do not at all understand her. It is a gloomy scene, but in its way indeed *comic*—Elia making little obscene insinuations, and holding onto nothing but her tough pride:

> There's my things drying in the corner;
> that blue shirt joined to the grey skirt.
>
> I'm sick of trouble.
> Lift the covers if you want me
> and you'll see the rest of my clothes—
> though it would be cold lying with nothing on!
>
> (p. 6)
>
> I won't work and I got no cash;
> what are you going to do about
> it?—and no jewelry—the crazy
> fools! But I've my two eyes and a
> smooth face and here's this, look!
> it's high! There's brains and blood in there!
> My name's Brobitza!
>
> (Pause. She looks up slyly as the officer makes a move as if to draw back the covers)
>
> Corsets can go to the devil and
> drawers along with them! What do I care.
>
> (She laughs coarsely. The man is convulsed.)
>
> P.M. [the Poor Master, one of the attendant characters]:
> You ain't got no clothes on?
> Well, damn your soul. You old she devil!
>
> (p. 7)

But following this rather crude scene Elia is miraculously visited by Flavi, a lover from the old country who appears in the window bearing gifts and presenting a far gayer picture of his "little sweetheart":

> My wild Elia! Just the silly
> little fool you have always been,
> with your tricks and pranks!
>
> (p. 10)

> Oh, the girls in that country were a
> brazen stupid lot. But here Elia is the wonder
> of wonders.
>
> (p. 12)

He offers her a grab-bag of wonderful things: paper flowers, a looking glass, a spool of red ribbon, slippers, stockings, a silver clock ("Don't be afraid of it, little country bumpkin./It won't bite you," p. 12). All except the clock have a special meaning, and evoke implicit memories of better times; but the clock only reminds the amazed Elia, now in peasant's dress and young, of "time passing" (p. 13). The fantasy is running down. Flavi attempts to explain his absence with a long story but only ends up telling an abbreviated version of "The Reeve's Tale" from *The Canterbury Tales.* At the end, with the clock ominously striking first one hour and next another, Flavi coldly gathers up his gifts—her youth—and at the stroke of 12:00 he is gone. As the light changes, men come to evict Elia, only to find that she is dead.

Elia Brobitza is remarkable in that it deals in a tentative way with a theme that would later occupy Williams in several of the major plays, in some of the fiction (including the Stecher trilogy and *The Farmers' Daughters*), and in many of the poems (including *Paterson*). This concern might be identified here as the dehumanization of one or both partners in love or marriage. "Elia Brobitza's metamorphoses," writes Guimond, "indicate that all the ages of womanhood are scarred by male inconstancy and brutality— Flavi's, Jim's, and finally the Poor Master's." What Guimond calls "the conflict between the male's need for the new and the female's need for constancy and responsibility"[48] emerges most clearly in *A Dream of Love,* but it is also central to *Many Loves* and *The Cure.* As shall be seen, the question later apparently becomes, at least in part, an autobiographical one for Williams: how does one apportion one's life? On *love,* Williams' position is a various one, at times highly sexual, at times almost ascetic; and *marriage,* he wrote in 1919, "is the great stumbling block of all commentators on love." He added: "They seem to think that one is in some way related to the other: no more so than a bird to the tree where it perches."[49] Adding his careers as physician and poet to those of lover and husband contributes to the textual complexity. In *Elia Brobitza,* however, there are only fragments of all this; Williams merely presents surfaces, kinetic shots of two or three moments in Elia's life and consciousness. The fact that it is called *The Comic Life...* is important as a prefiguration for the future. Williams thought of such plays as *A Dream of Love* and *Many Loves* as comedies despite their tragic dimensions, not really relentless in character or denouement. (In his working manuscript he had titled the former play *A Comedy of Love.* As for *Many Loves,* Williams told Julian Beck in 1957

[March 11] that "The whole atmosphere of the play is humorous, if that is not brought out and the lines recited with dash and lightness you are not doing with it what I have intended.") One also remembers the comic edges in certain passages of *Paterson,* and his statement in "Writer's Prologue to a Play in Verse":

> And how
> you shall laugh to see yourselves
> all naked, on the stage![50]

The comedy in *Elia Brobitza* is an ironic and bitter sort (excepting the ribald comedy of Flavi's tale), and Elia herself is the cynical and sad comic. She defends herself by laughing at her own hopelessness, and at the moment of her death she is, in fact, roaring grotesquely.

Williams has still not found his poetic voice in *Elia Brobitza,* even though his writing skills have been considerably sharpened since *A September Afternoon.* It is curious to note what he has done here with the poetic line. It is lengthened, apparently to slow it down and make it read more smoothly. Thus a somewhat choppy stanza of free verse from the poem—

> My two boys?
> —they're keen!
> Let the rich lady
> care for them—
> they'll beat the school
> or
> let them go to the gutter—
> that ends trouble.
> (p. 151)

becomes in the play—

> My two boys, they're keen!
> Let the rich lady care for them.
> They'll beat the school—or let them
> go to the gutter. That ends trouble
> (p. 7)

The change has really nothing to do with the quality of the verse, which remains uneven throughout. The best writing actually occurs in the scene between Elia and Flavi; here the lines evoke a kind of ecstasy of young love revisited. The monologue itself has a spareness which is characteristic of much of Williams' later verse. But Flavi's narrative points up the weakness of much of the poetry: it is in effect really prose strung out as verse, with almost none of the abrupt imagery and detail, and finally restraint, that Williams later consistently provided.

24   The Shorter Plays

Two More Washington Plays

It is difficult to date *Under the Stars,*[51] another short one-act sketch by Williams whose subject is again George Washington. It was probably written before his opera *The First President* (published in 1936 but begun four years earlier), perhaps closer to 1925 when *In the American Grain* appeared. But Williams was interested in Washington as a public and private figure at least 15 years before this latter prose "history," and *Under the Stars* seems, in fact, to be "early" Williams.

The complicating factor is a statement by Williams himself,[52] written in 1960 for a Wesleyan University double-bill reading/production of *Under the Stars* and *A Dream of Love.* He says: "This ten or twelve page dialogue was written for the Little Theatre. It was first being thought of in Rutherford, New Jersey but was never produced there or anywhere else. The World War forced us to interrupt operations." That would place the play in the late 1930's—perhaps possible—but additional notes by Williams raise questions:

> I was much interested in the production of plays to be given outdoors "on the lawns of the rich." The actors and their baggage to be transported about the country by automobile was at that time more or less of a novelty.
>
> Three short three act plays were rehearsed and produced by us, since lost. This Dialogue was to take its place in the scheme, but it was not to be.
>
> The play that came out of it, *Many Loves,* was produced by the Off Broadway theatre of Malina and Beck in New York.

The inconsistencies in this account are obvious. It is scarcely believable that an extended dialogue between George Washington and young Lafayette could have been assimilated into *Many Loves;* in point of fact, that play grew out of three far different playlets. *Under the Stars* was not written for the Little Theatre of Rutherford; Kathleen Hoagland, who was active with this group in its most productive years (1939–1941), has made it clear that *Many Loves* was Williams' single written contribution to that organization's repertory, even though the group never actually produced it.[53] Williams' mention of the possibility of presenting plays outdoors reminds one of the period from 1909 to 1921, when, as we have seen, at least one of his plays, *Betty Putnam,* was performed outside, and when Williams in fact built his own theatre.

But the uncertainty of the date is unimportant; the relevance of the play arises from one element, the play's subject, George Washington, who is once more discovered at the center of a moral dilemma. The time is a night in 1788, immediately following the quasi-successful engagement by American troops of the British at Monmouth, New Jersey. The two main characters, General Washington and the Marquis de Lafayette (barely 20 years old at the time), discuss the day's battle, and then turn to the conduct of an American officer, General Lee. Lee's "withdrawal"—in truth an unwarranted retreat in the face of Washington's order to attack—has cost the colonials a decisive victory. "He is a traitor," Lafayette argues, taking a solidly militaristic position. "He should be courtmartialed" (p. 3). Washington, quick to anger on the field, now acts and reacts with deliberation: "It may be...that our calmer judgment may move us to think otherwise" (p. 4). Before moving against Lee, Washington seeks to be scrupulously fair. And so the debate winds its way into the night, with Washington's cool reason finally rising firmly above Lafayette's hot insistence.

Under the Stars ends inconclusively, with no decision reached. Of course Williams intended nothing more ambitious. In a letter in February of 1960 to Clinton Atkinson,[54] then a director in the theatre at Wesleyan, Williams had called the work simply "an old dramatic sketch, a dialogue," and it is that and little more. He added, however, that the play—in manuscript it was titled *Monmouth*—"could be worked by properly selected young men into quite an attractive morsel." But it is evident that the play is static and not really possible as theatre. What is interesting instead is the psychology of Washington, who behaves with the same slow courage as the national leader in *The First President*. He is a thoughtful commander and kind (according to Lafayette) almost to a fault; this is a different view of the Washington presented in *A September Afternoon*. He is also uneasy remembering his first flash of anger directed at Lee in the field. There is in Washington a thoroughness—others would call it a failing—which drives him never to accept as truth the invincibility thrust on him; he is a human being, and is quick to recognize the possibility of human error or fallibility. Half to himself and half to the impatient Lafayette he muses:

> At least we drove them [the British] off. We might have lost. Be patient with me, my boy, I have a mind which is easily disturbed and must resolve itself, by back paths most often, in its own way. We might have lost had my plan been followed.
>
> (p. 5)

What we see is something not before encountered in the short plays: the interior development of character. This is much more than the presentation of a one-dimensional figure arguing against another of the same sort (although Lafayette is precisely that); Washington's position is ambiguous, darkening away from the light. As Koch observes, "the conflict is developed *within* a single person by a dramatic oppostion of various facets of his temperament."[55]

As art, the play is, as Atkinson quickly discovered, "a negligible piece,"[56] and not quite the "attractive morsel" that Williams had hoped it might be. The only movement occurs in the mind of General Washington. Both characters are sprawled on the ground in camp, "under the stars"; the scene is like a daguerreotype from a later war. There is little or no drama as such. It is as though Williams, thinking of Washington and troubled by the hypothetical question, *How does a man know when he is right?*, decided to write a short exercise or colloquy, and then be done with it. The prose itself is undistinguished. The fact that the play remains appealing is really due to the point of view Williams assumes: that a great man is more interesting (and even more heroic) when he is vulnerable or racked by doubt, when he has in fact suffered a setback, than when he is most triumphant. Only then is character revealed. Thus in Washington there is a potential story to be explored more satisfactorily later.

There is one other unpublished play to be considered here, and that is *The Battle of Brooklyn*.[57] Williams called it a farce, but it is difficult to judge it as that, or really as anything else, since only little more than one act was completed. (The list of dramatis personae is fairly substantial, and includes the usual American military personnel—called "Rebel Chiefs"— and a thief, a retailer of rum, a New England parson, and two women who open the play on a feebly comic, but nevertheless strategic, note. The scene was to be "partly within the rebel lines at Brooklyn and partly at Gwanas," p. 1.) The play is significantly introduced by a six-line epigraph from Samuel Butler's *Hudibras:*

> For as a flea, that goes to bed
> Lies with his tail above his head:
> So in this Mongrel State of curs,
> The rabble are the supreme powers;
> Who've horsed us on their backs, to shew us
> A jadish trick, at last, and throw us.
>
> (p. 1)

The Battle of Brooklyn, which was one of several engagements between American and British forces for New York in August of 1776, turned out disastrously for Washington and his troops. But the actual battle does not figure in the play as we have it. What Williams has attempted to deal with is the concern reflected by the passage just quoted from Butler: that the energies of Washington and his men will be undermined by a confused and unruly citizenry, and that the military and governmental leaders will eventually pay the price for leading their people to war. The problem is—and we have seen it before—almost Washington's alone, and he has again taken to dark thoughts:

> My apprehensions from the King's troops believe me are trifling, compared with the risque [sic] we run from the people of America at large. The tyranny, that our accursed

usurpation has made necessary which they now feel! and feeling, I fear will soon make them see through the disguise. Their rage no doubt will be heightened by the slaughter that will probably ensue, and we, as members of the Congress, fall the first victims of it.

(p. 5)

The substance of this incomplete play consists of two scenes, the first between Lady Gates and the servant Betty, the second involving Washington, Putnam, Sullivan, and Stirling "in Council in the Brooklyn Church" (p. 3). The former scene does not really, as Koch suggests,[58] contain conversation that is "brittle, witty and on the side of Restoration bawdiness." Rather, the early silliness of the dialogue, with Betty and Lady Gates ignorantly arguing the merits and apparent discourtesies of General Washington, shows how vastly difficult the task ahead for the Americans will be. The British are only one-half of the struggle. Washington must in the latter scene convince his own people of the rightness of the course, and allay their deepest doubts and fears. He will also have to work somehow through the incompetence of his other leaders. It is in the soldiers themselves that Washington ultimately places his confidence. They are, he thinks,

a standing miracle to me; they define sensibly upon matters that are unimportant to them, and resign their powers of thinking to us in a case where their all is at stake; and do not yet discover, that we make them the engines of our power at the expense of all that is dear and sacred to them as men!

(p. 5)

The problem is again, as Williams so often sees it, typically a Shakespearean one. Like Hamlet, Washington is often torn between action and reflection. To act is to risk everything, including honor and strength (and pride); to ruminate is a loving art. "My dear General," argues Sullivan, "the moments for reflection are elapsed and irrevocable" (p. 5). Washington later tells himself: "Avaunt reflection!" (p. 5). And yet as the stage is emptied Williams holds to the question, urging Washington to think it through again, to talk it out (in a very moving soliloquy):

Oh! could I congratulate myself, on finding my lost peace of mind! — on the restoration of my honor! O! cursed ambition! What have I sacrificed to thee? An ambition too of foreign growth; obtruded upon me by the most artful insinuating villain that ever enslaved a once free and happy country. To behold myself, against my principle and better judgment, made the tool of their diabolical determinations to entail a war upon my fellow subjects of America — Heighho! ho!

But Williams leaves off abruptly just a few lines into Act 3, with gunfire sounding near an American encampment. He is through with Washington until *The First President*.

28 The Shorter Plays

Fragments "In the Works"

In the meantime, Williams remained busy on at least three fronts: as poet, as pediatrician, and as traveler. His poems were appearing regularly in small magazines. He maintained a full private practice in Rutherford and had joined the staff of the Passaic General Hospital. In 1924 he sailed to Europe with Flossie and spent six months exploring, absorbing, and visiting. There he met among others the composer George Antheil, generous but perhaps unreliable; Robert McAlmon reports Antheil was possibly the man who first struck up the idea for *The First President*.[59] In Paris Williams speaks of seeing Jules Romains' brilliant comedy, *Dr. Knock*, the subject of which probably amused Williams, and Cocteau's *Romeo and Juliet*, "of which I remember nothing at all save that it in no way resembled Shakespeare's story."[60] In 1927 he went with Flossie and their two sons to Switzerland; he returned home to work while his family remained behind. It is somewhat later that Williams notes in his *Autobiography* (p. 238): "For I had returned to the play and was intent on doing a libretto for an opera on the theme of George Washington." Writing on this drama actually began about 1932, and culminated with the publication of *The First President* in 1936. It was Williams' first completed full-length play.

Sometime in the late 1920's or 1930's—Mrs. Williams did not recall exactly when—Dr. Williams, who was fond of giving home entertainments, organized a "theatre party" in a private home for New Year's Eve. A broadside playbill in the Williams collection at SUNY at Buffalo, obviously printed in fun, advertised the performers as "The Tyro Theatre Group." Williams was listed as producer, and a neighbor, Andrew Spence, was the manager. There were three playlets on the program. The first was called *Intimate Strangers* (*A Grotesque in One Sitting*), and included Williams and Flossie acting out the parts of Husband and Wife. It was, Mrs. Williams remembered,[61] about the protective "masks" worn by partners in intimate domestic situations, and grew from the Williamses' own experience. The script, undoubtedly very short and of a comic nature, does not survive. The second playlet or interlude was called *The Return from The Opera—Costumes of 1870,* and seems to have been a kind of *tableau vivant*. The final playlet, a scene taken directly from E. E. Cummings' long play *Him,* was called by Williams *Les Americans or What Have You* (*A Parisian Cafe* [sic] *Klotch*). *Him* was first performed by the Provincetown Playhouse in 1928 and, as George J. Firmage writes, "might be considered one of the first successful attempts at what is now called 'the theatre of the absurd.'"[62] Williams admired Cummings, although he was often puzzled by him (see the Mike Wallace interview in *Paterson,* for example), and would have known the play from his connections with old friends at the Provincetown Playhouse in Greenwich Village. The section performed was most of Act III, scene 3, which is largely taken up with the silly badinage of two American women (one played by Mrs. Williams). In the playbill for this segment Williams is listed as Sir Henry Irving—obviously he has done the directing.

From this time on, Williams seemed always to have a play "in the works." It is astonishing to see the variety of short, unfinished dramatic vignettes which survive in his unpublished papers at Buffalo and Yale, many (but not all) of them partially developed conversations between a doctor (obviously Williams) and a female patient. These fragments had appeared as early as 1927 with a short sketch Williams facetiously called "Sweet Land of Prurience."[63] It is a trivial little courtroom dialogue in which a doctor is called to testify against a man charged for disorderly conduct. The man was arrested on complaint of a woman for allegedly urinating against a tree. The doctor witnessed the act, but it is clear that he thinks the charge is absurd, that it is an example of American prudishness. In the 1940's, especially, Williams seemed to have been constantly working on brief dialogues and organizing plots. Many of these were jotted down on prescription pads, to be typed up later. The following is from a single page in the Yale collection;[64] it can be dated around 1947:

> Penthouse etc
>
> Finale:
>
> She's pregnant
>   (from First Act experience)
> —finally rejects him—anyway.
>   (rejects marriage, that is)
>
> "–let's hope your son at least
>   will not be such a
>   son-of-bitch
>
> You keep my mother out of this
>
> (She takes over practically
>
> "oh my God!"   "I'm moving in this afternoon"
>   says he.
>   "You've got money and you
>   don't have to live here."

It is not surprising in these little exercises to see Williams return again and again to subjects involving distorted love and sexual perversion, with their concomitant and various consequences. This is a theme that he was careful to note in life (he records many examples in his *Autobiography*), and runs through much of his work. It takes an important role in the fiction ("The Knife of the Times"), the verse (*Paterson*), and especially the plays (*Many Loves,* for example). So, for instance, on a page dated October 15, 1947,[65] we get this exchange between a doctor and a policeman:

> Have they caught those guys who were molesting little girls?
>
> We got one of them, the one on the motor cycle. We almost got the other one yesterday—but one of the boys was a little lax. He drives a gray car.
>
> What does he do?
>
> He asks them where the Rivoli is. Then he says, come on in and show me.
>
> I feel sorry for them, damn fools. We're all a little bit that way, more or less. I suppose they got him locked up.
>
> Yea, but when a 20 years [sic] old man starts fooling around with 8 year old little girls. There are plenty his own age he could get, they'd be glad to give it to him.

Sometimes Williams as examining physician merely records random conversations:

> If I had to take care of women like you, I'd go crazy.
>
> I suppose I'm helpless.
>
> No. That's exactly it. There's nothing the matter with you.[66]

Occasionally there is developed a short plot outline for an entire play; the recorded interruptions in the following case are obviously the workings of the doctor's office:

> Play
>
> Act 1 comes to a climax—with hurry, hurry, hurry (phone). Why in hell don't they go to someone else?
>
> Why in hell are we alive and what's it all about?
>
> Wonderful little girl.
>
> One act: baby screaming (concentrate on office hours)
>
> (1)

> An entirely different set of circumstances
> night (alone or anything)   (11)

Elsewhere there are more elaborate plots for dramas that never would be completed. One is for a work called *Never Bore a Woman,*[68] and contains a sketch of a man discussing his marital troubles with a doctor. It is not in any sense a realized scene, but nevertheless contains a speech by the troubled husband which in a way prefigures the theme (woman as predator) of some of the later full-length plays, especially in *A Dream of Love:*

> Woman is the destroyer of the inessential, the unguarded, the improperly palissaded [sic]. If you hold a thing dear it teaches a man to protect it, with armies, with cunning — with deceit. Especially with deceit. Never be candid, never at least allow a woman — no matter whom — to catch you off guard in a moment of confidence. In the middle of the night, in the morning — waking from a nap, never answer directly but think! Think how at some future time it may be used against you.

In the Yale manuscript there is a sketch of another play, noted earlier in this chapter, which is worked out even more fully, but again was never written. This one is titled *No Love or What Use to Grow Old;* it is frankly autobiographical, with many characters apparently drawn directly from the Williams family. But there are other persons included as well — a Princess, the Count of Miramar, and "Various Young Men, all with half-told secrets." Williams states his "Argument":

> Approaching her 92nd birthday, the old woman wants to see young Dr. Bill married, Ingrid as well. She is virtually blind and deaf and cannot walk: but she is relentlessly alive.
>
> She does not scheme. She believes she is being deceived and that the truth is kept from her. She believes Dr. Bill is married and that a man has asked Ingrid — and cannot understand why, why, why these things go on.
>
> Incidentally, she has been 'told' of a war between Mexico and the U.S.
>
> So she fills her life. As 'arry fills his — with drink and sleep and dreams.
>
> What happens at the end, if anything, God only knows. But the Old Woman puts much stock in the future life. Which is the hero — if there is one.

There are more fragments, including a partial beginning to a play on Benedict Arnold called *The Fifth Star or No Love.* (The subtitle "No Love" is a favorite one of Williams, used more than once, and suggestive of the problems which he considers.) Another is rather abrasively titled *Women are Such Fools.* Most if not all of these seem to have been born during spare moments in the doctor's office, and such was the beginning of many of the full-length plays — the writing appearing first on prescription pads, note papers, and on envelopes, and gradually evolving through countless reworkings and retypings.

Thus we finally come to the major plays. Following *The First President,* the next drama was *Many Loves,* the most important of all of his writings for the theatre. It grew partially out of his association with the Little Theatre of Rutherford in the late 1930's and early 1940's, and was finally published in 1942 by New Directions. The version in *Many Loves and Other Plays* is slightly revised, and follows more closely the text used by the Living Theatre in its New York production of 1959. *A Dream of Love* was the third long play, published in 1948 (again by James Laughlin at New Directions) and first brought to the stage a year later by a New York group called "We Present." Williams' work on the Salem witch trials, *Tituba's Children,* was long in the preparation, but at last completed by 1950. It was not published until it appeared in *Many Loves and Other Plays. The Cure* was finished in 1960 and also published in the volume *Many Loves.* [69]

The Productive '40's and '50's

The 1940's and '50's, with Williams now moving into the fullness of old age, were wonderfully productive years. In addition to the plays there were *Paterson, The Collected Later Poems, The Pink Church, The Desert Music,* and *Journey to Love,* to name only a few of his books. Now a recognized man of letters, he lectured a great deal, gave readings, traveled from one campus to another, maintained old friendships (even with Ezra Pound), and continued to write whenever his health permitted. That his plays were attracting admirers from within academia and without was gratifying, and productions of his work, as we shall see, delighted him, especially the Living Theatre's *Many Loves.* Williams had kept up with the theatre as best he could, wrote about Lorca (whom he greatly admired), reviewed a production of John Ford's *'Tis Pity She's a Whore,* worried about the economics of the theatre in New York, encouraged new Off-Broadway activity, and extravagantly praised productions that he liked.

The following letter from Williams to the Becks regarding their production of Gertrude Stein's play *Doctor Faustus Lights the Lights* in 1951 is relevant here, because it gives one a sense of the passion Williams still maintained, at almost 70 years of age, for the stage. *Doctor Faustus Lights the Lights* is, to say the least, highly experimental. Written in 1938, it is a short three-act work which includes, along with the usual devils of the Faust story, a ballet and a speaking dog; the dog has a duet with Doctor Faustus. It is interesting to see in the letter Williams' continued interest in poetic drama as well (an inclination he would partly realize in *Many Loves*):

December 15, 1941

My dears Julian Beck & Judith Malina:
    I'm walking in a dream, the aftermath of what I saw and heard at your Cherry Lane Theatre last evening—in all that snow. I'd be there tonight if I didn't have a firm grip on myself—if I were younger nothing could hold me back. I belong there tonight but I dare not let myself go. And tonight is the last night of your play, of Gertrude Stein's Doctor Faustus Lights the Lights. To me it was a wonderful a truly wonderful experience to have witnessed it.
    I want to tell you everything at once: about the excellently chosen cast, the evenness of their performance, the way they kept the interest up among them as well as the integrity of their individual performances (I was thrilled!) but there was something else that overshadowed all that. It concerned the stage itself, the overall conception of the play as something elevated, as pure entertainment, as something so well sustained, so far above the level of the commercial theatre that I tremble to think it might fade and disappear. I swear it lives in a different air from the ordinary Broadway show, it is as fresh as a day in the country, the first really serious, really cleanly written, produced and acted play that I have seen, well, in a long time.
    I say I feel as if it was something that someone were going to snatch it away from before my eyes—that is one reason I am so driven to go again tonight. I can't believe it possible that that cast, in those parts, just as they were acted, is going to be dispersed. I don't trust my contemporaries. Such a beautiful thing. Such a truly entrancing experience! It's going to be let die without anyone having adequately celebrated it. I want you to know that as long as I live I'll never forget it.
    I realize that I'm speaking in hyperbole. I'm doing it of a set purpose. If I did not use the figure I could not show you how far above the usual conception of the stage you have set your mark and how I appreciate it. It's an almost impossible shot. But you've succeeded in communicating to me what you all together, as a company, have set yourselves to do and I want you to know and never forget that you have succeeded. You HAVE succeeded and it is important, I do not want you to forget, any of you, that you did communicate to me the elevated achievement you had in mind when you first conceived such a theatre as you placed before your audience last night.
    I don't know whether you'll succeed in the fiercely competitive field which the theatre in New York represents. There is a sordidness which corrupts playwright, producer and actor alike yet which somehow, and sad to relate, brings in the coin while it strangles the entire range of what is offered. We all know this vulgarity, we all detest it. The only protest to make is to stay away from the performances—but there are plenty that go and so the appearance of success is achieved. I want to tell you that everywhere people are conscious of this state of affairs, that they long for something more satisfying to their sensibilities than these fifth rate appeals to their emotions and intelligence represent.
    You are young and, apparently, incorruptible. You know that there is a whole range of plays (not just Ibsen repertoire) waiting to be created for a public, actually to be created. And if you can maintain yourself by the skin of your teeth writers will write more plays for you, poetic plays, excellent plays, the plays that an enlightened audience calls or will call for. I can't tell you how important it is for the theatre that you want to

> CREATE new plays. It is the most thrilling thing that can be done on the stage today.
>
> I wish I could give you a million to start at once on your plans to build a theatre housed in the walls of a brownstone. I can't do it. But to begin with you've got the thing, the practical energy to have made a beginning at the Cherry Lane. May all success be yours.
>
> Sincerely yours,
William Carlos Williams

With such a letter as evidence it becomes impossible to overestimate Williams' interest in and fascination for the theatre. The question of Williams as *dramatist,* however, is more difficult. On the one side, we have such partisans as Clinton J. Atkinson: "It is possible that William Carlos Williams may be one of our better playwrights," he wrote in *The Massachusetts Review* (1962).[70] But there are also those (they are legion) who have ignored his plays or have held them in contempt. Reviewing *A Dream of Love* in 1949, Arthur Pollock called Williams "a novice who got his only training in play-making by writing naughty words on fences and sidewalks with a piece of chalk."[71] That kind of misunderstanding is scarcely defensible, and surely does little to focus attention on the real merits or demerits of the plays. Nor does Williams himself always seem to have a very clear idea of what the value of his plays is. In a letter to the Becks (May 26, 1948) he wrote:

> BUT are my plays "suitable" for any sort of performance. The doubts rise like a fog creeping over the sun. Is my first play [*Many Loves*], the one that appeared in the issue of New Directions, *witty* enough to carry the dialogue? I had hoped that it was so and perhaps the ability of the actors may be able to add just that edge that would make the lines successful—but I am scared! scared to think that what should sound light may sound heavy—to the unwilling. In other words, it's a battle I see before me, a battle to sell myself to you and a possible audience.

Janes Laughlin addresses precisely this point:

> WCW did set great store by his plays and was always disappointed that they weren't more often produced.... You ask how Bill "valued" his plays. He was modest about all his work, never really grasped, I believe, how good he was, yet had such a strong compulsion to write, he would have gone on, I think, couldn't have stopped, even if he had had no recognition at all.[72]

In any event, if Williams the playwright deserves a reputation at all, it must come from the five major works, and not the interesting but very flawed shorter plays already considered. It is thus time to turn to *Many Loves and Other Plays.*

2
The First President

Preparing the Libretto

By almost any objective standard William Carlos Williams' first major play, the libretto for his opera on George Washington, is unsuccessful. *The First President* (1936)[1] was not performed until 1979.[2] Lacking a traditional narrative line, it is clearly a cumbersome artifact for the stage. Oddly, the poetry is without much distinction—odd because some of Williams' best verse comes from the volume *Adam & Eve & The City,* published in the same year. In addition, the opera lacks significant motivating action and is thus open to the charge of "being dull." And what action there is—the ballet in Act II, scene 2, for example—is subject to parody; it somehow seems false, a bit antiquated, and foolish. There is no question that the work is in several ways an advance over his earlier plays, but this fact alone would not be sufficient motivation for considering it at length.

The real reasons for looking at *The First President* closely are elsewhere and of a special importance. The first is that Williams himself so obviously admired it, writing at least one rather long explanatory essay in justification. Such self-conceit, while perhaps the normal pride of any creator of any work of art (whatever its worth in public), points to a naïveté in Williams which is discernible throughout his life. It is manifested in his striking inability to judge very clearly what it is in his own writing that is valuable and what is not, and when. Anyone who reads Williams at all will face this question sooner or later, and it is well to keep it in mind at the outset. Thus, to judge *The First President* fairly one must take into account what Williams' *intentions* were regarding both Washington as a character and the opera as a medium. Only then is it possible to make the proper distinction between conception and execution. The second reason is that the libretto provides a good chance to see Williams in the process of creating. He is the artist in the laboratory, and he is nursing a very complicated experiment. Third, some of the issues that Williams does raise are important and revealing as they relate to the rest of his work. What he writes about history, for example, and about the American hero and the American temperament, reflects on Williams the poet and fictionalist. Finally, I would like to record what I think are the modest intrinsic achievements—and there are some—of the work as it stands.

That Williams' first principal work for the stage should be the libretto for an opera on Washington is not surprising. He had anticipated aspects of *The First President* in certain of the unpublished plays, especially *Under the Stars* and *The Battle of Brooklyn*. A brief chapter of *In the American Grain* (1925) had been devoted to Washington. Here the emphasis was on the man's steadiness, his reserve, and his toughness. To quote several passages:

> Washington was, I think, the typically good man: take it as you please. But of course, a remarkable one. No doubt at all he, personally, was ninety percent of the force which made of the American revolution a successful issue. Know of what that force consisted, that is, the intimate character of its makeup, that is, Washington himself, and you will know practically all there is to understand about the beginnings of the American Republic. You will know, also, why a crown was offered this great hero at the conclusion of hostilities with Great Britain, and with what a hidden gesture he rejected the idea. Therein you have it: it was unthinkable—or he might have taken it.
> Here was a man of tremendous vitality buried in a massive frame and under a rather stolid and untractable exterior which the ladies somewhat feared, I fancy....
> Patience, horses or a fine carriage, a widow to wive, a sloping lawn with a river at the bottom, a thriving field, an adopted daughter—that was as far as his desire wandered. All the rest he accepted as put upon him by chance.
> Resistance was, I believe, his code. Encitadeled. A protector of the peace, or at least, keeper of the stillness within himself. He was too strong to want to evade anything. That's his reputation for truth-telling. It was a good scratching to him to take it on and see himself through. He knew he would come through.[3]

Further, Washington appears as counterpoint to the more easygoing Aaron Burr in "The Virtue of History," published in that same volume (pp. 188-207); and in his essay "The Writers of the American Revolution" (in *Selected Essays*, pp. 38-54), Williams again refers to Washington. He is also mentioned in some of the prose passages in *Paterson*.

What attracted Williams to Washington? "Actually," Mrs. Williams has remarked, "he probably admired Jefferson more, but Washington was, after all, the first president."[4] One remembers what Williams would say in the Introduction to *The First President* (in *Many Loves and Other Plays*):[5]

> There is an inevitability of strange proportions that seems to have preordained that there be an American opera and that its first theme be this theme; the character, the subdued but terrifically effective character, of Washington could be released in no other way. And it is a force which cries to be released, insistently, as if it would brook no denial. It is very definitely an Occasion for Music.
>
> (p. 307)

One also recalls, in the passage quoted above from *In the American Grain,* just how crucial Williams felt Washington was to the country. Williams was as inexorably drawn to Washington as he was to the origins of the United States. As librettist Williams looks back to first causes, to the literal Father of the Revolution, to the Hero, rather than to the more democratic and brilliant, and more complex, Jefferson. Washington was, indeed, our beginning, collectively sustained by the national psyche. In that sense, then, he was both a visionary and a practical success. Again Williams writes in the Introduction:

> It was an imaginary republic he created and defended with a very real army, as a servant of the people. It was a country he pasted together — a good deal out of shoddy — to represent the thing we still labor to perfect. His labors and our labors are the same, granted differences and varieties in the tensions involved. Could we know, deeply, what he faced and performed we should be the better able to realize what we have still to do — and what we are.
>
> (p. 303)

Thus the purpose of a play or an opera on Washington, Williams here declares, is to "project the figure of Geo. Washington across the panorama of American History so that it would galvanize us into a realization of what we are today...." (p. 303). Accordingly, such history instructs; but history in the artist's hands is given an added meaning. In "The Virtue of History" Williams elaborates:

> But history follows governments and never men. It portrays us in generic patterns, like effigies or the carvings on sarcophagi, which say nothing save, of such and such a man, that he is dead. That's history. It is concerned only with the one thing: to say everything is dead. Then it fixes up the effigy: there that's finished. Not at all. History must stay open, it is all humanity. Are lives to be twisted forcibly about events, the mere accidents of geography and climate?
>
> (pp. 188-89)

Washington's reputation among historians and students of the American past has waned in recent years,[6] but in the 1930's (and even to Charles and Mary Beard after the Second World War) he was still regarded as a strong military leader and a very competent president. The year 1932 was in fact the bicentennial anniversary of Washington's birth, and it was taken respectful note of by the nation. Maxwell Anderson's melodrama about Washington as soldier, *Valley Forge,* was successfully produced two years later by the Theatre Guild. Half in prose and half in verse, the play was extravagantly praised by the New York critics. (Burns Mantle judged it as "probably Anderson's noblest drama."[7]) But Williams, not satisfied in this case with the ordinary conventions of the stage, was to turn to another dramatic medium, the opera, to shape his story. In his Introduction he discusses some of the reasons for such a choice:

> Music must be the answer. The character creates a music—it must have created a music for its escape. A music accompanying action. It is a music to be uncovered by action, to be discovered and translated to our world of today. It was a music which Washington must constantly have felt from the beginning to the end of his life within the secrecy of his shuttling thoughts. It is a music which must be sought, borne upon which only can he affect us. His taciturnity might come out in poetic drama but there is no poetic drama today. All attempts to lodge him there must push him back into a turgid history which dulls us, defeats its purpose. It dates him, binds him. It deals with the past. He becomes at once of the past.
>
> But the music, created out of the identity of our interests, makes him of today. He becomes a contemporary in the inventions which prove our souls, in a common setting, to be the same as his. With it we mingle with him. Without it we remain apart and considerably bored.
>
> A grand opera which would be based on Washington's struggle toward realization of a world that is new and free might distil from his character a powerful element. It would have to be, as well, a contemporary element resting its weight fairly in the things which Washington rested in. He cannot become a real figure and remain wholly in his own day. He must be musically conceived; that is, essentially liberated from the confinements of his particular actions. He must go up and we alongside him into the imagination to which music is a natural language.
>
> How to keep recognizable features of an historical character, his local significance, and still make of him a fit figure for the universality which music can treat? Shakespeare did it for man and woman. But he did it in an accepted convention of his day. In this case, since the times will not permit the same wordiness, a greater stringency must be resorted to. Opera offers its effects, a convention still more remote than Elizabethan drama. For opera has a primitive side to it related to the sagas. Group singing is tribal. It must have had Greek tragedy as a child. That is the mood of grand opera as sought here. It is a convention which, if accepted, will permit the freedom of movement necessary to the play of the forces involved. It can report history exactly while draining it of its essence by substituting music for a coarser time.
>
> (pp. 304-5)

J. C. Thirlwall's notes in Williams' *Many Loves and Other Plays* give further elaboration on several of these same points, and fill in more of the specific detail. Thirlwall quotes Williams speaking in 1961, two years before Williams' death:

> The sesquicentennial of Washington's presidency—these were great years for me. My brother was a prominent architect in New York. When it began to be talked about that an opera was to be written on the theme, I proposed to Ed that he get busy on the Flushing Meadow site where the Fair was to be held and design me a setting—which he did and we were off.
>
> An opera. Tibor Serly, musician and composer, was introduced to me. I also met his father, a most interesting old man, a friend of Bartok. We began to have preliminary auditions in an apartment overlooking Riverside Drive and it seemed hardly any time before something more material toward the opera of my dreams began to be realized.
>
> In one of my earliest prose books, *In the American Grain,* Washington was strongly mentioned, but no more than mentioned. Now I was ready to dwell on the figure of our first President and make much of him as the primary figure of our nation. The only

trouble was that Washington was a silent man; it was hard to conceive of him as a figure in an opera. Despite his stature and heroic demeanor, Hamilton despised him. That placed Hamilton. But how to give Washington the figure he must have on the stage—to be taken seriously? There was a story involving the young people of Mt. Vernon during some merrymaking they had initiated—they were in the thick of it when the figure of the great man appeared down the stairs. At once all merrymaking ended and a great silence fell upon all of those present. The gaiety was killed. Washington was upset because basically he loved the raucous if crushing humor of horseplay. But he couldn't enter into that humor.

That could be shown on the stage but once only. So the role of Washington had to be conceived wordlessly. I accepted that, but it made for a figure that appeared mostly at intervals or in the background; the 'operatic' had to be mainly with the women and the lighter young men who were his aides.

Few realize how much the growth and development to manhood of George Washington was identified with the development of the country itself. But the country knew it, and he himself knew that a failure on his part would have meant the total collapse of the cause of the colonies themselves. When he said that if he were defeated on the general front he would have no choice but to retreat into western Pennsylvania to carry on the war as a guerilla, he meant what he said and the country knew that he would do just that. He was a grimly dedicated man. From his first devoted love for his friend's wife, pursued failingly for all of his youth, that was made clear to him. He was a tough man to beat. He could not give in without losing everything. But he had nevertheless to take a second place, even if his heart would be broken. His Sally must have disappeared in the end.

The intimate story of his development is forecast in detail from this point to his death. We shall be forever left in a quandary by Martha's decision to destroy their correspondence to the last item, which she did. We should have known more of George Washington had she not stuck to her decision. But his letters were the best part of him.

(pp. 429-31)

That Williams should begin with an opera is thus not unexpected. He had seen, as noted earlier, the work of many of the medium's great practitioners in Europe and in New York. His friend Ezra Pound had written an opera of sorts, *The Testament of Francois Villon,* which was presented in 1924 in Paris. That same year in Paris George Antheil had confided to Williams that he wanted him to write the libretto for his "American opera." Antheil, then just 24 years old, was a brilliant young composer whose *Ballet mécanique* would be a Paris sensation in 1926. (Williams himself defended this work against the critics when it was performed at Carnegie Hall in April of 1927. See "George Antheil and the Cantilene Critics" in *Selected Essays*.) But there was a certain lack of credibility about him as well, as McAlmon busily notes:

> William Carlos Williams was back in Paris, and he sat one day with Hemingway, and me, and two other writers, and confided to us that George Antheil had appointed him to write the libretto for his American opera. He, Williams, Antheil had said, was the one writer most certain to get into it the spirit of America. Hemingway and I exchanged knowing glances, and I noticed that the two other writers also looked "so that's the way

it is." For George had talked warmly and with much enthusiasm about how I was the logical writer to do this libretto. His innocent and childlike ardency about the quality of my work was heart-appealing. The others had thought his fervor about their work most pleasing too. I wonder if he had read anything any of us had written.[8]

Nevertheless, Antheil apparently did remain "in the picture" through at least the early part of 1932, for in the Williams collection at Yale there exists an apparent first draft of the libretto, dated February 24, 1932, with the notation: PLAN FOR AN OPERA IN COLLABORATION WITH GEO. ANTHEIL.[9]

But Williams does not even mention Antheil in the statement printed by Thirlwall, passing instead to another young musician, Tibor Serly. Serly was the same age as Antheil (both were born in 1900), a native of Hungary, a friend of Pound, and a violinist and composer with a minor reputation. Williams had admitted that he was collaborating with a second composer in a letter to Marianne Moore dated May 2, 1934.[10] He rather unflatteringly calls the new artist "an unknown," and then adds:

I admire him. We have made a few more or less futile passes at each other so far but by next fall the work should be in full blast. It should prove an interesting engagement if we don't fall apart from each other in disgust before we accomplish anything.

But the partnership with Serly did not succeed either, and in a letter Serly explains some of the reasons why:[11]

During the years 1935–36, B. W., myself and several others became very much interested in material for an opera on the subject of the first President. At that time, researches which went on for months gathering historical data in Wash., D.C. and Philadelphia, Pa., led to the preparation of a complete draft for an opera. The first act of the so-called libretto was presented and I actually commenced the opening sketches, including the first scene between George Washington and Martha. The manuscript is still intact.

Then things began to happen: first, I realized that Bill Williams had no practical comprehension of the stage and theatre. I suggested that his material (much of which was poetically, historically and dramatically superb) be done in collaboration with a reputable librettist with whom I could work constantly together. Bill turned down the idea. Second, B. W. had no reputation at all (except as a small-town pediatrician) — my own name was slightly known in the music world. Neither of us had any finances and we had even less access to influential people. Working on such a project would have meant at least a year of exclusive hard work which I could not afford. Third, we put out several feelers as to what interest there might be for an opera on George Washington. The reaction was not only nil — but remarks made like "Who the hell is interested in G. W. — the most unromantic, unglamorous character, even if he was the greatest of all Americans, etc. Lincoln — yes; perhaps even Lafayette; but General G. W. — never!" Add to this that a full-blown American opera by two virtually unknowns, without being commissioned — or even if so — had about as much chance of getting into dress rehearsal in the USA of 1936, as a snowman would have in hell.

After several conferences with Ezra Pound and several other of Bill Williams' colleagues and well-wishers, with great regrets and sadness the project had to be abandoned.

Williams went on with his work, however, and finished the libretto by 1936, when it was published in the *New Caravan*. It went virtually unnoticed. But he was still eager for production, and not long after turned to Virgil Thomson. The following account is from the *Autobiography*:

> The World's Fair of 1939-1940 in New York was over. I had again wanted to write the libretto for an opera on the theme of the heroic life of George Washington. Tibor Serly had half-agreed to do the music, and since the theme of this World's Fair was, in fact, Washington's life, with a heroic statue of Washington himself featured on the esplanade, I thought this was my opportunity. Grover Whalen couldn't see it!
> After Serly backed out, I went to Virgil Thomson, whose music to Gertrude Stein's *Four Saints in Three Acts* had been so superlatively good.
> I met Thomson at lunch in the restaurant of the famous old Hotel Chelsea on West Twenty-third Street. He was really very nice.
> "You don't know anything about the stage, do you?" he said.
> "No."
> "Then what the hell do you bother with it for? All these scenes and directions.... You're a poet, aren't you?"
> "Yes."
> "Then write your poem and forget it. But what about this ballet? All these 'snow maidens' you've got here."
> "Well, that's a ballet of the snow at Valley Forge."
> He laughed. "Imagine me doing a ballet of snow maidens!" he said and snorted. "What would they say of me?"
> I said nothing.
> "Who is this Washington? Who is he?" he said.
> "I am Washington," I told him.
> "That's different." And he cooled down a bit. "Well, write your poem then and when you're ready with it I'll do the music."
> Maybe someday I'll take him up, if we're not both dead or incapacitated by that time — *it'll be good, too, the way I have reconceived it — without snow maidens!*
> (pp. 300-1)

The above passage is a good example of how Williams occasionally misremembers facts or dates in his own life. Serly had clearly dropped out of the project by 1937. Williams' feelings about Thomson's music for *Four Saints in Three Acts* in the *Autobiography* are in part contradicted by what he had written earlier in "A 1 Pound Stein":[12] "To me Virgil Thomson's music is of doubtful aid to Stein's prose." In any event Thomson's version of the meeting (at dinner, not lunch) is somewhat more restrained:[13]

> Williams sent me the George Washington play in, I think '37 tho it may have been '40.
> I read it and we had dinner on the subject.

> He wanted me to make it into an opera. I said no. I didn't think it would make a good opera.
> Various reasons, none of them questioning his excellence as a poet.
> No unfriendly feeling resulted.

Years later a full score was finally written by a composer from Brooklyn, Theodore Harris, but according to James Laughlin the opera did not enjoy a production until Kean College produced it in concert version.[14]

The Nature of the Opera

What kind of opera on George Washington did Williams intend to write? We have already looked at some of the clues. As usual, his notes and early manuscripts are also enormously helpful in discovering the creative process at work. Some of these jottings would indicate that Williams held brainstorming sessions with a party of one; he simply wrote down the various directions from which he might begin the development of the character of Washington:

> Prototypes (suggestive) Shakespeare: Henry the IVth. Meistersinger. Verse? Prose? Wotan. "Sing something simple." The music of the times[15]

We have already seen, and will later have a chance to observe in greater detail, how important Shakespeare was to Williams; the same is true of Richard Wagner. Suffice it to say here that there are elements of both Shakespeare and Wagner in *The First President,* and Williams himself suggests in his introduction how expertly the tragic aspects in drama can be borne by the music of opera:

> No one could call this a pageant. No one could say there was not a plot. It is the moment of fruition of the man's life. His whole life has contributed to it. He dislikes his fate, he has fought it. But against his desire for retirement, for peace, for pastoral exercises which must have released his private mind upon itself—he must go. He is compelled to it, tragically, to serve—again.
> The plot cannot be a superficial playing with emotion, some stupid dawdling with this or that. The plot enforces itself beyond that. It is the destiny of a man following his fate among a distraught, conglomerate people, bent upon being themselves, whose great word, "freedom," has infected him as well.
> It is definitely a function, and should be the chief burden of the music to express this. There is no other way in which it can be expressed. A movie wouldn't express it. It would miss it. It couldn't make the tragedy apparent since the photographic reality of the scenes would be constantly in the way. The tragedy is not for the most part in what the protagonist is doing; it is over all he does, it encloses him, it trips and turns him about. It must be the music. It must be an opera. A grand opera. The music must move toward the inevitable end of all love—to rest.

Well-chosen scenes appear in sequence, revealing the man struggling against unfaithfulness, incompetency—resigning all desire for self to win for the others and with the others a liberty which, if it were possible, he might have enjoyed like a supreme savage. Washington was a primitive more than any about him in his resources of fierce energy but he kept it under heavy check his life long, subdued by an oppressive destiny.

(pp. 305-6)

Over and over in this Introduction we notice how much importance Williams attaches to the *music*. "There is no other way than the music" (p. 306). "Nothing but music can do this with a sufficient feeling of inevitability" (p. 307). W. H. Auden, with much experience in these things, would probably have agreed with Williams, and rightly claims in his essay "A Public Art"[16] that there are ways opera, with music at its center, can function to better advantage in modern times than mere drama or verse drama:

There are two kinds of stage-work in which a poet can have a hand, verse drama and opera.... Human egoism is such that no poet will prefer the subordinate role unless he prefers opera to any verse-drama, even one he might write himself. He must be convinced, that is to say, that there are two things opera can do which verse-drama cannot, and that these are more valuable than anything which could be done in the latter medium. He is thinking, of course, of the present, not the past, of what can and cannot be done *now*.

For what it is worth, my personal conviction is this. Drama is necessarily a public art. To be of public interest a human being must be heroic; his or her actions, sufferings, emotions, must be exceptional and in the grand manner. For a number of reasons the Public Realm is no longer a place where speech can be authentic. Speech, the medium of the poet, is now the expressive medium of the intimate: the singular can address the singular in poetry, but poetry cannot appear in public without becoming false to itself. In our age there are only two public dramatic arts, opera and ballet. Ballet is wordless, but opera requires the singable word. (Let us not presume to call it poetry.) Outside his own proper sphere of the intimate, there is still something a poet, if he is prepared to submit to a librettist's limitations, can contribute to the Public Realm.

Dramatic poetry, to be recognizable as poetry, must raise its voice and be grand.

(pp. 129-30)

One of the advantages thus enjoyed by opera over conventional drama is that, by raising its voice and being grand, it produces a general *elevation of feeling*. Williams anticipated that this would happen in *The First President,* but unfortunately such was not the case.

In any event, Williams was in 1932 making tentative beginnings, drawing together threads that eventually would be assimilated or discarded, bringing into the action characters who would either evolve or disappear as the material was reworked. "Wrestling with himself is characteristic of Williams' method," Koch has pointed out,[17] and it is true: Williams literally exhausted the potential of all alternatives as his libretto took its shape, screening out the dross from the whole. Early in 1932, for example, he had considered (see the Yale folder) the option of intruding frames of appropriate film into the stage action, anticipating to a point the various mixed media approaches now often seen in the contemporary theatre:

> *Notes:* Use of the silent movies? — on a sepia screen — his past on horseback — telling moments — interspersed — as he sits waiting. Orchestrated. He gets up. Paces. Joins the scene, living again the action which — evaporates as it has arisen.

It was an intriguing possibility, but Williams finally discarded it because, as he wrote later in the Introduction, "the photographic reality of the scene would be constantly in the way" (p. 306). (We will see later that reality in a conventional sense is what, in this opera, he wanted to avoid.) Two years later, in addition, he was still struggling with the *plot* of the opera; in what he called a "detailed synopsis" of Act III he had sketched out a narrative line which dramatized the life of George Washington against the cyclorama of a vulgarly urbanized Washington, D.C. Williams elaborates on this odd setting in his notes:

> 1. The large, high main hall of a modern Duplex Apartment, Washington, D.C., in about the year 1925. It is somewhere above the tenth floor of the building. Glass doors at the back open upon a balcony disclosing a view of the Washington Monument in the distance. There is a large couch or divan in about the same position on the stage as that occupied by the bed in the first act.
> The two main protagonists of the scene, an older man, a legislator, and a young woman, his mistress are buffeted about to their destruction — over against the devotion and solidity of Washington's life which appears as the troubled, remorseful imagining of the man. The woman tries to pacify him (as did Martha her husband in the first scene) but he succumbs.

In this scheme, by the end of the first scene in Act III, which takes place while a party blares in the background, the man has shot himself with a pistol. It is all very lugubrious, and Williams wisely dropped it.

Meanwhile, the George Washington sequences began to take shape on paper, scrawled out by hand and then rapidly typed on any available paper. Williams had at one point in 1934 titled the opera (in the Yale folder) *The Indestructable* [sic], based on his writing of a fragmentary speech for Martha (Mrs. Washington) which was to be an encomium to her husband: "you are as you have been — /the indestructable..../Fortune working/in you." This passage is deleted somewhere along the line but it is helpful in that it intimates Washington would be inexorably driven by some force through the dangers and bitternesses of the Revolution to a destiny marking him as President. To Martha and those who loved him, Washington's strength was unassailable; he was guided by a special providence. Washington did not choose to lead; he was chosen. And yet this largeness of character brought about a serious problem in the opera with which Williams had to contend: how can an artist make his hero *human*? He worries in the Introduction:

> A first difficulty is that people think the man to have been stolid—a cold rod of no subtlety of interest, certainly no emotional appeal. He worked, he married and he died. He was indeed a voluminous writer, one of the world's most prolific writers. But his exterior was frigid. He spoke, it is commonly believed, seldom and formally. What in the world, retaining his obvious vitality, can you do with a character like that?
> (pp. 303-4)

Again, one returns to the music, or to Williams' conception of the music; it is that itself which gives Washington enough wind to draw breath:

> The character of Washington itself, in this case, forms the libretto, forms the nature of the word-music relationship. A revolutionary relationship. The inner character creates the necessity for the opera being like none heretofore produced.
> (p. 308)

> The man moves, not through the scenes as in a pageant—this is not a pageant. He himself moves the scenes, as revealed by the music, and to a fixed end, relentlessly. The genius, rather, that moves him is seen operative in every scene and always the same—power in leash, selflessly, for a common purpose of freedom.
> (p. 309)

In his Yale notes Williams significantly adds: "The opera is to give the *impression,* curiously enough, of his silence—of his silence and isolation (surrounded by music) a music." Thomas R. Whitaker is thus partly correct when he writes that "Washington is less a dramatic character than a controlling imagination, brooding over the events of his own life."[18]

In the completed text of *The First President* there are three acts, each with three scenes. Williams explained the final design in the Introduction, which again serves as a valuable source of information:

> Scene after scene might be used. But this is governed by the convention of a musical performance which should not go beyond a hundred minutes. Many scenes might serve to reveal the situation as it existed, but that would not be for opera. I should suggest that it begin with personal betrayals, stand upon the faithful namelessness of common men who worshipped Washington and end with the furies and uncertainties of office, largely frustrated, softened by a note of happy retirement.
> (p. 306)

In the Yale papers he had planned that "All the scenes must be extraordinary but *natural.* No faked choruses, etc. especially." The intended evolution of the opera is thus quite clear. Numerous scenes from earlier manuscripts were later discarded wholly or in part; Williams discovered that ornament and surplusage were not consonant with the forthrightness that he demanded. To present Washington directly, sparely, as an internalized man, in a manner similar (in some ways) to the Washington of *Under the Stars,* was Williams' intention. The extra baggage was ruthlessly dumped from the wagon. For example, short scenes between Negro slaves or slaves and their masters cluttered up the early drafts. They were obviously included to serve as background, to provide a stock Southern ambience, but they strike one now as being quite as false as, say, *Show Boat,* especially the dialogue (see the Buffalo manuscripts):[19]

Colored Girl: Get away from here you good for nothin'

Colored Boy: What you been doin' here all mornin'?

Girl: I been knittin' That's what I been doin'—

Boy: You can't knit—

Girl: I can so, look what I done knitted—

(A large colored woman with a dinner bell comes from the house, she sees the boy)

Woman: Get around back to the kitchen with that basket. The cook's been waitin' bout an hour for you to bring that fish up from the river. Lemme see. You mean to tell me it took you all mornin' to ketch them three little fishes?

(Martha comes from the door. The slaves change their tone)

Woman: (to boy) Move along, boy. Move along—(he goes)

Also discarded from a Buffalo draft is the scene in which Charles Thompson, the secretary of the Continental Congress, arrives at Mt. Vernon (in a real phaeton, of all things) to tell Washington he is now the president. It is wholly superfluous.

In completed form there are three acts, each with three scenes. The cast ultimately remains rather large, but none of the speaking/singing roles, save Washington's, is particularly strenuous, and even Washington exists more as a "Figure...brooding over the action" (p. 325) than as an active character. Washington is conceived of as a baritone voice, Martha as a contralto, Alexander Hamilton as a tenor, General Gates as a basso, and Mrs. Arnold as a soprano. There is actually a chorus, first designated as an "Invisible Chorus" (Act III, scene 2), then in the final scene of the play (Act III, scene 3) as the Chorus, " in full evening dress, black and white, with a full light on it" (p. 358).

The Character of Washington

It is clear from the beginning of the play that Williams admired Washington—indeed, this is apparent from his other writings on the man as well. But, as I suggested in my discussion of *Under the Stars*, the admiration was more for Washington as troubled public servant than for the man as legend. Williams conjectures in the opera that it was out of loss and occasionally shattering reversals that Washington grew to his undoubted but peculiar greatness: "The wealthiest man in the colonies, the most successful, most important and the most richly deserving, Washington had been all his life used to defeat—so that it never surprised him and out of it he built his genius" (Introduction, p. 319). And it was this instinctual grittiness, Williams discovered after months of reading about and reflecting on the man, that eventually won the people over. Forced to make certain unpopular decisions as President,

> In neither case did Washington swerve one iota from what he thought right, writing, "These are unpleasant things, but they must be met with firmness." Eventually the people always came back to their leader, and Jefferson sighed over the fact that "such is the popularity of the President that the people will support him in whatever he will do or will not do, without appealing to their own reason or to anything but their feelings toward him."
>
> (p. 318)

Thus the first picture of Washington in Act I, scene 1 is of a man who is sleepless, at war with himself, pursued by his conscience, haunted by both "the evil dreams of seven years" (p. 322) and the restive soldiers at Valley Forge—and finally, most pointedly, deeply disturbed by the betrayal of Benedict Arnold. Tomorrow Washington is to go assume the new office of the presidency, but it is to him wholly a joyless task, and it is Martha, alarmed at her husband's depression, who must assuage his doubt. She sings, in stilted lines and with odd rhymes:

48   The First President

> Faint and wearily the wayworn traveller
> plods uncheerily, afraid to stop,
> wandering drearily and sad unraveller
> of the mazes toward the mountain's top.
> Doubting, fearing while his course he's steering,
> cottages appearing as he's nigh to drop.
> Oh, how briskly the wayworn traveller
> threads the mazes toward the mountain's top.
>
> (p. 324)

It is in the second scene of Act I that we first encounter what might be called the expressionism of the play, expecially in Williams' use of the psychology of dreams. That Williams was unsatisfied with simple imitation as a way of approaching truth through art had always been clear, even though he is, because of his directness, often called a realist; in spite of his admiration for Shakespeare he has written in his *Autobiography*:

> Certain "stories" from the past held us back. We had Apelles, the Athenian, painting cherries so lifelike in appearance that the birds pecked at them when they were exhibited — in the Athenian light, let it be added. We have, above all, for our own Occidental thought, Shakespeare's, "To hold the mirror up to nature"—as vicious a piece of bad advice as the budding artist ever gazed upon. It is tricky, thoughtless, wrong. It is NOT to hold the mirror up to nature that the artist performs his work. It is to make, out of the imagination, something not at all a copy of nature, but something quite different, a new thing, unlike anything else in nature, a thing advanced and apart from it.
>
> (p. 241)

In his attempts to get beyond the immediacy of the senses (and one can see the intensity of the struggle in such a laboratory work as *The Descent of Winter*), Williams had used the dream or vision throughout his career as artist, calling it a kind of complement to the imagination. We have already seen the centrality of the vision in *The Comic Life of Elia Brobitza*. Dreams will become most important, of course, in *A Dream of Love,* where Myra Thurber, through dreams, both recreates the past and suggests the play's theme.

Music—the core of the opera—is, as Williams remarks, one way to allow the writer greater freedom to present the sense of the facts rather than merely the facts: and in *The First President* the structuring of dreams through the extended flashbacks is intended to add to this objective, and therefore more penetrating, exploration of character and scene:

> Practically, reality, or the odor of it, is still further broken by laying the whole action in a world which is familiar and which yet permits liberties—the dream, the mind casting backward over things past. The world of recollection is real. The mind of Washington, which knows its own history, is seen doubling back upon itself at a moment

of overwhelming importance—the moment in later life, when Washington is going up for the presidency.

(Introduction, p. 305)

If this sounds more like a memory play than a projection of Freudian dream psychology, it is intentional. In Act II, scene 2, the beginning of Washington's dream, Washington himself appears hovering like a spirit over the Arnold residence:

> This Figure appears above the usual plane of action, as in a dream—an imaginary witness to the events that take place below. The feet remain in darkness so that the Figure seems floating, brooding over the action.
> The music mounts and becomes agitated. The Imaginary Figure assumes almost the function of a "chorus" in the older interpretation, but in a simple, direct manner—the single figure of a man. It is the personification of Washington's recollecting, feeling spirit as he recalls his bitter moment of his life.
>
> (p. 325)

This is obviously neither wish-fulfillment on Washington's part, nor repressed experience arising from his unconscious. And yet Williams' handling of the matter is still Freudian in essence, since experiences remembered in sleep through dreams, Freud says, are often more detailed and therefore more accurate than those merely recalled while the subject is awake. (This statement of course does not even take into account the symbolic meaning of the dream memory.) The dream is seen, the author hopes, as the more profound rendering of experience, bringing understanding to the dreamer (and in this case, to the reader or the audience).

And Washington in *The First President* is both symbolic observer and anguished participant. In scene 2 he sadly invokes Arnold, his old compatriot:

> Arnold, the day has come, the moment
> of betrayal. Once more the scenes rise
> bitterly before me. Arnold, if you
> whom I so deeply loved and trusted
> could betray us, whom can we trust now?
>
> (p. 325)

Washington watches, pained, as Arnold, discovering that he himself has been discovered, flees the country rather than face the accumulated charges or the accusations of his old comrade. Washington is now both a character in the action and commentator upon it, giving us the advantage of the double perspective:

> A countryman of mine! Your country
> Arnold, and my country. You
> or me. Which way? It cannot follow both.
>
> The skiff is waiting to conduct
> him down the river and he's gone. . . .
>
> And this *my* Arnold—he to whom, at
> Morristown, remembering Saratoga,
> what he did there like a soldier and
> a brave man—
> admiring that headlong valor, that
> tenacity, that gifted soldier's heart,
> with my own hands I gave a general's
> uniform. Here, I thought, is an example
> for the Army! And here's the same Arnold,
> sneaking away. Oh coward! Oh disgraced,
> unmanned! Not even daring to pause
> and say to a young wife, good-bye.
> (p. 326-27)

From this experience, now being relived and deepened by the dream, it is Washington's own charge for the remainder of the scene to comfort Mrs. Arnold, to relieve her fears for her husband's safety. The Imaginary Figure of Washington has by this time dissolved into the "real" George Washington; the light is up, but Washington, avoiding the unpleasant, enlists young Alexander Hamilton, a colonel, to report Arnold's fate.

And so the dream-history continues, focusing on the few key scenes Williams hopes will give the spectator critical insight into his suddenly ambiguous hero. But in point of fact we soon forget that the dream still is operating, since Williams does not effectively cut his action back from the dream itself. He merely holds it in place, and then the dream, after all of Williams' theorizing, becomes superfluous. For example, in Act II, scene 1 we have displayed before us the ramifications resulting from an event considered elsewhere by Williams—General Charles Lee's shameful retreat at Monmouth. Instead of allowing the spectator to see Washington from inside (as in *Under the Stars*), Williams here presents the circumstances from a far different vantage point. A group of Americans, including Lee, are gathered in an inn at Englishtown. It is the evening of the Monmouth battle. The action is, as a normal flashback, before us; there is no sense of it being anyone's dream. What emerges most tellingly here is the awesome wrath of Washington:

> *Jones:* What happened in the West Ravine this morning?
>
> *Grayson:* They say His Excellency cursed

and swore at him. Is that true,
Fitzgerald?

[Fitzgerald shakes his head, refusing to speak.]

Jones: You were there, Harrison. What
did he say?

Harrison: He was in a fury,
but I couldn't hear him.

Fitzgerald: It was his manner more than
what he said.

Grayson: But what *did* he say? Out with it.
That's not like you, Fitz—
let's hear it.

[Fitzgerald takes another drink before he speaks.]

Fitzgerald: It was just across the bridge.
Lee was coming in behind
the Jersey troops
when His Excellency, who was
busy, saw us and rode up
directly in our way. He was
in a rage. I never heard him
speak like that before.

(pp. 328-29)

If Washington's self-control had become, even by this time, almost legendary to those who followed his banner, the wild anger of the confrontation with Lee, never presented in full view by Williams, suggests depths of passion (and perhaps insecurity) that make the scene particularly revealing and important. Williams is therefore including it consciously, but objectifying it by keeping Washington on the outside. He writes of the meaning of the scene in his Introduction:

> Such an action as Lee had permitted himself once more passed beyond the boundaries of Washington's comprehension. And yet the fury of his own life, biting upon itself, is revealed in Washington's consuming wrath at Lee. But whether in proportion or out, the overpowering anger which caused Washington as a boy to kill a horse in attempting to break him asserted itself. Old Lord Fairfax had told him then that he must learn to control his temper if he would succeed in life. But this time it boiled over in spite of him. The dormant fury of a volcano cannot be self-contained forever.
>
> (pp. 310-11)

And yet one is justified in asking of this scene, as one is often tempted to ask of some of Williams' other work, why the confrontation is not shown dramatically. Would it not be proper to display Washington's rage openly, to let the reader see it fully uncovered in all of its ugliness? Williams himself responds to this point, again in the Introduction:

> It is impossible to show this moment as it occurred. First of all, the men were on horseback, at a crossroads in the middle of a battle. But that aside, the emphasis would be overpowering and out of all proportion to the balance of effects desired. It would throw the whole construction out of scale. So Washington's anger is reported in a narration of the incident by a young officer.
>
> (p. 311)

Another tentative answer would be that it is never the action so much as the thoughts about the action that are important in Williams' work; and these thoughts, as we have seen even in the earlier plays on Washington, are carefully and often dramatically presented—only this time they are not Washington's thoughts, but the reflections of others. Another response would be that Lee's short speech halfway into the scene makes it dramatically unnecessary for Williams to do more with the *real* encounter: Lee's incompetence is firmly established, and his vanity probably would have excused Washington's earlier temper. Lee speaks:

> Sit down, young men, it's too
> damned hot to stand on ceremony.
> Fitzgerald, have they seen my dog?
> Where the devil is that dog?...
>
> What? What do you say?
> But the temerity, folly and
> contempt of orders of General Wayne—
> separated eight miles from
> our main body—I said that it
> was madness to attack!
> We could not be successful
> *in a level country...*
>
> We were outnumbered—especially
> the cavalry, which was at twenty
> different times upon the point
> of turning our flanks.
> This naturally *obliged* us
> to retreat.
>
> To these maneuvers the success
> of the day was wholly due,
> 'Twas I gave him the only
> victory he ever had. Washington
> had scarcely more to do in it
> than strip the dead.
>
> [He drinks the water they have been holding for him.]

> Five pounds I offer
> to the one who finds my dog.
>
> (pp. 337-38)

The technique is a familiar one in the plays of Williams, and even in *Paterson* (the Corydon and Phyllis episodes in Book 4, for example): the characters are defined, or define themselves, by their discourse and soliloquies. The drama is mostly in the verse.

And yet the very next scene of *The First President* (Act II, scene 2), the ballet, contradicts just that very notion. It is all movement, all action, noiseless. Oddly, the silence is fitting, since it affects the subject like a dream—visually, without language. Here Williams is attempting to intensify our feelings about General Washington in a ritualistic way, isolating him further from ordinary human experience, even making out of him a kind of American folk giant. I have already remarked how deep was Washington's devotion to the soldiers in *The Battle of Brooklyn;* in this scene one sees how that feeling was reciprocated though its return was like that of son to father. Williams partly explains the purpose of the ballet:

> It is important to note that this is intended to be a "true" ballet, a serious and essential part of the opera, representing the lot of the common American soldier and his relation to Washington. The characteristic of the ballet is that it is *not,* in the old sense, a mere diversion, a distraction, but an important functional part intended to delineate a situation in order to clarify and dignify it, to endow it with its full emotional power.
>
> (p. 341)

The ballet was not choreographed, although Williams' directions for it are quite explicit. The setting is Valley Forge, with the obligatory snow, cold, and general misery. A Sentry is the main protagonist. He has fallen asleep, to be awakened by the Queen of the Snow Maidens (who have just been dancing) as Washington and his generals briskly appear on a tour of inspection. Will the Sentry be punished? No. The men are in fact delighted to meet the lovely maidens, and everyone soon pairs off and dances, Washington choosing the Queen as his partner. The implication is clear: if Washington is not a king—and he would have hated the idea of being a monarch—he is at least (to the popular mind) kingly. But a good monarch is also a gracious leader, and Washington, in a touching gesture, offers the hand of the Queen to the Sentry. The soldier is timid, and only accepts after his General urges him to it. There is a moment of genuine happiness. Williams writes:

> The man is shy, conscious of being in the presence of his superior officers. He can't dance. Washington urges the Queen to encourage him. She plays with him, teasing him.

> Everybody laughs good naturedly. Then the man rouses. He becomes excited. Awkwardly at first, then with more and more skill, he outdoes himself before his Commander-in-Chief. He is the real dancer and does all sorts of complicated movements to show his joy and appreciation.
>
> (p. 342)

Yet the third part of the ballet, aptly called the "Tragedy," darkens quickly. The fantasy of the folk game gives way to sudden catastrophe. When the Sentry spots some British soldiers stealthily approaching, he tries to warn the party but is not quite fast enough. The British surprise the soldiers, seize the maidens, and are about to kill Washington. The General is only saved from death by the brave sacrifice of the Sentry, who has positioned his body between Washington and the jutting bayonets.

The rest of the ballet finds the reinforced Americans quickly gaining control of the situation, averting a general rout, and then paying homage to their slain Sentry. It is a moving if not very plausible interlude. But what is most significant about the ballet is what it suggests of Williams' method of composition: if verse through music is often more suited to the protrayal of *character* than action, then the most overt *action* is itself developed through pantomime, or wordlessly. For in terms of action the ballet scene and later Washington's inauguration (Act III, scene 1) are the climactic moments of the opera, and yet the first is carried out without any speaking or singing whatsoever, and the second with only a few token speeches. Williams has written, as we have seen, of Washington's "taciturnity" (p. 304); music loosens that to a point, and mime and dance contribute a visual dimension which, in the end, projects (even with the flaws) a good deal of the subliminal tone of the entire work. Williams' conception of the theatre was an encompassing one, and involved a desire to use the resources of all of the arts on the stage. But if music was to be even more important than language in this opera (at least in theory), this ballet reminds us again that Williams was aware of the visual as well. Clinton Atkinson writes perceptively on this very point:

> It is in the knowledge that the theatre is a place where things are seen differently, where visual impact is as important as the aural, that Williams operates as a true playwright....
>
> That Williams knows the essence of theatre lies in a visual conception of story is shown in his use of the ballet in this play.... the whole becomes a moving evocation in visual terms of the winter at Valley Forge, its horror and heroic beauty. It is worth noting that the use of a story ballet came a number of years before Broadway acclaimed the original use of ballet in a musical comedy, *Oklahoma!*
>
> ...the ballet in *The First President* indicates how far ahead of contemporary theatrical thought Williams is capable of writing....[20]

Williams writes in the Introduction (p. 312) about Act III that "The catastrophe begins with the inauguration of the first President." But in fact it is initiated earlier than that, in the final scene of Act II (that is, scene 3), when Washington, harassed, bitter, threatened by inefficiency all around him and by envy from superiors, wants to resign as commander-in-chief. The question becomes one of duty, a central concern to Williams as dramatist (and as a writer of fiction). To whom is a man responsible, to himself or to those who demand his allegiance? The tragedy of Washington—and we see the beginning of it in this flashback, although we have already encountered it in earlier plays—is that he is unable, because of fate and self-sacrifice, to make a personally satisfactory choice. Washington has his resignation drawn up, ready in his pocket, but General Knox reminds him of his obligations:

> You were always to obey
> your superiors. You were commanded
> to lead this army. No one
> has commanded you to cease
> leading it.
>
> Whatever lack of courage,
> whatever knavery—if it exists—
> would leave us here to starve,
> we have no one else to turn to.
> Congress have put you here
> and you have sworn obedience
> to them. There is no choice.
> You must obey. You have sworn it
> to Congress and Congress alone
> can free you from that oath!

Washington weakly replies:

> There is something in that—
> I will think it over.
>
> (p. 346)

And he of course cannot say no. With all of his heart he wants to return to Mt. Vernon, but he submits, stays, and leads. Unwillingly, inextricably, he is thus lured into first one position of authority and then another, all in retrospect pointing to the presidency. To Williams, then, Washington qualifies as a true hero; that is, he is someone who, far from thirsting for power, has it thrust upon him, and is propelled into leadership not out of ambition but out of self-imposed responsibility. The presidency to Washington is sheer drudgery, finally an albatross, but he discharges his responsibilities as best he can, he carries on. It scarcely matters to Williams whether he performs well in the job—the heroism is in performing at all.

Thus Williams is concerned in his short libretto with showing only the end results of Washington's ascension to the presidency, not the detail of the job itself. He must accordingly leave out much. And yet the principal event he does select from Washington's years in office, the working out of the Genêt affair, is perfectly suited to Williams' purpose, which seems designed to show how lonely is the exercise of power, and how badly the world honors its great men. The Genêt affair had grown out of the efforts of the radical Girondists in France to topple all European monarchs; by 1793 the French were at war with England, as well as other continental nations. In such circumstances, must the United States honor its 1778 treaty with a now bellicose France, which at the time provided for American defense of French territory in case of attack on France herself? "Citizen" Edmond Genêt was dispatched to this country to see that the government of the United States assumed its obligations. Once here, however, he really undertook more dubious enterprises when Washington coolly issued his Neutrality Proclamation which said, in effect, that the United States would have nothing to do with the French Wars. But in *The First President* Williams gives us none of this background. He merely presents the apparition of Genêt exhorting the crowd before the executive offices in Philadelphia:

> France was your friend in time
> of need! England the common
> enemy! Citizens! Brothers!
> Lock fraternal arms in mine!
> Revolution bred you! Revolution
> made you strong! Revolution
> calls you to the side of France.
> Who is George Washington
> to block the people's will?
> A doddering old man, who served
> you once, it is true. But a tool
> of England now. Rise up, be free
> again and let all tyrants die
> beneath your trampling feet!
> (pp. 351-52)

The mob acts as a good mob should, foolishly and unreasonably, unable to make discriminatory judgments. Jefferson and Hamilton are respectively cast in the matrix of the old Good and Bad Angels, offering to Washington temperate and intemperate alternatives to the dilemma of what to do with the Frenchman. But Williams cheats us, in a way, by not showing Washington's resolution, and instead turns the President ahead to more general speculation:

> Gentlemen, let me plead with you
> for more forbearance and charity.

> Differences of speculative opinion
> within the Cabinet should not
> be pressed when we are encompassed
> on all sides by avowed enemies.
>
> [He pauses.]
>
> All our late accounts from Europe
> hold up the expectation of
> a general war. I ardently wish
> we may not be forced into it
> by the conduct of other nations.
> If we are permitted to improve,
> without interruptions, the great
> advantages which nature
> and circumstances have placed
> within our reach, many years will not
> revolve before we may be ranked
> among the most responsible and
> happiest people of this globe.
>   (pp. 354–55)

The final scene of the opera (Act III, scene 3) actually takes shape near the end of that which precedes it ("In a dreamlike transition, approaching darkness, Washington is left alone near the window," p. 356). The President, anticipating his return home, sings his only conventional aria of the opera, backed by the Invisible Chorus:

> All dangers changed
> to pleasantness,
> my happiest
> reward
>
> to live to know
> without alloy
> the sweet
> enjoyment
>
> of good laws
> among
> my fellow
> citizens—in all
>
> the dearest object
> of my heart
> this soil
> where I was born.
>   (p. 356)

The scene itself opens on a subdued note, with the chorus giving him a welcome home:

> Welcome wanderer home from a
> tempestuous ocean to that
> well-resorted tavern
> of your heart's desire, the
> vine and fig-tree under whose
> benignant shade that heart
> has longed to rest in peace.
> (p. 357)

And *The First President* ends on a curious crescendo with these directions:

> [Washington and Martha have disappeared from the scene. Then boldly the shadowy character of the scene ends abruptly and the Chorus—in full evening dress, black and white, with a full light upon it—fills the scene. The effect is to bring the whole, with a tremendous sweep, out of the past, up to today—the uncertain fruits of Washington's labors—in a music of blended voices.]
> (p. 358)

The First President as Art

How to judge *The First President* as a whole, as art? "The objective in writing is, to reveal," Williams would argue in 1947. "It is not to teach, not to advertise, not to sell, not even to communicate (for that needs two) but to reveal, which needs no other than the man himself." Then he adds significantly: "Reveal what? That which is inside the man" ("Revelation," from *Selected Essays*, p. 268). Williams accomplished nothing if he did not reveal, by objectifying, moments in the experience of the soul; and one cannot read a poem like "Asphodel, That Greeny Flower" (in *Pictures from Brueghel and Other Poems*) without respecting the purity of such revelation. Yet note the ambiguity of the statement: to reveal something which is *inside the man*. The question is, of course, *which* man—the subject, in this case George Washington, or his creator, William Carlos Williams?

Naturally the problem of autobiography is present in any creative work (and especially in literature), but it is particularly thorny in Williams' art. Thus he writes of Shakespeare in the Buffalo manuscript of "The Descent of Winter" (later published in part as "Notes in Diary Form" in Selected Essays, pp. 62–74):

> The drama is the identification of the character with the man himself (Shakespeare—and his sphere of knowledge, close to him). As it flares in himself the drama is completed and the back kick of it is the other characters, created as the reflex of the first, so the dramatist "lives," himself in his world.
> (p. 20)

Therefore his seriousness and his accuracies, because it was not his play but the drama of his life....
When he speaks of fools he is one; when of kings he is one, doubly so in misfortune. He is a woman, a pimp, a prince Hal—....
He is Hamlet plainer than a theory—and in everything.

(p. 36)

One remembers Virgil Thomson's question to Williams, quoted in full earlier in the chapter: "Who is this Washington? Who is he?" And the reply: "I am Washington" (*Autobiography*, p. 301).

Thus any evaluation must take into account at least two revelations, one of Washington and another of Williams himself. But a consideration of the former is severely handicapped by a lack of information on the music. "Music must be the answer" (p. 304)—the injunction is, as we have noted previously, Williams' most important clue to the character of Washington. "It would only be in circumjacence to the music which Williams conceives as *prior* to the opera that any final judgment could be made," cautions Koch of *The First President*,[21] and she is quite right. Without the benefit of a full-scale production it is impossible to judge fully the contribution of the music to the opera, except to emphasize once again how much Williams, in his Introduction, valued its potentialities. But it should be pointed out that there is a discrepancy between the Introduction and the text of the opera itself; the latter actually appears to call for *less* music than Williams had anticipated. There are very few arias (as we have noted, Washington has only one). The chorus sings only occasionally. As a matter of fact, unless some of the incidental speeches and dialogues were originally planned as recitatives, the work seems to contain fairly substantial nonmusical segments. (The same is also true of *Tituba's Children*.) In a way, then, one must ultimately return to the language itself, the verse, as an alternate means of identifying the conception of the character of George Washington. What does the poetry reveal about him?

Koch says that the libretto is "written in a stiff, archaic and deliberately anonymous blank verse," and adds: "The special genius of Washington's temper so clearly perceived in Williams' notes does not come through in the play."[22] Whitaker more or less agrees, rating the verse quite low and speaking of "the somewhat stilted verbal line."[23] The deficiencies— lack of tonal consistency is another—are clear and not arguable. And yet to one who has read the at times agonizingly slow dialogue of the early plays, the writing in *The First President* seems, within a rather narrow range, almost refreshing, like moving from Williams' doggedly rococo early poem "The Wanderer" (1914, reprinted in *The Collected Earlier Poems*) to any number of selections in *Adam & Eve & The City* (1936, also reprinted in *The Collected Earlier Poems*). It is important first to note that the poetic line is not blank verse. Rather, the metrics are simply a less sophisticated example of what Williams termed his "variable foot"—or, as John Malcolm Brinnin interprets it, "his name for a vague entity meant to delineate a unit of language that might carry into formal expression the tilt and accent of natural speech."[24] This is not, Williams insists, mere free verse. In the essay "Against the Weather" (1939, reprinted in *Selected Essays*), he writes: "Verse is measure, there is no free verse. *But* the measure must be one of more trust, greater liberty, than has been permitted in the past" (p. 212). Still, as Guimond points out,[25] during the late 1920's and 1930's Williams worked toward tightening his verse; he was continually speaking of the necessary *constraints* on the poetic line. In all of the earlier plays there is scarcely one speech which suggests depth of passion as well as Washington's one aria in *The First President* (see pages 101-2 in this Chapter), aborted as it may at first appear. The restraint is matched by a spare but gentle humor in several of the scenes. In Act II, scene 3, for example, Washington, addressing certain disgruntled officers of the army (who believe Congress is neglecting them), is able to bring the men to order and sense by first assuring them of the government's concern, and by then beginning to read a letter "corroborating testimony of/the good disposition/in Congress toward the Army." But as he sets out to read the letter he finds that he can no longer see well enough without his spectacles. He fumbles in his near-sightedness, the men wait, and finally, "In a pleasant and altogether natural voice" (p. 332) he remarks:

> You see, I have grown grey
> in your service.
> And now I find myself
> growing blind.
> (p. 332)

The joke is on himself; it is a remarkable event. Williams has created in one brief moment a human being. The men are won over.

In life Washington was not comfortable as a speaker (his Farewell Address was never delivered orally, merely printed in the newspapers), and Williams justly endows him with more courage than eloquence. Washington's strength is his toughness under fire, and in, for example, the Genêt scene this quality is displayed most vigorously. Washington, aggressively on the attack, challenges the slander of a writer whose verse has appeared in a newspaper:

> With what malignant industry
> And persevering falsehoods
> I am assailed, in order

> to weaken if not destroy
> the confidence of the public.
> The result, as it respects myself
> I care not—for I have consolation
> within no early efforts can
> deprive me of.
>   (p. 352-353)

But more important than this *real* ability to take the initiative, even more important than Washington's undoubted courage, Williams shows the man—the doubting hero—most poignantly in moments of inertia, pride, and procrastination. There is a petulance and self-righteousness about him, for example, in the same Genêt scene which graphically illustrates his volatile nature, the following speech comes hard upon the one quoted above:

> By God! I cannot stand
> this personal abuse that's heaped
> on me. And I defy any man on earth
> to produce a single act
> since I have been in the government
> that was not done out of the purest
> motives....
>   That Rascal Freneau
> sends me three papers every day,
> as if he thinks I will become
> distributor of his papers. I can see
> no more in it than
> an impudent design to insult me—
>   (p. 353)

That Washington was a decisive man is true, but that he was also a victim of his own insecurity about these decisions is made clear by Williams:

> Like a man going to the gallows
> I am willing to put it off
> as long as I can.
>   (p. 355)

The metaphor—and there are very few of them in this libretto—is particularly appropriate, since the idea of Washington imprisoned is implicit throughout *The First President*.

To show this in a way that is both thematically consistent and dramatically viable requires even more than inspired verse (which Williams here only occasionally musters). Thus we must look back briefly to Williams' use of the dream. His goal is, I think, a modest one: to make Washington's personality not likeable or even defensible, but merely *believable* in the historical context. We have seen before that the dream both helps us understand the subjective past of *The First President* and provides (perhaps) a way for the artist to approach the deeper reality of the character. To go one step further, the dream can be also allied with the concept of the *descent* in Williams, a psychological approach and ordering technique which became increasingly important in his work. Whitaker, noting the Jungian elements of such journeying toward discovery, writes perspicaciously of this process:

> It is a risky movement downward into an unknown realm of actuality and potentiality which has been excluded from the conscious synthesis of the immediate past, and which may now be experienced as flowing from the personal, racial or ultimate "source" or "ground" of one's being.[26]

Thus the plunge downward. The drop out of time and into the unknown is important in other ways to Williams, but it is particularly crucial to the plays—especially *Many Loves* and *A Dream of Love*. It is one of the ways the dream in Williams can be linked to the plays of Strindberg and to the dramatic precepts of Antonin Artaud, and certainly it is a crucial meeting ground in the relationship between Williams and the Becks (and the Living Theatre). "Time sequence is abolished and place sequence, as in a dream, can be put aside," he wrote in the Introduction (p. 307). So the scenes of *The First President* float before us, spontaneously, almost randomly, as Williams presents not the satisfied thoughts of a powerful man who is dozing, but the deepest fears of an insomniac trying to get through the troubled night. "Hours till morning, you must sleep again" (p. 322), Martha gently reprimands. Washington replies:

> Sleep? Sleep and let
> the evil dreams of seven years
> bring new doubt, new fears?
> (p. 322)

The dream is thus *real* life, according to Williams.

The American Inheritance

The other revelation of which I spoke has to do with Williams himself, and with his feelings about America. The latter is a complex business, as we will see in a later discussion of *Tituba's Children*. But in *that* play he dealt with the shattered remnants of the American dream, with a bitterness that went even beyond the disillusionment of the later Whitman; in *The First*

President Williams was yet trying to affix our place in the sun. For this opera is, despite its sharp criticism, a sympathetic appreciation (if not celebration) of the American inheritance as surely as is *In the American Grain*. But as Benjamin Spencer points out, the United States of *In the American Grain* is a more complex amalgamation than that of Williams' opera; it is, he writes, really three Americas, not one:

> ...a kind of Platonic idea of America historically expressed in the American dream; a covert America intuited by poets like Poe and Whitman; and finally an existential America, vulger and recalcitrant in its temporal pursuits.[27]

The First President gives readers more of the dream in America than the existentialism of it, and it conveys almost nothing of the hidden America about which Spencer speaks (except as Williams, himself a poet, intuits it). To be sure, the dream is hardly perfect. A New World for De Soto, it was no longer quite so golden for George Washington. There was something grasping and meanfisted about 18th-century Americans, haunted by their Puritan past, which at once robbed their lives of joy and was destructive. Williams had written in "The Virtue of History" (from *In the American Grain*):

> The acute delight Americans have always got from denying themselves joy and maiming others that they might be "saved" from some obliquity of moral carriage is only lately understood. One step further and it leads to persecutions. The world is made to eat, not leave, that the spirit may be full, not empty.
>
> (p. 205)

In that same essay, Williams, in a moving tribute to the calumniated Aaron Burr, writes that Burr knew "what a democracy must liberate.... Men intact—with all of their senses waking" (p. 206). Instead the American democracy delimited, closed off, blocked—and Washington, scarcely aware of how these pressures worked within him, retired "disheartened to his farm to breath the air" (p. 204).

Such impecuniosity of spirit and narrowness of vision are indeed part of the American grain. Williams—Unitarian, Democrat, Liberal—contended with it all of his life, in all of its forms, but learned to plan against it, live around it. One thus reads in the *Autobiography* (in the foreword): "Once, in great excitement, we took the train for Philadelphia late in the day to be present at a performance of *Lysistrata* before it could be censored." It was almost as if he expected such action from American officials; and yet he could not really predict the ideological violence that would arise in part from similar behavior in the tragedy of the early 1950's and Senator Joseph McCarthy. For *that,* though, there would be *Tituba's Children*.

In *The First President* the American landscape is still bathed in soft light. It is mostly appealing, and so are its people. If the common folk and soldiers of Englishtown are abrasive and insensitive, unable to discern Washington's strengths for what they are (Act II, scene 1), they acquit themselves much better in the ballet. "The common man warmly reciprocated Washington's devotion to him with a love equally as strong," Williams remarks in the Introduction (p. 311). The crowd is duped by Genêt, but Washington reestablishes in them proper sense through his authority, and wins the people back. Washington believes there is a solidity about the country, and we are led to concur. Taking the oath of office, he is moved by the sweep of it all, not because the new country was without blemish but because it offered hope, a future. America was, Williams wrote, "a country he pasted together—a good deal out of shoddy—to represent the thing we still labor to perfect" (p. 303).

That Williams felt Americans did not succeed and have much work left is at the core of his writings about his country. In his short essay on Lincoln from *In the American Grain* he speaks of "the brutalizing desolation of life in America up to that time; yet perversely flowering" (p. 234). And of course there are those peculiar American grotesques like the raper from Passenack and sad Elsie, broken by circumstances and loss, littering the countryside like abandoned scrap. But the future, of course, was still in the people, the heroes of the country like Washington, Jefferson and Lincoln, and those others—the Indians, the old women, the children. All is not despair. If in *Paterson* Williams could write—

> But Spring shall come and flowers will bloom
> And man must chatter of his doom....

he could also say, only a few pages later, with faith, that

> Clearly, it is the new, uninterpreted, that
> remoulds the old, pouring down.[28]

In a strict sense *The First President* is less autobiographical than any of Williams' other principal works for the theatre save *Tituba's Children*. By analogy, of course, there is something to the statement that Williams is Washington: there is a sense in Williams' letters and the *Autobiography* of the kind of reserve which he ascribes to Washington as something "deep within himself...which refuses to be liberated" (p. 310). But this is of token importance to *The First President*. What instead is revealed here about Williams is the nature of his art. One would today probably greet a play about George Washington with much the same dubiety as Virgil Thomson did years earlier. Thus the question: is Washington of sufficient interest? I think that Williams does in fact make him interesting, given the special limitations of the short opera form he has chosen, by discovering himself what is most durably interesting about the man. Washington is a formidable hero torn by uncertainty, stumbling at length through a world that guarantees nothing for even its most remarkable inhabitants.

So Williams convinces us that there is life in his George Washington. But such an assurance only makes one more aware of the opera's most serious shortcoming: Washington, alive as he is, seems to move in a vacuum, in a world that is only vaguely palpable and scarcely real. Now this unreality is partly due to the functioning of the dream—circumstances are purposely shadowy. But what makes the opera much less satisfying is that there is not one secondary character worth caring about, no one to act the real antagonist. The forces at work against Washington, like the character of Genêt, are presented briefly and superficially. Thus in his attempt to focus on Washington, Williams slights the surrounding figures, which in turn makes us feel less concern for the President himself. Hamilton and Jefferson move as puppets. Even Martha Washington, despite a pleasing aria now and again, has almost nothing to do. What this says about the opera has been also true of most of the earlier plays: Williams has not learned to fill in the background, to create a world with depth or range, to extend horizons. Consequently, while readers may finally believe in Washington and sympathize with him to a point, he fades from memory quickly because we are given no one to whom he can be related. It is thus astonishing to turn to Williams' next play, *Many Loves,* and see how much he had learned about managing all the elements in proper dramatic proportion. *The First President* is a provocative libretto with a plausible central character at its core, but Williams as playwright would do much better in the time to come.

3

Many Loves

Genesis of the Play

Many Loves (titled *Trial Horse No. 1* in 1942, revised as simply *Many Loves* in 1959)[1] is Williams' most ambitious play. Its complexity lends itself to various critical approaches. For one, the work is, along with *A Dream of Love,* Williams' most exhaustive analysis of both the pain and promise of love, in a variety of forms. "The theme of each 'playlet,' and of the counterplay, is love—of a sort," he had written in the synopsis (p. 3). Domestic, heterosexual, homosexual, adulterous, naîve, comic, tragic—all the possibilities are here. Thus, of course, the title *Many Loves*. For another, it is as perceptive a consideration of the potentials of language, and especially of verse in dramatic form, as Williams ever wrote. "Of course my chief interest as always where the theatre is concerned is the language, verse first of all if it can be swung," he had told Vivienne Koch.[2] Third, *Many Loves* reveals more about Williams' understanding of and attitude toward the theatre than any of his other plays, and allows him to display his somewhat radical (for the time in America, at least) innovations in dramaturgy. C. J. Atkinson writes: "It is possible to look at *Many Loves* as Williams' theatrical manifesto; in it he acknowledges the lure of the avant-garde in the traditional theatrical appearance, he plays with form, he creates a poetic diction for his characters, and in the triangle situation he resolves his final attitude toward the theatre."[3] Finally, the play is on the one hand a serious existential exploration of the futility and frailty of modern human experience; and on the other it presents this experience as farce, as comedy. (Williams had titled the play in a Buffalo manuscript *The Comedy of Love*.) Both aspects are nicely balanced throughout.

Many Loves consists of three acts, or as Williams writes, "three completely unrelated sequences, written in prose—one forming the substance of each act—and a counter-plot, in modern verse, which binds them together" (p. 3). Actually, the prose sequences are unrelated only in plot, for

68   *Many Loves*

as the poet/playwright Hubert (who has ostensibly written the three sequences) insists in the body of the counterplot (or framing action), *Many Loves* presents

> Three short sketches on
> a general theme, of which each is a facet
> casting its own aspect of the light.
> (p. 11)

The various dimensions of love (and of its absence) provide a many-sided perspective on sexual passion. These sequences, which were specifically written for the Little Theatre of Rutherford *before* the counterplot, can be quickly summarized by quoting Williams in his synopsis:

> In the first sequence, a young man loves an older, married woman. In the second, a young man and a young woman of high school age—comparable to the lovers of Romance—are assailed by the girl's father. In the third of these prose playlets, an older man and a younger woman engage in mild intrigue.
> (p. 3)

Finally, there is the Pirandello-like rehearsal action, written some time later, which frames all of this:

> In the counter-play, the love is between two men, an elder and another, young one. Here the dramatic action hinges on the necessity for the younger, who is the author of the three short pieces, to get the older man, his presumptive backer, to finance the production of his play—but without concessions. For the poet-playwright is in love with and about to marry his leading lady, a fact which he tries to keep secret from his enamored backer. The discovery of this love by the backer supplies the climax and catastrophe of the play.
> (p. 3)

The genesis of *Many Loves* arose from Williams' association with Clayton and Kathleen Hoagland and the Little Theatre of Rutherford (or the Rutherford Little Theatre). Williams recalled for J. C. Thirlwall (in 1961):

> *Trial Horse No. 1,* or *Many Loves,* was taken on as a project for the Little Theatre of Rutherford twenty years ago as a group of three one-act plays. They were too difficult to perform. At this time, Noel Coward had a group of three one-act plays which he was producing on Broadway with considerable success. I saw them and it gave me an idea. Why not take my own three plays and combine them under one title? This I got to work on at once and completed the play *Trial Horse No. 1.*
> (p. 431)

In *I Wanted to Write a Poem* Williams had told Edith Heal:

> The plays were too stiff for Rutherford, not that they were sexy or too modern, just hard to produce. They didn't want to play any of them and didn't so I was left with three plays on my hands and what to do? I had been to the theatre to see Noel Coward's *Tonight at 8:30* — I thought it was a wonderful idea. I took my own three plays and tried to link them, found a situation I thought took care of all three. The program began with two men on the stage talking about putting on a program of plays. One was the angel of the play, in love with the producer. The other, the producer, was in love with his leading lady, kept secret so the angel wouldn't find out. The plays themselves were unrelated, all taken from my experiences in Rutherford with people I had seen or known. The play was set as a dress rehearsal — that was why the angel was allowed to be present. The script was straight theatre prose, not poetic drama. In the end the angel — or the fairy — turns generous and lets the producer have his leading lady. I still think it's a producible play...small theatre groups have tried it and it seems to work.
> (p. 69-70)

The Little Theatre had been extraordinarily active in the years just prior to World War II, performing regularly at quarters in a former motion picture theatre on Ames Avenue and occasionally in the local high school auditorium. Williams was actually never an official member of the group, nor did he ever act in any of its productions, but he did give occasional poetry readings at monthly workshop sessions. In May of 1939, Kathleen Hoagland, by then a good friend of Williams, staged a one-act dramatized version of his short story about marital unhappiness, "To Fall Asleep" (from the collection *Life Along the Passaic River,* 1938). It was retitled "Mallows in the Moonlight." In his *Autobiography* (p. 305) Williams implies that the nature of the play offended some of those who attended, and as a result lost the theatre "the support of some influential but conservative subscribers." But Hoagland writes:

> Bill Williams was enthusiastic; his wife and her sister Charlotte Earle attended. We had a crowded house. When the audience called out, at the curtain, "Author, author!" Bill Williams rose and declared that it was Kitty Hoagland's play, from his story — *she* was the author — and called on me to stand.

She added: "Bill Williams thought the RLT was doing a fine job in trying to give the avant garde some recognition in a community that was a bulwark of conventionality and tradition."

In the meantime, Hoagland had suggested to Williams that he himself write something for the Little Theatre. For it

> was, after all, endeavoring to produce original plays as often as good ones appeared. I even suggested a theme to him, from a story he had told me about the hermaphrodite rabbit. Later this was incorporated, from his first draft, in the final version of "Many Loves."[5]

This short play, the first of the three which was eventually placed in *Many Loves,* became in that play the second scene in Act I, the "Serafina" sequence. By 1940, Mrs. Hoagland continues, "he worked out a play for two particular actors in the RLT whom he knew well could do the parts, about a woman ironing, and gulping wine, while talking to the man.... an episode later in 'Many Loves.'" (This scene turned up as "Talk," Act III, scene 1.) The third, called "The Funnies" (Act II, scene 2), was written shortly after. Mrs. Hoagland, who had herself continued to write plays for the Little Theatre, hoped to put Williams' works into production, but the war, a resulting loss of manpower, and a fire which wiped out the theatre on Ames Avenue all led to the dissolution of the organization before anything could be accomplished. The lack of a production may have been just as well, for Williams had come to believe that the plays were too difficult for the Rutherford performers, all of whom were amateurs. He told Koch later that he realized "it was impossible for me to write for any local group of this sort for the moment I became serious it got wholly beyond the actors...."[6]

In any event, Williams had the three one-act plays at home in manuscript. He had worked hard at them, and wanted to see something come of it. But how, and in what form? It was Noel Coward, of all people (as we have observed from *I Wanted to Write a Poem*), who unknowingly helped him make up his mind. Coward's play *Tonight at 8:30* had opened in New York at the National Theatre on November 24, 1936, and had run for 118 performances into 1937. Coward himself was a member of the cast, with Gertrude Lawrence and Alan Webb. Williams attended (he does not say when) and was, as he reports, enchanted. The play consists in book form[7] of three groups of three short plays each. In production on any given evening only one of the groups would be presented; apparently the plays were also interchangeable from group to group. The plays were all comedies and farces, all self-contained, almost all about men and women who were in love happily or unhappily. But other than that, the plays were not at all related. The beauty of this for Williams, remembering *Tonight at 8:30* some five years later, was that since he initially felt his one-acts were unrelated, why could he not simply put on a production of "Serafina," "The Funnies," and "Talk" in the same manner? It would be a straightforward evening of three one-act plays. And yet, mulling over the possibility, and going through the plays carefully, Williams finally decided on something even more satisfactory, and certainly more imaginative. The one-act plays, as Williams discovered and as Hubert says, *did* indeed share something in common, were reflections of each other. Koch writes: "Once Williams perceived that they had a related theme, the depiction of various kinds of love, he appears to have constructed the verse play which, in the final version of

Trial Horse No. 1 (published by New Directions in 1942) runs through the three prose plays and welds them into a finely soldered unit."[8]

To begin the framing or rehearsal action, Williams started with a memory of another kind of love, a specific instance of homosexuality (or transvestitism) which had impressed him when he was an intern at the old French hospital years earlier. Thirlwall has recorded Williams' recollection:

> I had been a physician all my adult life. During these years I had encountered many cases of aberrant sex. One case in particular created for me the character of Hubert [does Williams really mean Peter?], which I wove into the play in the course of the development of the plot, making a dramatic contrast between him and the normal characters. It interested me to remember the incidents which had developed between my nurses and this flagrant deviant as he appeared among my patients in the old French Hospital on West 34th Street in New York. I had to invent a character to fill out the contours which interested me and make three acts of it. It was fun and excited me no end.
>
> (pp. 431-32)

Williams has, in the *Autobiography,* given a remarkably full picture of his encounter with this man and another as well, and it is a curious story:

> The old hospital...was one short block away from the excavation then being made for the new Pennsylvania Station. We had sandblast victims in the clinic every day. But one day they brought in, unconscious, a big lump of a man in dirty overalls. He'd been dumping broken stone from a wheelbarrow off the end of a trestle to the pile below when for some reason he'd fallen, barrow and all, onto the heap twenty feet down. When we saw him he was messed up generally, bleeding from the mouth and nose and, as I say, unconscious. I looked at him, smelled whisky and told the girls to undress him. I wasn't sure whether he had a fracture of the skull or was malingering. It isn't always easy to make a snap diagnosis in such a case.
>
> I went to sit in the chair at the chart desk but almost at once heard the girls cry out and come piling from beyond the screen.
>
> "What's up?"
>
> "Come see."
>
> I went and was not a little astonished at what they had discovered. The man was a big guy, a plump specimen in bloody clothes, but when they had begun to remove the outer clothing, they found he had on a woman's silk chemise with little ribbons at the nipples; that his chest and finally his legs were shaved; that he wore woman's panties and long silk stockings.
>
> ...His wife was notified of the accident and when told of her man's unusual dress, said merely that he liked that sort of thing, that he was a good husband and that she had no complaint of him. She was genuinely broken up by his critical condition and went away weeping.
>
> The next morning—the man was still being unconscious with an obvious skull fracture—a magnificent open car of the 1907 breed, something of unusual luxuriousness, pulled up in front of the hospital and out of it stepped a figure which cannot be forgotten. He was over six feet tall, erect and so dressed that everyone about him looked like a lackey. He inquired for his friend, the injured workman. I saw and spoke to him

in the lobby. His hair, pure white, was worn in tight curls covering his really fine head. He was quiet but insistent. I reported the condition of his friend and told him how the cards lay.

"Have him moved to a private room. Give him the best there is." No, he didn't want to see him. "Send all the bills to me." He gave me his name—which was one of the most prominent in the state—and came every day thereafter to inquire about the man's condition. When the man died, the body was returned to the wife for a decent funeral.
(pp. 81-83)

But more went into the conception of the counterplot than this. In 1918 Ezra Pound had complained morosely that "it is hopeless sighing to imagine that there is going to be an interesting 'theatre' in our time."[9] Williams, who had learned much from Pound, fortunately did not acquire his friend's despair about the theatre. His reservations about modern drama were tempered, as Pound's was not, by an obvious recognition and understanding of such contemporary European playwrights as Pirandello, Yeats, Cocteau, and Lorca, and of such theorists as Artaud. (Williams' appreciation of O'Neill's work has already been noted.) His criticism of the insipid fare on and off Broadway during the 1940's and 1950's was harsh but selective (one remembers his praise of *Doctor Faustus Lights the Lights,* for example); and he did not blame the medium, but rather the timidity of current playwrights and audiences. Sometime around 1949 he wrote in explanation to Professor Norman Holmes Pearson, who had tried unsuccessfully to get *Many Loves* produced:

> I don't really believe a 'serious' play can be produced in the U.S. in our time; there is no audience for it. I don't think our world is interested in accuracies. It hurts too much to hear discussion of 'real' situations, and people just don't go to the theatre to have themselves shown up, that is, to be caused pain.
> (Thirlwall's *Notes,* p. 434)

In 1959 Williams told Julian and Judith Beck in a letter:

> The taste of the commercial theatre is not your dish. The technique of some of the plays I have seen is too childish, just a catchy plot involving a rapeable female   with no inkling of *theatre* is all it amounts to; no brains.[10]

Williams' critical position was thus positive, since he used it and would continue to use it as a stepping-off point to what he hoped would be a new American drama with an indigenously American idiom. Accordingly, it is really Williams himself, speaking through the persona of the character of the poet/playwright (who will be named Hubert) whose indictment of Broadway is an exhortation to forge ahead and open up the future. Williams, weighing the possibilities of his new play, had typically dashed out a score of tentative beginnings for the "framing" action. The as yet unnamed poet is, in one outline,[11] apparently speaking to the producer (the man whose name later will be Peter):

> The stage today is completely without imagination (of major sort)—dominated by box office wit and women's legs. Now, you are a producer of intelligence, I am the dramatist. Let me show you some of the possibilities. I have an idea. Did I say one? I have saved one as it rushed by me in the crowd, one of the more tameable so as to be able to domesticate it. Imagine three deadly acts. Not 4 for complacency mind you. That is taboo. Nothing serious, really, or too awfully true—just enough packed and wrapped to offend shrewdly—in the first act, so that if no one gets up and leaves, license is granted for abortions. Where is poetry? where is daring of spirit—where is—not mind! that would be too remote—but brains. Little pins of amusement to prick the pigs guts of laughter.... I propose a temple to exclude all noise. Don't you really think we should have a national theatre where a good company could produce stock—even if only ten interested patrons were present. Imagine the exquisite pleasure of such an occasional snowy night. Marvellous, like a half empty plane starting for the moon.

Then to the play itself, which is apparently to serve as a kind of trial horse:

> Take a theme! Something simple. The Comedy of Love—that old stalkin [sic] horse and let's see how we can refurbish it. I'll show you. Just an example of what might be done. We begin.

Thus Williams has, on two typewritten pages, formulated the vague outline for a play, with the poet and producer functioning as both commentator upon the three one-acts and characters in their own "fourth" plot:

> CHORUS: Two "men" (the poet and the producer) somewhat formal, in evening dress throughout (?) and definitely *verse*—if possible, poetry.
>
> 1st play They walk up the street, ignored by the "young man" and talk about the plays about to occur (etc etc) "No imagination, no understanding, especially no poetry. Without which there is no play. (etc etc) Let me show you what I mean.
>
> (after it has started and before the girl comes in) (?) Very briefly—if at all
>
> 2nd play They walk all over the stage as the characters on the porch just sit there, no [sic] immobile—even go in and out but not speaking as yet.
>
> This is a device I think of great possibilities. You see the word [sic] as a complex place, not the numbsculls kindergarten of ROMANCE and BATHOS—they (Shhh!)
>
> At this corner is a picnic table. Over here a desk. That is a sop to the feeble imagination of the audience—but babies will grow, I hope to wonderful proportions.
>
> And so, take this chair (near the front) and let's watch them a few minutes.

3rd play	They lean in at the door while it is going on. As the good Doc is kissed one of them say, Mymy!—then speak, coming forward at the end

> Yes the idea has possibilities
> But needs more wit and certainty
> Then if we consulted Kaufman
>
> Oh my God! (Curtain)

It was truly to be a revolutionary play, in revolutionary form, and the playwright (Williams/Hubert) was to be a kind of demonic force who would move the audience as if by magic, with a sweep not seen before on the American stage. Hubert's verse was to be new and fresh, an experiment. Indeed, there is a single typed sheet in the Yale folder which shows Williams to be closer technically and ideologically to the European dramatists of the period. Williams had written:[12]

> The audience is the play: the play is to be written looking from the stage, not at it, into the minds of the audience where it is really taking place. That is the thing to represent on the stage as it occurs.
> The playwright watching it there in its physiologic, wholly poetic jumps and stops and expectations—merely transcribing the scenes that take place there out of hand—beyond his doing.

Thus in *Many Loves* Hubert repeats, "The audience is the play" (p. 33). Such an announcement sounds new for its time, even radical, and one is reminded of what Julian Beck would say much later, in 1959: "If we want to revolutionize the theatre it is because we have lost faith in a modest mystical awareness we have of things that could happen in the theatre, things no one has yet imagined, things that could happen in the theatre and in life as well."[13] The goal of both Williams and the Becks was to break down walls, to bring the audience closer to the world of the drama, to destroy our expectations of illusion and reality, to blur the distinction between art and life, and above all to intensify the experience. It is, as a matter of fact, another kind of descent, promising the unexpected, a way to get at a deeper level of consciousness. In an unpublished fragment of "Writer's Prologue to a Play in Verse"[14] Williams warns those who would be the audience for such a theatre:

> We are not here, you understand
> but in the mind, that circumstance
> of which the speech is only poetry
> —it would be unnatural to speak
> otherwise. Or would you prefer
> not to enter? Perhaps so. Sorry
> to say there is a distorting mirror

> which, with your permission, must
> be broken at this place—we beg
> your tolerance if we break it—
> called, a stage. Ignore it, an accident
> an impertinence, clumsy and in fact
> lifeless. But look, we beg, try
> and look rather within yourselves.
> Yourselves!

And what is inside is, as he says in the same poem, "the undiscoverable/ language of yourself, which you avoid," a language which is,

>   if you will open
> your minds and let us tentatively dig
> the metal which is there for our
> construction....
>   to make what is not seen
> visible.

    It is clear by now, of course, that Williams' conception of a new drama in *Many Loves* was not really new, certainly not in Europe. If Williams was one of America's first avant-garde dramatists (to revive the cliche), on the continent the avant-garde was almost old hat. In post-Ibsen Europe—and even before in a play like Alfred Jarry's *Ubu roi* (1896)—many of the early steps had already been taken by such writers as Pirandello, Artaud, Cocteau, and others. To these Williams is directly indebted. Pirandello is a perfect example. There is no positive evidence that Williams knew Pirandello's work at first hand,[15] but it is entirely possible since, for example, *Six Characters in Search of An Author,* written in 1921-1922, had been presented in New York in 1922, at a time when it was Williams' habit, as Thirlwall reports, to go into the city for the theatre every Friday that could be spared.[16] It is perhaps too facile to ascribe the play-within-the-play structure in *Many Loves* solely to Pirandello—the device had been around at least as long as Beaumont and Fletcher's *The Knight of the Burning Pestle* (circa 1607-1608). But without the work of Pirandello, which had already broken down barriers, it is hard to imagine that *Many Loves* would be quite the same. Even the relationship of Hubert and Peter is in some ways similar to that between Pirandello's six characters and the theatre manager in *Six Characters in Search of An Author*. There is, moreover, a resemblance in philosophic attitude of Williams and Pirandello: for both artists life is flux, the personality is inevitably changing, and because fallen man ultimately lacks final control over his own actions and his own fate, human life is at once a tragedy and comedy. Finally, there is also a practical toughness about Pirandello which Williams would have respected. "In a world of suffering humanity," Thomas Bishop writes of the Italian dramatist, "he would seem to subscribe to whatever action relieves misery."[17]

Artaud, the French surrealist, is a different case, but no less important to the European theatre and finally, perhaps circuitously, to Williams and the Living Theatre. Williams knew Artaud's work (at least his poetry) and approved of it, citing him in *Paterson:*

> Salut à Antonin Artaud pour les
> lignes, très pures
> *(p. 164)*

A true revolutionary, Artaud turned away from old modes and orthodox perceptions, calling for a new theatre in *Le Théâtre et son double:*[18]

> The action of theatre, like that of the plague, is beneficial, for pushing men into seeing themselves as they are, it causes the mask to fall and reveals the lie, the moral inertia, baseness, and hypocrisy of our world....
>
> For the theatre as for culture, it remains a question of naming and directing shadows: and the theater, not confined to a fixed language and form, not only destroys false shadows but prepares the way for a new generation of shadows, around which assembles the true spectacle of life.
>
> To break through language in order to touch life is to create or recreate the theatre....

There were others, of course, who were sharing these ideas—Lorca (a favorite of Williams'), for one, in Spain. But as Jacques Guicharnaud writes, "while Artaud is not the only influence, he is the center of an increasingly generalized movement toward creating a theatre intended, more than ever, to shatter the spectator."[19] There were other common interests shared by Williams and Artaud: both were attracted to Ford's *'Tis Pity She's A Whore,* a play that does, if nothing else, "shatter the spectator"; both favored the use of music and dance in productions wherever possible (Artaud incorporated elements of both in his play *Les Cenci*). And both were interested in selected aspects of history—not so much the events of history as the men. Artaud had even drafted a play on Montezuma.

There is no hard evidence to show that Williams was inordinately interested in the work of another French dramatist, Jean Cocteau, even though Williams met Cocteau in 1924 in Paris and reports having seen his *Romeo and Juliet* (*Autobiography,* pp. 224-25) the same year. But that play left no impression on him. Kathleen Hoagland writes that Williams "was *most* enthusiastic" about Cocteau's film *Beauty and the Beast,* remarking especially on its fantasy and technique.[20] Once again Cocteau's influence on European drama was so pervasive that it would be difficult imagining Williams writing *Many Loves* without some sense of what Cocteau had done and was trying to do. The interests of both were in many ways close. Both were friends of Pound. One of the most versatile artists of the twentieth century, Cocteau wrote his first two works for the theatre as ballets, *Le Dieu bleu* and *Parade* (with music by Erik Satie and settings by Picasso). He wrote operas. He was a painter, interested in Cubism. Francis Fergusson points out how a play like *La Machine infernale* (1934) is in the new Pirandello style—"the stage as an art-medium like that of the painter or musician."[21] Julian Beck considered himself a disciple of Cocteau. To Cocteau, the theatre was, as it was for Williams and the Living Theatre, a temple where all the arts were worshipped.

Changes from *Trial Horse*

So Williams, with perhaps many of these notions in his head, with suddenly a new opportunity before him, was ready to finish putting *Many Loves* together, to make it into a whole. The job was initially completed in 1942, when the play *Trial Horse No. 1* was published in New Directions 7, and subtitled, "An Entertainment in Three Acts and Six Scenes." A revised acting version was readied for the Living Theatre production which opened in New York in January 1959.[22] There were slight revisions in that text for its inclusion as the lead play in *Many Loves and Other Plays* in 1961, but the essence of the play had remained intact from 1942 on.

The only major change in all of these versions was in Williams' handling of the opening of the play. In the 1942 version he starts abruptly, with Peter turning on Hubert:

> But what is your plan? What?
> You haven't given me your plan.
> What are you trying to do?

That speech does not appear until 11 pages into the action in the text (p. 14) in *Many Loves and Other Plays*. For that version and for the Living Theatre production, the Pirandello-like rehearsal action at the start had been much expanded, with the actual scripted dialogue taking over almost imperceptibly, and only after much shuffling about by technicians and actors. Certain speeches had been transposed in the framing action closer to the start of the play. What is true here is true throughout the rest of the play: most other changes in *Many Loves* from *Trial Horse No. 1* on—and they are slight—occur in the poetry of the counterplot. Once Williams was done with the three sequences for the Little Theatre, he was essentially satisfied with them all the way through. The only other difference between the 1942 and 1961 versions is in the number and length of the stage directions; there are many more, and in greater detail, in the latter version.

As usual the working drafts[23] are extraordinarily helpful to anyone interested in following the development of plot and character from their origins to the 1942 and 1961 publications. In "Talk," for example, the play written for possible performance by the two actors Williams knew in the Little Theatre, the dialogue between the vaguely dissatisfied housewife (called Ida in early drafts, Clara in published versions) and "Doc" is more brutally frank, the delineation of the needs of each character more direct, than in the final versions. In *Many Loves* Doc is somewhat mellowed, and clearly less antagonistic. But in early Buffalo drafts he is even cruelly blunt to the neurotic Ida/Clara. The following speech does not appear at all in the published text:

> I'm no psychiatrist but it doesn't take any supreme training or experience to tell that you're sick. Probably nothing in the world the matter with the child but a slight cold. You're the one, a schizophrenic if ever I saw one — walking around in some honest, distorted sort of world thinking God knows what.... A lazy good for nothing female. Can you either type a letter, sing, play the piano, simply, musically, naturally — or even cook a man a decent meal? I doubt it. You might succeed in ironing a few napkins once in a while between neglecting your child and a bridge game but could you do a day's washing? No.

The candor of dialogue in early versions reminds one that when Williams is ready for publication he sometimes acts as his own censor. (One remembers the vulgarisms of the prose passages in *The Descent of Winter,* not one of which is retained in the extrapolated "Notes in Diary Form" in *Selected Essays,* pp. 63-74.) In the Buffalo "Talk," Clara and Doc are speaking of women:

> Doc: ...practically any woman interests me.... I like them in good health and independently inclined.
>
> Ida: Sex, huh?
>
> Doc: Slightly more selective than that — but in the main, yes.

That same passage (the woman is now Clara) in *Many Loves and Other Plays* reads:

> Doc: Let me tell you some of my own little weaknesses. Women! They fascinate me. All kinds of women. I'm an absolute fool for them.
>
> Clara: Sex, huh?
>
> Doc: I admire them profoundly. What a marvelous job they do with the equipment they have.

(p. 80)

Williams (and certainly Hubert) works to give *Many Loves* itself, in the counterplay, the impression of being a workshop, an improvisation, a *trial horse*. Hubert says to Peter, who has just arrived at rehearsal: "You've come into the garage—the hood's up...these are the odd parts lying around, the mechanics, the grease" (p. 7). He is a new playwright, and

> lacking experience, as you know,
> I have adopted this method
> of a trial-horse to approach it.
> (p. 92)

Actually, as we will see, the trial or experimental emphasis in *Many Loves* is one of the engrossing things about the play, and one of the reasons that its production at the Living Theatre was called avant-garde. And yet in microfilm #24 there is even more of this insistence on the process of invention, the experiment, the making of the drama as a creative learning experience for all concerned. "I would like to demonstrate a dramatic/mode capable of present day/development," Hubert says. And what will be developed from the laboratory, he hopes, is a refreshing language adapted for the modern stage. Hubert says:

> I'd like to be
> a dramatist. I've no interest in
> thinking or prose, that hides us
> as a man might wear shorts. I
> despise prose almost as much as I
> do poetic language. I want coarse
> daily language lifted up by the stage
> to movement, as if you were looking
> up at the underparts of a mechanism....
>
> So I have arranged the present
> entertainment with this in view—to
> learn something of the mechanism of
> the thing; words to sound, to perform
> independently of the insignificant
> flesh and blood. I want the actors
> to speak the words. And let the words
> drag them about—the mere humanity of
> it is a secondary matter—

We are not to be fooled by such a task—it will be enormously difficult, as Williams had anticipated in his struggles years earlier in *The Descent of Winter* (the following passage is reprinted in "Notes in Diary Form" in *Selected Essays,* p. 71):

> The difficulty of modern styles is made by the fragmentary stupidity of modern life, its lacunae of sense, loups [sic], perversions of instinct, blankets, amputations, fulsomeness of instruction and multiplications of inanity. To avoid this, accuracy is driven to a hard road. To be plain is to be subverted since every word is tricked out of meaning, hanging with as many cheap traps as an altar.

In the back of his mind Hubert has a plan for another play, a truly superior work with wonderful poetry that was expected to grow out of the present experiment. In theory, the labors of *Trial Horse No. 1* are an apprenticeship, preliminary to what is ahead. Thus Hubert says to Peter, trying to stave off his impatience: "All this is introductory, a prelude." But in #24, especially, Peter, who has put up the money for what he thought would be a "conventional" play, does not care what will come later. He only sees chaos and a box office disaster now: "This is all shoddy/every bit of it."

Accuracies

Turning to the play as it appears in *Many Loves and Other Plays,* one is again struck by the almost bewildering possibilities of approach to and definition of it. Julian Beck has said,[24] "i once asked him [Williams] what many loves was about and he answered 'accuracies.' it wiped me out, that answer. it has had its affect [sic] on my whole life, in and out of art." Vivienne Koch writes of *Trial Horse No. 1* that "it is a play, a comment on what a play is, and a demonstration of how a play gets written."[25]

On the other hand, Raymond A. Kennedy says, with tongue only halfway in cheek, that *"Many Loves* probably is not a play at all." He adds:

> A play has a single motivating principle which should be advanced relentlessly by even the most remote incident, word, or gesture. Few plays succeed in this; but a play does have to sustain and ultimately satisfy my curiosity about that one idea. No one is so avant-garde that he can overlook that.[26]

But Kennedy misses the point completely. *Many Loves* has not one "motivating principle" but two or three, and these several do move the play—but, except in the narrative of the counterplay, not forward "relentlessly" but rather cyclically, backward and forward, like a meandering tide, covering some of the same territory over and over again, but with the changed perspective of a new season.

The first major theme of *Many Loves,* as Williams has already said, is love, which, as Thomas R. Whitaker comments, serves Williams perfectly "to lift our attention from linear plot to a multifaceted situation."[27] The playwright takes us everywhere while in effect going nowhere. Hence we have three playlets, in prose, with three sets of characters and three quite different situations—but all directing our attention toward love, or more to the point, the consequences of a lack of love.

In some ways the ambiguities (and perplexities) Williams saw in love grew from his own contradictory experience of it.[28] Fifteen years after his marriage to Florence Herman he had tried to arrive at a definition of the word from their own special relationship:

> What "love" is I don't know if it is not the response of our deepest natures to one another. I went direct to you through my own personal hell of doubt and hesitation and I have never changed the millionth part of one inch since that first decision.
>
> You know and I do not deny my irrational—and I still believe necessary faults—but the result of whatever I have done to lessen myself in your eyes has merely brought me back to you the stronger. All my life I have grown from that moment when I asked you to marry me, always into a clearer and more satisfying realization of what really took place at that time. I love you and you love me and so only at the end will I know what love is—and that is my answer to the world and to you.
>
> (*Selected Letters*, p. 81)

Yet in *Many Loves* one scarcely senses this kind of commitment—that is, the response of the lover's deepest nature to that of the beloved. The epigraph to the play, "Let me not to the marriage of true minds/admit impediments" (Shakespeare's sonnet 116), is almost wholly ironic. For the play is, in truth, a pessimistic prediction about the possibility of love to work out its grace in the lives of those who live according to its demands. "In all three playlets," writes James Guimond, "love is defeated...."[29] "Three sketches of useless love," the Italian newspaper *Avanti* said after its reviewer watched the Living Theatre production in Rome in June of 1961.[30] Such judgments are not very far off the mark, although Williams is of course showing the inadequacy of the many loves for important redemptive reasons. In the first of the three sequences, "Serafina" (Act I, scene 2), the direction is established quickly. The subject is the brutalization of love. The setting is "the poorer section of an Eastern mill town" (p. 17), and there are four central characters: Serafina, her husband, her boyfriend, and Laddie, an ingenuous admirer. Serafina is, apparently, the neighborhood tramp, noisome, possibly pregnant (not by her husband), who drinks away the afternoons in a local bar. The husband is a nondescript factory worker. The boyfriend is a no-account who is leaving for Georgia and the army the very next day. But he is involved with Serafina in the central episode (Detail 2) which takes place in the bar. We discover that he had arranged to have a pregnancy test for Serafina, but that the test failed because—and here we remember Kathleen Hoagland's story—"the Goddamned rabbit was a queer" (p. 20). The boyfriend, who probably is the father, continues:

> He [the doctor] says he thought it was a she when he shot the stuff into its ear, but when he come to open it up and see if you was pregnant it turned out to be her boyfriend — that hadn't come of age yet.
>
> (p. 21)

But there is no consternation, no alarm: it is treated as a joke by both. And the boyfriend merely picks up and leaves. "So long, kid. You'll be all right.... I'll send you a post card" (p. 23).

Detail 3, the final episode of this sequence, is the best of the lot, for here we are introduced more fully to Laddie, "a blond young man of Polish or Russian descent" (p. 17), who has been secretly in love with Serafina. The situation has precedent in American literature, and is like something out of Thomas Wolfe. Laddie, tongue-tied, not very healthy, turned down by the draft, is a sensitive Eugene Gant type who confesses to Serafina that he wants to raise "a couple of hundred bucks" to become a writer. She is slightly incredulous:

> Laddie, honest — are you? That's marvelous. Write books — you mean like Hemingway and all that?
>
> (p. 27)

But his other admission — that "I'm so damn sick crazy in love with you" (p. 27) — never really leads to anything. Serafina feigns an interest, but Laddie pulls back, and the sequence draws to a fitful close. Serafina returns to her apartment ("Good-bye, sucker," she says to Laddie), and then, in a rather intrusively symbolic finale, "Someone throws a bunch of stale flowers down at Laddie's feet" (p. 29). But Hubert moves to the stage — one must remember that all of this has been welded into the trial horse — and tells the cast that "the business of the flowers" will be cut. Peter grumbles about the whole: "I can't see the point. Is it related to something I should know about?" (p. 30).

The second major sequence, "The Funnies," seems almost to have begun in Williams' mind as an improvisation. In the Buffalo manuscript there is a preface to a fragment of "Play" which is an early version of this same work:

> The players are doing no more than to try to interpret what the audience is thinking. This makes it difficult for them since they have to be alert to discover what is in the mind of the audience and present it rapidly.
>
> They, the players, have set the scene, that at least is the first act. Then they give the audience a key to begin on. From then on the audience has to be watched....

This approach, a vague descendant of the old *commedia dell' arte,* was not maintained, and Williams soon fleshed out the skeleton episodes in some detail. Hubert explains the scene to Peter:

> A picture
> I saw one day last summer
> driving up through Jersey. A
> Sunday afternoon. Just some farm
> people sitting on a porch. It
> seemed full of malignant tension and
> I conceived the play. I had already
> passed and had to stop and back up
> a distance to make my notes on it.
> Something suggestive of the Greek theater.
> (p. 35)

The title of the play comes from the fact that, as the scene opens, George, the disagreeable patriarch of the household, is monopolizing the funny pages of the paper. There is boredom, hate, envy, and indeed "malignant tension" on all sides; the only thing lacking, predictably, is love. George, about 70 years old, is the owner of the farm which consists of the house, a barn, a garage, and 20 acres. His lame nephew Pete, who manages the place, "is a rather lean, tough-looking individual with a sour face"; he desperately wants to sell the farm, which to him is worse than hell, and move away. He takes sadistic delight in taunting George by occasionally displaying a "For Sale" sign and threatening to put it up. "You ain't a gonna put no sign on this house," George cries. Pete mutters that "for two cents I'd knock your teeth down your dirty throat".

But Pete is spiteful not only to George. It is to his teenage daughter Ann that he behaves most execrably, wildly accusing her of promiscuities which have no basis in fact (he addresses her as "that slut," or "the little bitch"), separating her from Horace, her boyfriend, and in general acting viciously. In the Buffalo draft there is a suggestion that his loathing of Ann comes from the fact that he doubts whether the girl is really his daughter— which might also explain his abuse of Mattie, his wife—but this inference is not present in *Many Loves* as it now stands. What *is* suggested, however, is that Pete is incestuously jealous of his daughter, sexually attracted to her in a way that arouses in him an even greater hatred, not only toward Ann, but also toward those who would take her away. (The theme has had uncommon attention in American drama, with Arthur Miller's *A View from the Bridge* the most obvious example of the incest play.) Pete's insults to Ann are in the main sexual:

> You got legs—walk. Yeah, you got legs, plenty!
> (p. 42)

> I'll warm you good one of these days, young lady, big as you are. I'll take 'em down for you in a way you ain't used to.
> (p. 44)

> Tell me what you were doing in that car last night. Or do you want me to tell you? Go ahead—how far did he get with you?
>
> (p. 59)

Suspicion, jealousy, possessiveness, greed—all play a part in Pete's psychosis. As a matter of fact, these feelings are accentuated even more in microfilm #24, with Peter (the producer) actually identifying the central problem, something he does not do in the published *Many Loves:*

> You have
> a lame father, ignorant as
> you are yourself in your duller
> moments—in love with his own
> daughter. A timid sort of incest
> that he takes out in bluster.

Driven apart from Horace, misunderstood by the rest of the household, nearly defenseless, Ann is easy prey to Miss Agnes Breen, "a young business woman" who intends to buy "a small place in the country for my personal use" (p. 51). When Miss Breen appears in Detail 5, Peter (the producer) calls from just off the stage, "She looks like a man!" (p. 50), and as the situation develops, and it becomes clear that Miss Breen will buy the farm, it also becomes evident that she has designs on Ann and that she is, as Peter says in #24, "an undeveloped Lesbian." (In the Living Theatre production she was actually played as a rather aggressive lesbian.) For her part Ann imagines in Miss Breen a way out of her horrible situation. She wonders to Aunt Kate:

> What kind of a woman do you suppose she is, Kate? Do you suppose it's someone like Helen Hayes—some woman like that? Because if she is, Kate, you never can tell what might happen. Do you think it is, Kate? Oh, that would be marvelous.
>
> (pp. 63-64)
>
> Oh, Kate, do you think I could ever get to be like that, so lovely, so thoughtful—and so clever. She must be clever. I feel different just to be near her.
>
> (p. 66)

At the end of the play, old George—thought to be sleeping in a chair on the porch—is discovered to be dead. All is suddenly thrown into confusion, but Miss Breen, "taking Ann in her arms," says to her: "It's all right, darling. I'll take care of you" (p. 68). This is, perhaps, love, but scarcely the kind which has Williams' approval.[31]

There is no banter between Hubert and Peter to stand as an interlude before "Talk," the final prose sequence. Harold Clurman was right when, reviewing the Living Theatre production, he said it was the most interesting of the three playlets.³² It is most interesting because we are given a much closer documentation of the frustrations of the people: Clara, the bored wife, and Doc, a fiftyish physician who is helplessly infatuated with women: "Women! With their small heads and big lustrous eyes. All my life I have never been able to escape them" (p. 84). The scene is vintage Williams as a dramatist. There is no real plot, just conversation, at times repetitious, with not very much happening, but with a whole world revealed in it, like the very best of the short stories. "Oh, let me talk!" Clara cries. "I'm just getting to what I wanted to say" (p. 78). "Talk, talk, talk! Everything runs out finally into talk," grumbles Doc (p. 85). But that is precisely the point — that men and women are closest to exposing and expressing themselves in what they say and how they speak. Thus, of course, Williams' obvious concern with the language — Williams has raised the point before in *The First President* and he will raise it again.

The sharp dialogue in "Talk" is, in fact, carefully directed toward this end, that is, of incisive revelation. There is nothing remotely dramatic in the action except, at the end, with Clara throwing her arms around Doc, her small child comes in and screams, "Daddy!" (p. 86). Williams tells us that Clara is "aghast," but the surprise is not followed up and the scene ends. (One unfortunately is reminded of the conclusion of any episode from the current television soap operas, with much of significance hanging fire.) But the real drama in the scene has come earlier, dragged out in the unhappy contrapuntal exchanges between the two. Clara's complaints seem to be the usual ones of a housewife suffering from domestic malaise: the child is a nuisance (she is apparently ill, ostensibly the reason for the doctor being there in the first place), she is bored with the housework, sexually troubled, irritable — and, as a final requisite for *Many Loves,* unable to love. This last deprivation helps explain the other problems, and makes the situation much more serious. "I haven't got an ounce of mother love in my whole carcass," Clara complains. "What do you suppose is the matter with me?...I don't love children" (p. 76). She is divorced from her first husband because she did not want babies, and is no longer sleeping with her second (after having had a child). Her gropings toward love have been futile: "I thought I was in love with a swimming instructor" (p. 80). Finally she comes to the hard truth: "I don't think I'm capable of love" (p. 83).

For his part, Doc seems, like Dr. Daniel Thurber of *A Dream of Love,* to be a victim of self-love, sexually attracted to women but not willing to assume the obligations which follow.³³ Although Clara really dominates the scene as a talker, it is Doc himself who is most fascinating as a character. We are given little of his background; his marital state is uncertain, although one guesses that he is married. His most important revelation in the narrative, which is conveyed in the tones of a mock horror-comedy, is his remembered story of himself as "a kid," planning to seduce "a little girl of the neighborhood" (p. 83). He plotted the assault as elaborately as Tom Sawyer did the escape of Jim in *Huckleberry Finn*. Yet it was not to be ruthlessly carried out, with the brutish lust of a criminal, but tenderly, and Doc speaks as though the girl were to have been the recipient of special fruits of his loins:

> My plan was, of course, to try first to induce her to come willingly for after all I had no desire to harm the child but merely to enjoy her and to endow upon her those things I had so abundantly to give. But if she would not yield, I would carry her off, come what may.
>
> (p. 84)

Earlier (pp. 80–81), Doc has compared women to the *retiarii,* the netmen, in the gladiatorial competition in early Rome, doing battle with the *mirmillones,* the combatants with swords. "Oddly," he adds, "it never occurred to me before that the matador plays the part of a woman!" The metaphor is, of course, a violent and therefore apt one, but ambiguous as well. For Doc women are the hunted, the preyed upon; and yet the netmen, through cunning, often held the swordsmen to a standstill in the arenas (as Williams tells us), and clearly the matador ultimately has the advantage in a bull fight. The man may seduce and rape, but it is a dangerous game and if played *he* is assuredly the loser. Williams himself remembered from his experience as a young man: "I didn't want to indulge in sex so much that I lost my head."[34]

Thus far *Many Loves* has been really a chronicle of many inadequate loves, or, as it were, love on the skids. In the framing action—the counterplay or fourth scene, which runs concurrently with and around the rest— this premise continues, only with a greater urgency and complexity. Here the *kind* of love is even more curious than in the prose sequences: Peter and Alise both love Hubert, but Hubert loves only poetry and the theatre, although Williams limply says he loves Alise in secret. No one is apportioned satisfaction. Peter, instinctively suspicious from the beginning, loathes and distrusts Alise, who is of course a threat to him, cutting her at every opportunity:

> May I tell you something, my
> dear young lady, whoever you are? Anything
> you have to say is not of the slightest
> interest to me.
>
> (p. 11)

Even before the Serafina scene he querulously accuses Hubert of being interested in the girl, and the jealousy is only fanned by Hubert's evasive response. "I am passionate/about her voice," he says. "A marvelous/ facility for modern meters, completely/unspoiled by English" (p. 12). (Williams' bias for what is American forces its way in.) But Peter will not let it pass:

> She's much too mild. Not the one
> for you, Hubert. There'd be no
> contrast in your lives.

Hubert, parrying clumsily, only replies:

> She's a very clever actress.
> I wanted someone to do the complicated
> innocent. I don't know anyone to
> equal her, to give the signature, the
> emphasis which, after all, is
> I—and what I want to do.
> (p. 13)

The insults exchanged by Peter and Alise continue apace. "I could spit in his face," Alise says of Hubert (p. 16). Then to him directly: "You're worse/ than a dog in heat" (p. 94). "Don't be vulgar, Alise," Hubert cautions, not wanting to lose the backing for his play, but Peter breaks in with his calling card: "She's a woman" (p. 95).

Hubert is thus the man in the middle, the object of love and focus of displeasure. The imaginative author of many loves, he is caught between two that are not of his making, and he is uncomfortable. But how to maintain the financial support of Peter, the usefulness of his leading lady, and the integrity of the play all at once? For it is obvious that his consuming passion is his work, his drama:

> My purpose is
> to write for the stage such verse as never
> has been written heretofore.
> (p. 14)

The goal is, of course, not realized—the three short plays are entirely in prose. In the meantime, however, Hubert must, following the "Talk" sequence, make up his mind how he will see the work through. Peter has grown more captious, and Alise, always anxious, is now becoming temperamental. To Peter he finally summons up his courage and, surrounded by the din of the scene-shifters, blurts out a hasty solution:

> I might as well tell you first
> as last—Alise and I are to be married.

88   *Many Loves*

But the jostling for position and priority has not quite ended. Back and forth go the contestants: Alise, finally urging Hubert to forget the play and leave with her ("He's too strong for you," she correctly warns of Peter, p. 98), and Peter, chagrined, now ostensibly planning a marriage ceremony on the set, but really devising a new strategy to win back the poet:

> Don't sulk, Hubert. Look—this is my
> last evening. I claim it. After
> the ceremony is over we'll take Alise
> and pack her into her little bed—
> so she can get her beauty rest
> against tomorrow evening.
>   She'll
> agree, and you and I shall steal
> away.... It is my privilege!
> *Le Droit du Seigneur!* For just this one
> night! We two, together.
>   (p. 99-100)

The end of the play collapses in Pirandello-like confusion, with Peter desperately pulling out all stops, apparently without embarrassment (but not with quite the candor of microfilm #24):

> As a husband, this man isn't worth
> a woman's hairpin—completely
> wasted. I'd like to break his neck
> rather than see him do it....
>   There is
> something in this man—as in
> any man—not to be benefited by a marriage.
> And he knows it thoroughly.
> This thing that you see here, that you,
> Alise, imagine is your lover,
> this complexity about whom you
> will never in your entire life
> learn anything to the purpose, this man,
> as you are a woman, will remain....
>
>   [The company is amused and laughing
>   at Peter's mock heroics.]
>
> as cold as ice in his heart—toward you,
> as toward every other feeling
> thing about him, completely cold...
> except—as interpretable to him through
> his writing! Do you think he loves you?
> Don't make me laugh. He doesn't even
> love himself. He is as specialized

> as a foxhound. He waits only to
> be loosed by his writing.
>
> (pp. 101-2)

Hubert is dazed, even frightened, but he manages to dismiss it as "Heroic nonsense.... Just the/relief I needed. Very funny" (p. 102). Meanwhile, Alise has gone backstage for a pistol, and in a remarkable confrontation almost shoots Peter—but decides not to. At the end the company, more amused than anything else, is in an uproar. The bemused minister enters to perform the wedding ceremony ("This is preposterous," he groans, p. 104), champagne is flowing, and a piano is being played.

What Williams thus says about love in the counterplay is quite clear. Peter loves Hubert to the extent that he will provide money for his play (although as "angel" he appears to be something less than happy with the results), and will even fight hard for him. But as Williams sees it, this love, while apparently quite sincere, is not "real." For not only does homosexual love apparently subvert the normal growth of intimate human relationships; it denies the individual, in this case Peter (it is doubtful whether Hubert is in any sense a homosexual), the opportunity to discover his *own* real self through the "proper" sexual expression of his person. Gay love becomes, at least in this instance, a kind of selfish self-love; it is ultimately sterile, giving nothing (and getting nothing). One remembers Peter's aside in "The Funnies":

> I find I have very little power
> over you any longer, Hubert.
>
> (p. 53)

Hubert says in return: "I believed that you would look beyond/self interest" (p. 62). And that is the key: when love (homosexual or not) is based on control, when the lover wants to maintain a kind of position over the beloved, such feeling is in itself unnatural, already past the point of love, dehumanizing to both parties, and ultimately leading to discord and separation. Alan Ostrom writes: "Where sex is normal, it unites the human and the natural in an image of harmony. But where it is perverted, it becomes a sign of 'divorce.'"[35] Peter of course has tried to control Hubert economically as well, which merely adds to the inappropriateness of the affair.

But both Alise and Hubert are at fault as well. On Alise's behalf, one must first point to her faithfulness and courage; she *will* wrest Hubert from Peter. And yet there is finally a lack of real understanding in her love for Hubert, too: she demands of him the one thing that he can scarcely afford to give up, his play:

> *Alise:* Come...*now!*
>
> *Hubert:* But the play.
>
> *Alise:* Oh, damn the play! I know what I'm talking about. Now. At once. If you love me, Hubert.
>
> (p. 99)

It is this posed choice that can only be for Hubert a defeat, and Alise, who has understood the importance of his play up till now, misses the point at the critical moment. *One or the other, either this or that*—the impossible ultimatum for a man, Williams will imply in *A Dream of Love* when he explores the incompatibility of domesticity and art. In a sense, if Alise had really loved Hubert she would have saved him but then let him have his freedom; she does not make the sacrifice.

Hubert is no homosexual and has apparently never loved Peter, and he does not seem really to love Alise either, even though Williams has told us he does in the synopsis. Hubert says he will marry her (simply to avoid trouble?), which is, as Peter correctly observes, a most gloomy prospect:

> Marry him
> and become his jailor—you'll find
> him thoroughly contemptible,
> not even human. This is the way
> it is—and you shall have, tomorrow,
> no part whatever in his life.
>
> (p. 102)

So Hubert loves nothing but his work:

> There's nothing else
> that in the least concerns me, neither
> to eat, nor drink, nor sleep—either alone
> or with a woman—or anything
>
> (p. 32)

But he is a failure, as far as we can tell, in that—where is the verse play?—and he is also a failure as a human being. Guimond says that "Peter's and Hubert's lives have the limitations as well as the advantages of a well-made play. Their passions are satisfied in art and talk, not life."[36] The remark applies to Hubert but not to Peter: Peter has life's passion, call it what one will; he shows it for Hubert. (And so does Alise.) But there is something noticeably missing in Hubert, a dimension of feeling, a sense of compassion for another human life. This lack puts him in company with some of his own characters from the playlets—Serafina, Pete, Clara, and Doc. But more than that, Hubert, who is psychologically perhaps the weakest of the three main characters in the counterplay, does not even, as Peter says, love himself.

Language for a New Theatre

As much as the counterplot suggests of love, it is more important for what it says about a new language for a new theatre. "I wanted to write plays — plays in verse," Williams had written in the *Autobiography* (p. 51), referring to his early inclinations at the University of Pennsylvania. But we already know that despite Hubert's aim to write

> Verse. That
> is the drama of words — words in love,
> hot words, copulating, drinking, running,
> bleeding!
>
> (p. 33)

— he never was able to accomplish this goal. The only evidence we have of verse in *Many Loves* is clearly that of Williams himself, who is fitting the counterplot around and throughout the play. But Hubert's *intentions* are ambitious. Along with Williams, he wants to get beyond the prosaic sense of things as they appear to a deeper consciousness of things as they are or might become; thus he says verse "is what says/what I am saying beyond the words" (p. 32). In microfilm #24 Hubert had elaborated on the point:

> I am a writer
> and I take
> great satisfaction
> from it
>
> I like to time
> my phrases
> balance them by
> their sensual
>
> qualities and make
> those express
> as much as
> or more
>
> than the merely
> literal
> burden of the thing
> could ever tell

One recalls in this connection Pirandello's question about *which* reality is real, and Cocteau's use of fantasy as an instrument to uncover truth. Especially, one recalls Artaud: "To break through language in order to touch life is to create or recreate the theatre...."[37]

Williams puts this another way to the dubious Peter early in the play. The miracle of his hoped-for verse is that it will

> give the word a metaphorical twist by the position it assumes, the elevation it induces — without pictorial effects — by the force of its meaning; a similarity to daily speech, the miracle being it sounds so, but by the awakening experienced is proven otherwise, charged to raise the spirit to a full enjoyment.
>
> (p. 9)

("Perhaps so," says Peter in #24, "but can it be/put over on Broadway?") One remembers Williams' preoccupation with language in *The Great American Novel*. And in 1942 he had written:

> The thing has been with me to find what new may be done with it.... Not merely does one chase after newness for the sake of sensation or abandon the old because it is stale. There is a necessity to reinvestigate our means of expression in every age.[38]

In *Many Loves* he continues the argument:

>   A new
>   conception, more suited to ourselves,
>   our times — which wants to use
>   its brains....
>
>   —those who would think in
>   their own terms than borrowed ones....
>
>   —and in the same terms
>   celebrate our achievements — but
>   elevated to a distinction which, with
>   genius, may be invented to astonish
>   them.
>   (pp. 14-15)

And in *Paterson* Williams had claimed that

>   without invention the line
>   will never again take on its ancient
>   divisions when the word, a supple word
>   lived on it, crumbled now to chalk.
>   (p. 65)

The key word here is invention; it is to be an entirely new language for the American theatre. But, Peter complains, "We don't/like verse in plays." Hubert replies:

> I know that. But I know more.
> There is no verse, no new verse
> to write a play in. That's why. Invent it.
>
> (p. 16)

Since "There can never be/a play worth listening to except in verse" (p. 32), Hubert sets out to explain that verse. And as we have seen from *The First President,* the dramatic power is to be in the words themselves; it will be a drama of its own within a play:

> The words must carry a special meaning
> a special dramatic structure of their
> own. What is the dramatic structure
> as it occurs in words? Verse.

He continues to speak of verse, this time in contradistinction to prose:

> No one knows what poetry
> should be today. It should be the
> audience itself, come out of itself
> and standing in its own eyes, leaning
> within the opening of its own ears,
> hearing itself breathe, seeing itself
> in the action — lifted by poetry to
> a world it never knew. A world it has
> always longed for and may enter for a
> few precious moments never to be known
> in prose.

Then he adds something that has been heard before, calling again for a kind of reshaping, in almost a spiritual way, of the audience:

> The audience is the play.
> And it is pure poetry — unless one
> fails to imagine it and lift it beyond the
> dirty boards into the empyrean.
>
> (p. 33)

Thus the experience, galvanized through the invention of an original and vigorous verse, can reach out immediately, can seize participant and audience alike, can shake up the old formulations of reality and modes of thinking. One remembers Artaud's manifesto: to name and direct shadows by not holding to a fixed language or form, finally preparing the ground "for a new generation of shadows, around which assembles the true spectacle of life." To those familiar with Williams' poems, and especially with

Paterson, much of this is not a surprise; he calls for a "redeeming language," an American idiom which will unblock the language. And most important for the stage is the sensory quality of this language, somehow transformed into life, revealing, as Brinnin says of Williams' poetry, "emotion as a process—a living document of experience rather than a delayed report of experience."[39]

" 'Can prose/do that?' Hubert asks?" (p. 33). Perhaps not, but the question at hand is really the one posed by Peter: "Can you do that?" (p. 33). The answer, as we have seen, is no, at least not in this trial horse. (We will look at the verse of the framing action itself shortly.) In that sense, then, Hubert is a failure. But as a spokesman for Williams, the would-be-poet for the American stage, he has clearly not failed (and for the Becks he has not); and more than that, Hubert sounds a kind of rallying cry (for Williams) in his efforts to ring the changes for this new, "avant-garde" American theatre. And here is where Peter, worrying about the conservative Broadway audiences, is no angel at all:

> Poetry? To them?
> Something like—a handkerchief, to blow your
> nose on. They smell. They talk during the
> pauses. During key speeches they cough.
> They're not people. They're not even
> representative. You can't imagine an
> audience. They don't exist. They merely
> have tickets. That's all they are. And
> you'd better entertain them. They don't
> come here to be elevated—by the imagination
> or otherwise. They're tired—you've heard
> it. This isn't an affair of state—or taste.
> This is the modern commercial theater. If
> the play isn't interesting, they leave.
> (p. 34)

> What is this here?
> No heat, no lifting of the scene,
> no tension—no romance!
> (p. 88)

> It won't do. Let some idiot—in
> the usual arty fashion—make
> a book of it. But don't seek to produce it.
> (p. 90)

But Hubert refuses to be budged. Of the audience he says: "Excite their curiosity/and you can do anything you please with/them" (p. 34). And later he tells how that audience may be excited, with the poetry making its own sparks, irradiating the darkness:

> I say: when we see,
> on the stage, what we expect to see —
> I'm not speaking of circuses
> but something to turn our minds a little
> to the light — it should project
> above the coarseness of the materials...
> something else, in the words themselves,
> tragic without vulgarity. Seen —
> in the mind! The mind itself... today,
> without firearms and other claptrap,
> in its own tragic situation. We can't
> do this at once but must restudy
> the means.
>
> (p. 92)

Tempo and Direction

The nature of theatre in the past two decades has changed so much — it is yet too early to say for better or worse — that it seems strange in evaluating the total contribution of *Many Loves* to call it a revolutionary drama. And in point of fact Williams had been in earlier drafts much freer in presentation and experimentation, with the audience being even more closely involved. In microfilm #24 Williams had written:

> Note: Vote at the box-office as patrons enter which end they prefer — light or tragic.

The idea was intriguing. If, after the votes were counted, those who desired a tragic ending were in the majority, then the audience would see something like the following: subsequent to Peter's long speech which tells of the unsuitability of Hubert as a husband, Alise really does draw a pistol and attempts to shoot Peter. But Hubert dashes to her in order to prevent what would be a murder. "There is a muffled, Plop! like the bursting of a rubber toy balloon as she is shot and killed." From this point Williams has suggested two possibilities: one, that Hubert take the gun and himself shoot Peter (but only wound him), and then sit down before anyone else can act and kill himself. The second is that Hubert be disarmed while aiming the gun at Peter, and that a minister enter to intone an ironic speech:

> how fortunate for this young man
> in his time of trouble
> oh Lord, that he has such a good
> kind and resourceful friend
> to assuage his lonely heart —
> in some measure for what he has lost.

The light and more orthodox ending, on the other hand, is what Williams has apparently retained. Alise does not shoot anyone, but turns the gun over quietly, and the carnival-like preparations for the wedding proceed.

Eliminating the possibility of audience choice, Williams has locked himself into a more conventional conclusion, though still an unusual one. Many questions remain unresolved: Will the marriage really take place? What will become of Peter? Will the play—the three sequences—actually be performed, or has Hubert's spirit been broken? "It's unresolved,/ floating, silly. The old goat/gets nowhere," Peter himself complains (p. 88). This irresolution or unwillingness to untangle ambiguous relationships is what confused and annoyed some reviewers, and yet one confronts the same problem in Pirandello and Cocteau, and even more so in the works of Beckett, the novels of Robbe-Grillet, the plays of Harold Pinter or Tom Stoppard, and making the full circle, perhaps the work of James Joyce (whom Williams admired). And yet, as Guimond points out,[40] there really is a kind of resolution of character in the way Williams deftly relates the counterplot backward to the playlets. "When the articulate characters of the counterplay recognize their situation in the coarsely authentic medium of the prose playlets, they can respond to it and resolve it" (p. 151). As Guimond observes, in Peter's asides and increasing involvement in the three sequences he is transformed "from a detached spectator to an unwilling participant" (p. 152); he thus sees in Horace's exploitation of the sadly unattractive Lil (in "The Funnies") his own possible humiliation at the hands of the toughening Hubert. That is, he sees for once his love as greed; it is illumination, but the awareness does not save him.

Williams employs the same strategy forward as well. In "Talk," for example, Doc complains to Clara: "Talk, talk, talk! Everything runs out finally into talk" (p. 85). We have noticed before that in Williams, dialogue (language) reveals truth, and in this case it tells us in context much about Clara. But the implication of the statement can be taken further as an indictment of Hubert. Hubert talks a lot about writing a verse play, but does not get the job done, and the irony is clear: Williams has talked his whole life about writing plays in verse, and yet, save in the counterplot, what one encounters is prose. In addition Doc's speech which follows sets up not only the theme of "Talk," but helps put in order the entire play:

> And pretty soon we'll all be dead forever and never have opened our eyes wide once— wide, that is, to see what actually...starved as we live, because we never, never, never, never took a chance among the five or six thousand or million people of our small personal world to know them actually and individually...what actually the creature in the next bin is doing or feeling. And all the shyness and all the prudery and all the moral carpings are no more than so much heartburn from our chronic emptiness.
> (p. 85)

The speech is almost an artistic credo of Williams, who took time to look at "a poor Old Woman" on the street "munching a plum" or to discern fragments of life that "No one/will believe..../of vast import to the nation" (*Collected Earlier Poems,* pp. 99, 121). As a doctor Williams had treated somewhere around a million-and-a-half people and had delivered 2,000 babies;[41] and as his poems and short stories show, he had looked long and deep into "the next bin." But in all of *Many Loves* scarcely anyone has gotten outside of himself or herself to pay attention to the detail of another's life or notice another's need. This is the irony of the sequences in *Many Loves:* Hubert can hardly write of love when he himself has never experienced it. Peter, deadly accurate, asks him:

> Have you ever
> been in love? I doubt it. That anguish,
> that insistence, that mad fatalistic
> plunge!
> (pp. 88-89)

Thus the sequences are derived clearly from Hubert's limited and cynical assumptions, and we are better able to understand the whole play as the framing action sheds light on the sequences, and vice versa. It is finally the responsibility of the members of the audience to tally up in their minds the play's meaning, and discover within themselves (as Williams writes in "Writer's Prologue to a Play in Verse") the rest of the secret.

But the question arises: how seriously is Williams taking all this? "It is a little difficult with *Many Loves* to decide how much of it is supposed to be a joke," writes Gerald Weales.[42] One remembers that an early title was "The Comedy of Love." In a Buffalo draft Hubert tells Peter: "This is/a comedy, not the tragedy of love." Williams himself told the Becks not to miss "seeing the humor of the situation" (March 11, 1957). Some of the humor turns, as we have already seen, on irony: Hubert claiming to be a poet but writing in prose, and so on. But there are other genuinely funny moments throughout—in "Serafina," the confusion about the hermaphroditic rabbit, in "The Funnies" the exaggerated outrage of Pete, in "Talk" the neurotic confessions of Clara (supposedly Judith Malina's best portrayal in The Living Theatre production). Of "Talk," Koch says, perhaps overstating the case: "The comic interludes in the park, devoted to the younger generation, are unbelievably funny in their crude American fellowship.[43] Much of the verse dialogue between Hubert and Peter is witty and rapid-fire, somewhat in the manner of Coward, and directed inward. And yet, it is obvious that Williams wants the audience to take much of this same material seriously indeed. His manifesto for a new theatre is one example, the urgent need for verse onstage another. The word tragedy or tragic is occasionally used, as in Hubert's explanation to Peter:

> The mind itself...today
> without firearms and other claptrap,
> in its own tragic situation.
> (p. 92)

There is ultimately something hopelessly despairing about "The Funnies," something meanly vicious about "Serafina." The end is broadly ironic, even with elements that intimate farce, but there is considerable pain as well, and some shock: what is in the future for the three characters? One suspects that without love, the cure, there is little that is very promising.

It must be admitted that Williams' poetry in the counterplot is not nearly as exciting or vigorous as that promised by Hubert. But Weales is not right when he says the verse is, "except for a few mock-rhetorical passages, indistinguishable from prose."[44] There is, again, no fixed metre, but there is, as is usual in Williams (and these are his words), "the *tune* which the lines (not necessarily the words) make in our ears." He continues (in this letter to Richard Eberhart, May 23, 1954, from *Selected Letters,* p. 326): "By measure I mean musical pace." And the pace of the verse seems slower than the prose—it interrupts, after all, the main thrust of the sequences, and should be more accented—and much more literary, occasionally winding up in a flourish, as in this speech of Peter to Alise:

> You'd be fortunate if he
> had that much feeling in him for you.
> He has none. It is only
> the machine grinding toward its end.
> To break the walls and let him out.
> To escape, to write, to realize,
> to come through the obscurity
> of his surroundings to the flame—
> of himself, not you—a light
> he, poor fellow, thinks he sees.
> (pp. 102-3)

The language is more metaphorical than in the prose as well, which suits the characters who are intoning it. The poetic line is longer than in most of Williams' shorter lyrics, and about the same length as in *Paterson*. Because of this line, drawn out slightly, there is a sense of leisureliness about the counterplot which in the prose is only felt in "Talk."

I will speak more fully of Williams' prose in the next three chapters, but suffice it to say that, having by 1942 already written *White Mule*

(1937), *Life Along the Passaic River* (1938), and *In the Money* (1940), he had come a long way from the early unpublished plays. As Emily Mitchell Wallace points out, he in fact took his prose quite seriously, and worked hard to perfect it,[45] even though he judged he was a better poet than prose writer.[46] In *Many Loves* the prose serves as a medium of expression for the "lesser" characters as in some of Shakespeare. One notices this in the dialogue of those persons appearing in the three one-act plays. One also observes about the prose a kind of toughness reminiscent of Eugene O'Neill's, although Williams' dialogue is much less wordy. Colloquialisms, vulgarisms, and clichés abound, reflecting the sense of the characters:

> Jesus God! Is that what he said? What was that again?
>
> (Serafina, p. 21)
>
> You got too much lip, that's what's the matter with you.
>
> (Pete, p. 43)
>
> I'm no blushing violet.
>
> (Clara, p. 76)

"Williams' ear has always been agile and delicate," writes Koch. "It tells here in his genius for cadences that are at once generically American, and at the same time highly individualized."[47] The prose moves at a running pace, sometimes with a kind of violent lurch. George, reading the funnies, cries:

> By guy! She wants to chuck the baby in a tub of icewater to cure the hiccoughs. Then she starts hiccoughing herself! So what does Popeye do — he grabs her around the neck with one fist and...oh boy.
>
> (p. 37)

The major improvement over the prose of the early plays is in its spark, in the dramatic interplay that is established in the dialogue. This is particularly true in "The Funnies" and "Talk" — there are a tempo and a direction which bring the characters beautifully to life. The actors have something solid from which to build their roles.

4
A Dream of Love

"Masterpiece" in the Making

If *Many Loves* is William Carlos Williams' most ambitious work for the theatre, *A Dream of Love* (1948, revised in 1961)[1] is probably, as Norman Holmes Pearson suggested, his best all-around play.[2] Clinton Atkinson, who directed a staged reading of the drama at Wesleyan University in 1960, agrees, calling it "his masterpiece."[3] Margo Jones, the late founder of the experimental theatre in Dallas, saw it in production and was highly enthusiastic. Mrs. Williams has said that her husband valued this play above all of his others;[4] and according to Vivienne Koch,[5] Williams had even ranked it "in importance" with his major poem *Paterson*.

There are several reasons for these opinions. First, the principal concerns of *A Dream of Love,* love and domesticity, have been developed in part from the discoveries in and possibilities of *Many Loves,* and the play's dramatic technique (the use of the dream, for example) can be traced as far back as *The First President*. But *A Dream of Love,* composed almost entirely in prose, is much more finished in form than the earlier works and there is a unity of purpose about the themes which is absent from the others. Second, Dr. Daniel Thurber, the wayward husband/lover/poet/ physician, and his troubled wife Myra are two of Williams' most achieved dramatic characters. They are also the most complex, since each has his or her own special dream of love which is at once agonizing and consoling. There are elements of the tragic in Dr. and Mrs. Thurber and of modern tragedy in the play because of them. Finally, the question of autobiography emerges most forthrightly in *A Dream of Love,* with Williams revealing a good deal about himself and his writing; these revelations have continuing interest.

The origin of *A Dream of Love,* and its growth from random idea to completed play, is again a complicated but fascinating story. In his *Autobiography* (p. 307) Williams wrote of himself during the busy war years that, "A whole play would work itself out and not a moment for its scribbling." One of these plays—perhaps *the* one—was probably *A Dream of Love,* since notes and fragments (and scribblings) on the project are dated in the collection at SUNY at Buffalo as early as April of 1945.[6] Williams wrote to J. C. Thirlwall in 1961:

> Having written one play more or less successfully [*Many Loves*], I was tempted to follow it up with something which would be, at last, a major work aimed at Broadway. As usual, it came from incidents in my practice as a doctor—a middle-aged man in the suburban community where he had been successful, on the outskirts of New York City. The wife was very much in love with her husband and he with her, but that did not prevent this surreptitious poet from indulging in affairs with his women patients. But his poems which the wife knew and on occasion read aloud to him (she was an understanding reader) caused them both misgivings. The love of the man for his wife was unquestioned, but what man can be unconscious of the world of women which surrounds him?
>
> At the point where the doctor dies, the character of the play suddenly shifts to tragedy, with the wife occupying the central role. It is her tragedy which has to be evolved. It ends in her victory—over herself—and the rescue of the doctor. They are reunited in a love which they, and particularly she, bring to a triumphant—but losing—conclusion. Lucky for his reputation as a poet to which she has remained true from the days of their youth—as in a dream which they have dreamed together from the first.
> (pp. 432-33)

What Williams implies here about his own presence in the play is not entirely clear, and will be looked at more closely later. (One might, for the moment, keep in mind an earlier clue from "Notes in Diary Form," *Selected Essays,* p. 72: "The drama is the identification with the man himself [Shakespeare—and his sphere of knowledge, close to him.]... So the dramatist 'lives' the character.") Mrs. Williams has provided additional information about the plot, suggesting that her husband took the motivating "action"—the married man, Dr. Thurber, dying in the bed of his mistress, Dotty Randall—from two sources.[7] Williams had at one time treated a patient who later had had a fatal heart attack while sleeping with a woman who was not his wife; and Williams also had known the story of a somewhat profligate actress who suffered the shock of a man dying in her bed. Thus the conception of the play grew from the suggestion of adultery, from a break in the marriage vow. Accepting this as the starting point, one may reasonably speculate that Williams moved *backward* to gather up remembrances of some familiar past concerns. One of these can be traced to a poem first published in 1936 in *Adam & Eve & the City* and titled "Perpetuum Mobile: The City" (*Collected Earlier Poems,* pp. 384-90). This rather lengthy poem becomes crucial to *A Dream of Love,* and sections of it are brought verbatim into the play and spoken by Dr. Thurber/Williams. Its controlling idea, that love is a dream and that this dream is likely to be false, is asserted twice by Doc:

>   —a dream
>   we dreamed
>   each
> separately
>   we two
> of love
>   and of
> desire—
>
> that fused
> in the night—
>
>   A dream
> a little false
> toward which
>   now
> we stand
>   and stare
> transfixed—
>   (p. 122)

The last stanza, especially, discloses the paradox for Williams, since in "Perpetuum Mobile" he had continued:

> Let us break
>   through
> and go there—
>
> in
>
>   vain!
> *(Collected Earlier Poems,* p. 386)

What preoccupied Williams as he began to write was the bitter realization, already suggested in the Doc/Clara episode in *Many Loves,* that love's desire made infidelity in mind and/or body unavoidable and even necessary (especially for the male), though it brought peace to no one. To recall Williams' own astringent definition of love in *Paterson,* "Love is no comforter, rather a nail in the/skull...." (p. 99).

That the play was in part conceived of as an extension of *Many Loves* is made explicit from an early typed outline at Yale. The projected title was originally *Trial Horse No. II* or *Off the Cliff;*[8] what is thus intimated is that the game will be now more perilous. The kind of estrangement one senses in the lives of Doc and Clara of *Many Loves* is in a way preliminary to the more dangerous "divorce" between Dr. Thurber and Myra. The form of the work was also, like that of the other play, to be quite free: "a play in three acts or one according to the tempo of the listeners." One is reminded of Hubert's prediction that the audience would be the play, that there would be a sense of the improvisational about what would take place.

In notes now at Yale, apparently written by a reader in collaboration with Williams, the play was to open as follows:

> CURTAINS PART ABOUT FIVE FEET. ENTER 1ST PROPERTYMAN.
>
> 1ST PROPERTYMAN (CLASHES CYMBALS) Pay attention. We are in the house of man. (HE EXITS)
>
> ENTER 2ND PROPERTYMAN.
>
> 2ND PROPERTYMAN (CLASHES CYMBALS) Compose yourself, that you may well consider what you are about to witness. (HE EXITS)
>
> CURTAINS PART TO REVEAL THE FULL STAGE. PROPERTYMEN ARE SEATED LEFT AND RIGHT DOWNSTAGE ON THEIR BENCHES. JO IS GOING ABOUT HOUSEHOLD DUTIES. SHE STOPS [,] WALKS DOWN STAGE.

Williams himself had in fact written set choral-like speeches (in verse) for the major characters, to be presented at intervals directly to the audience as ruminative soliloquies. Thus the maid Josephine, whose role appears much shorter in the published *A Dream of Love,* was to have confessed at the opening:

> My name is Jo, which is a man's name. I am no man but a woman whose heart is wrung for my mistress, Myra, whom I love. She is a good woman. So, God rest his soul, is her husband, Dr. Thurber, good. A practicing physician he has lived in this old home with Myra for a dozen years. The children are away at school. Myra has had her troubles with the doctor. For some reason strange to me he's taken to writing poems (many doctors, they say, have turned poets in the past) and surrounded as such men are by women who adore them he is not one to take things casually. No more is Myra! No, no, poor soul, she is not one to take such things casually, in the end. Why must he be so hot today from this quiet suburb to rush off like a dog under a mad moon to the city? I am uneasy for the welfare of this household.

Fragments dated April 26, 1945 indicate that the core of the play had been settled upon quite early, even though Williams would later do a certain amount of rearranging of the material. The play was to contain two scenes (in published form *A Dream of Love* includes three acts), the first occurring "3 days following his [the husband's] death":

> The wife is besieged in her kitchen at the scandal of her husband's death, in a hotel, with a woman. Lucy stays with her. The woman comes to make amends. She, the wife, struggles to reestablish her faith. She is [claustro?] phobic.

The second was to be "The night of his appearance in her dream:"

> Having had her bed made where she is — refusing to go into the rest of the house, she dreams. The Doctor comes home for supper, their children are away, it is Lucy's night off. She bakes a cake. He goes and comes — but she will not "in her dream" go into the house. Why not? (She has already gone into the cellar)

> She goes, finally into the office, to straighten it out. The woman appears (it is still the dream) She and her lover are in the hotel room, She is resisting. Finally she says, Yes (blackout) The wife is back in bed. She hears the lovers whispering.
>
> It is morning. Milkman. Lucy rings back door bell. The wife admits her. "I saw him last night." She goes into the *house*.

"Lucy" is obviously Josephine; the rest of the characters are unnamed. A running subtitle was "Tragic Phase." By May of 1945 Williams was considering the possibility of a chorus to begin the play by intoning the familiar speech, "a dream we dreamed/a little false/of love/and of desire, we two...." There are other clues throughout:

> End is "happy". She possesses him, dead.
>
> (May 19, 1945)
>
> Love, its persistence or destruction, with all that that implies, is the theme.
>
> The dramatic action hinges on whether or not she (who has long since understood his character and motivations and "forgiven" him) will harden her heart against him, whether love perishes or survives.
>
> (June 10, 1945)
>
> The dream is to be "natural" in interpretation—something screwy about the action but not exaggerated.
>
> (undated, 1945?)

In one earlier draft of what then was Act II, scene 2, the doctor is named Dr. Bill James, and with "Bill" quoting from his own verse in the script, it is difficult to know just exactly how "objective" Williams had really planned to be.

In any case Williams had in *A Dream of Love* the good fortune to excise, with one important exception, much that was superfluous and repetitious (or possibly even libelous: one remembers he was once sued for $10,000 after using the name of a real person in a short story published in the *New Masses*). For example, Williams had earlier determined to emphasize the role of the Milkman. In initial drafts that character is much more a presence, and even more intrusive, than he now is. In the dream scene of *A Dream of Love* as it appears in *Many Loves* (Act III, scene 2), where the Milkman cuts in on Dr. Thurber to dance with Myra, Williams had apparently planned the action to be more dramatically expressionistic. Thus the Milkman had become "a fantastic figure INTERCHANGING WITH THE HUSBAND—perhaps even a *very subdued* dance figure—erotic—with Tiger Jazz (heard earlier on the Vic.)" In the published script his meddling is much less officious. In the penultimate scene of the earlier version the Milkman, seemingly wounded by mysterious gunfire, falls on Myra's bed and she tends him, wearing a Red Cross cap. But it turns out that he is not injured, and Myra finally says: "Oh get up, you're not hurt. Not even touched." Williams' stage direction follows: "(She smiles and kisses him)." The implication seems clear but somehow unfitting: the Milkman, somewhat leering about sex ("She's a good-looking lay"), not very bright, generally coarse and unfeeling, will apparently assume a part in her life after the tragedy has been forgotten. But none of this, happily, has been retained.

In addition to that cutting, Williams has also de-emphasized the role of the nude woman who appears at several crucial points in earlier drafts and in the 1948 version. The woman is obviously supposed to represent Doc's dream of Dotty Randall in the hotel bathroom. Thus in the frenzied closing moments of Act III, scene 3, Williams had directed:

> When she [Dotty] says Yes! there is a flash, the lights go out and the nude form is seen in full light of its own—for a moment. Then the lights return.... She appears beyond them, silhouetted in darkness, posed in "the shower"—standing...in faltering light.

In the final version, the nude figure is far less sensational, and appears only once—at the opening of the dream episode in Act III, scene 2: "During this speech the sliding door of the alcove has unobtrusively opened, revealing, in the darkened recess, the nude figure of a woman—which quickly disappears" (pp. 191-92).

But the most significant change, and I think a change for the worse, occurs in the final scene of the play (Act III, scene 4). In the 1961 version, Myra is awakened after dreaming about the incident in the hotel. She answers the ringing telephone, and then walks into the front of the house. It is meant to be a victory of sorts, for she has now crept out of her shell and is actually ready to face the future. But the revitalization is presented without adequate motivation. Such an omission is crucial; the audience is not permitted to see the impetus for her transformation. In earlier drafts, however, including the 1948 edition, this scene is presented with the necessary supporting detail. The dream is suspended in motion through a page-and-a-half of revealing dialogue between Myra and Doc. Thurber has entered the house (it is his second and most dramatic appearance as "ghost"), complaining of "This pain, in my chest, here!" Death is obviously closing in. "I think I'm finished," he groans. "A thrombosis this time." There is a request for forgiveness; she grants it: "Of course I forgive you. I love you. I love you, my dear." Doc says, significantly, "I want to go to bed. Our bed." As the phone rings again, he gasps his final words: "My adored wife." Williams brings matters to a close with a note: "the phone insists. The dream melts away 'as a dream'." The result of the elaboration is that the conclusion of the play is clearer and more satisfying than it becomes in the 1961 script. The relationship, if not settled in full, is at least understood. Doc is exonerated at the moment of death, and Myra, facing the heartbreak at last, may go forward to live her life. Koch observes, "Dawn, when 'reality' asserts its sway, is automatically making everything seem 'normal' again."⁹ That is overstating it a bit, I think; life will hardly be the same for Myra. What is more to the point here is better reflected by another passage in Williams, this time from "Asphodel, That Greeny Flower." It beautifully suggests the healing power that is one dimension of love:

>   What power has love but forgiveness?
>   In other words
>   by its intervention
>   what has been done
>   can be undone.
>   What good is it otherwise?
>   (*Pictures from Brueghel*, p. 169)

A Phantom Rules

Things Greek were very much on Williams' mind in *A Dream of Love*— there is even a short discussion of Greek prosody by Dr. Thurber in the hotel scene—and Williams begins with a pertinent epigraph from Aeschylus' *Agamemnon,* taken from the J. A. Symonds translation in *The Greek Poets.* The passage concerns the abandonment of Menelaus by Helen:

> "She, leaving to her fellow-citizens the din
> of shielded hosts, and armings of the fleet with
> spears, bringing to Ilion destruction for a dower,
> went lightly through the doors, dishonorably
> brave; and many a sigh was uttered by
> the bards of the palace, while they sang—
> O house! O house, and rulers! O marriage-
> bed, and pressure on the pillows of her
> head who loved her lord! He stands by in
> silence, dishonored, but without reproaches,
> noting with anguish of soul that she is fled.
> Yes, in his longing after her who is beyond
> the sea, a phantom will seem to rule his
> house. The grace of goodly statues hath grown
> irksome to his gaze, and in his widowhood of
> weary eyes all beauty fades away. But dreams
> that glide in sleep with sorrow visit him,
> conveying a vain joy; for vain it is, when one
> hath seemed to see good things, and lo, escaping
> through his hands, the vision flies apace on
> wings that follow on the paths of sleep."
>   (*A Dream of Love,* p. 107)

The consequences of this abandonment (or abduction) resulted in the Trojan War. Williams is not suggesting that his work will explore matters of such consequence, and his play is about a *man* who leaves the marriage bed, but otherwise the passage approximates the sense of *A Dream of Love*. The key to the play for Williams lies in one sentence: "Yes, in his longing after her who is beyond the sea, a phantom will seem to rule his house." The phantom for Myra will be her husband, returned from the dead, and the memory of her husband's love. And yet her dream, like Menelaus' vision, is bound to disappoint, for love is elusive to these sufferers, giving of itself unpredictably and without faith. The love to which Williams addressed himself is domestic love, considered earlier in *Many Loves* but lacking there the fullness that one sees here. Approaching this subject, one remembers Williams' short and highly personal lyrics about married love ("I Would Not Change for Thine" and "Après le Bain," for example), and also his creation of Joe Stecher and his wife Gurlie from *White Mule, In the Money,* and *The Build-Up*. Myra is portrayed much more sympathetically than Gurlie—she is not "pushy"—but her attachment to honor at all cost is not wholly salutary. In his Socratic essay, "The Basis of Faith in Art," Williams, echoing the later words of Dr. Thurber, asks provocatively: "Did it ever occur to you that a marriage might be invigorated by deliberately breaking the vows" (*Selected Essays,* p. 188). From Thurber's point of view, the question becomes the touchstone of *A Dream of Love*.

Because Thurber hides little about his extramarital excursions, we find out early in the play that he has broken his wedding vows well before the affair with Mrs. Randall. "It's been going on all my life, since we've been married," complains Myra (p. 128). Like Doc of "Talk" in *Many Loves,* Dr. Thurber finds the opposite sex irresistible. A second passion is his poetry; his pursuit of both become as one. When the Thurbers discuss the possibility of the doctor's giving up his practice to write verse full-time—for he is, like Williams himself at the time, making a minor but steady reputation as a poet—Myra taunts him: "But what would you do without all your women, darling?" There follows this exchange:

Doc: I'd find one up a tree somewhere.

Myra: You sure would. And drag her down by the hair—if she didn't drop on you first from a low branch. I don't care—so long as I have my garden. Really, Dan. I'm getting awfully fed up with this routine. The same thing, the same thing, over and over and over.

(p. 117)

So Doc, now in his middle 40's, has his women, and the consequences have left scars on both husband and wife. But the most extraordinary thing is that Thurber is still very much in love with Myra. He fancies himself a good husband. "I love you!" he insists early in the very first scene of Act I (p. 113). Then, thumbing through "The Complete Collected Poems of Daniel T. — for Titcomb—Thurber," he finds a suitable poem written earlier to define this special love. It is actually a short lyric, "Love Song," from Williams' own *Al Que Quiere,* written to Flossie:

> I lie here thinking of you —
>
> the stain of love
> is upon the world!
> Yellow, yellow, yellow
> it eats into the leaves,
> smears with saffron
> the horned branches that lean
> heavily
> against a smooth purple sky!
> There is no light
> only a honey-thick stain
> that drips from leaf to leaf
> and limb to limb
> spoiling the colors
> of the whole world —
>
> you, far off there under
> the wine-red selvage of the west!
> (p. 126)

The poem is fitting because it conveys both the depth of Dr. Thurber's love for his wife, and the unhappiness growing out of it. Whitaker observes: "The controlling word, 'stain,' is both pictorial and sexual in implications, taking in both directions its devouring acid and its honey, its insubstantiality and its heavy body."[10] As the play begins, there is no doubt that the doctor is still physically drawn to his wife. There is genuine evidence of his attachment. Arriving home he wakes the napping Myra by addressing her as "Sweetheart," then goes on in complimentary fashion: "A damned good-looking woman. You always did have beautiful legs. That's why I married you" (p. 109). He reads poetry to her, is gently solicitous. But the first scene also sets up the areas of conflict. With an unspecified number of children away (at school?), the Thurbers are living a kind of modern-day life of quiet desperation. Doc, who longs for the time to write, is chafing at his medical practice, burdened by the inconvenient telephone calls and interruptions. He tells his wife: "One thing I know, my dear: we've got to get the hell out of this kind of life" (p. 116). For her part Myra is restless, irritable, at loose ends; she takes naps because her empty afternoons are filled with headaches and vast stretches of unoccupied time. She is hardly the model doctor's wife, in turn cursing "the God-damned thankless practice of medicine" (p. 116) and frequently hanging up on patients who phone in for advice. At the heart of these anxieties is Myra's worry about their own relationship, their compatibility:

> Now look. You know I always like to have you close to me. Almost always. I love you. You don't love me—not in the same way. But that's my affair. I love you and believe in you. I tremendously admire you. But I don't trust you.
>
> (p. 113)

What Williams wants us to see is that each yet believes he or she loves the other, only in different ways and on different levels, despite the problems. Thurber's love for his wife is the more complex of the two, of course, since he has a more complicated life. In that sense the play reaffirms the common-place from Byron: "Man's love is of man's life a thing apart,/'Tis woman's whole existence." For Thurber has his patients and his poetry as well as his responsibilities as lover and husband; Myra has only her husband, and has her fears about that. "If only I were sure of your love" (p. 124), she worries, and this theme—the need for a woman to be certain of being loved—is picked up again and again. In the meantime, Thurber can rest assured of *her* love, even though he is the one who seems not to want such security. In fact, as the drama unfolds through Act I, scene 1, it is evident that the prospect of permanence or changelessness horrifies him. That possibility is a burden, arousing in him only dread. He loves his wife, but not above everything, and he will not lie about his wishes and feelings. The initial definition of his love for Myra is thus sustained from "Perpetuum Mobile"; love cannot abide constancy. "What in God's name is our relationship?" Myra cries near the end of the first scene. He answers, almost brutally:

> Our relationship? Something horrible, in all probability—if it isn't magnificent. Perverse. Insane—of which we shall never know anything. Murderous perhaps, but inevitable... I love you!—the sacred word being an eternal lie. And you can omit the "eternal" too.... What does any man know?
>
> (p. 128)

But to understand further the nature of Thurber's "love" for his wife, one must look to Myra's dream, which covers the second and third scenes of Act III. The first of these involves the fantasized return of the ghost of Doc. Myra, abruptly "awakened," calls to him as he rummages for something to eat: "You're dead! So you're not dead. But we burned you up" (p. 190). In the 1948 version Doc replies, "Come on, get on the job here. I'm dead"; but in the 1961 edition he says, "Come on, get on the job here. I'm worn out" (p. 190). Sandwiches are made. The ubiquitous Milkman, hovering over the scene as a kind of invisible stagehand, supplies the milk, and the two settle down into a prolonged and emotional discussion. It is in part an elaboration of the first scene of the play, but with important new information. For one thing, we are given a full measure of Myra's resentments, not only those resulting from the recollections of Doc's affairs but also from the great blocks of time he has stolen from her to write. To Myra, Doc has thus cheated on her in two ways, by giving himself to other women and to poetry: "I don't think you've ever taken a mean advantage of a woman in your life—except me," she complains (p. 198). But to Thurber love and art—writing—flow from the same source of energy and inspiration, the creative imagination. As Williams would write in "Asphodel, That Greeny Flower" (*Pictures from Brueghel,* p. 179), "love and the imagination/are of a piece/swift as the light/to avoid destruction."[11]

Less than halfway into the scene Thurber, conscious of the dual role of husband/poet, tries to put the attendant responsibilities into focus for Myra:

> *Doc:* A man must protect his pride, his integrity as a man, as best he is able, by whatever invention he can cook up out of his brains or his belly, as the case may be. He must create a woman of some sort out of his imagination to prove himself. Oh, it doesn't have to be a woman, but she's the generic type. It's a woman—even if it's a mathematical formula for relativity. Even more so in that case—but a woman. A woman out of his imagination to match the best. All right, a poem. I mean a woman, bringing her up to the light, building her up and not merely of stone or colors or silly words— unless he's supremely able—but in the flesh, warm, agreeable, made of pure consents. That means they're not married, of course—unless he unmarries them by hard work for a moment now and then. Something—to that time unconceived by him or anyone in the world. Do you follow me?
>
> *Myra:* Is that all?
>
> *Doc:* When a man, of his own powers, small as they are, once possesses his imagination, concretely, grabs it with both hands—he is made! Or lost, I've forgotten which.... [He looks at her closely.] And just as a woman must produce out of her female belly to complete herself—a son—so a man must produce a woman, in full beauty out of the shell of his imagination and possess her, to complete himself also....
>
> *Myra:* [yawning]: The rape of the imagination.
>
> *Doc:* Good. It *is* a kind of rape. You often surprise me by your felicitous phrasing.
> (pp. 200-1)

Much of this is plainly reminiscent of *Paterson III,* written at the same time as *A Dream of Love,* and published only one year later in 1949. In Book III it is initially the search for the Beautiful Thing which inspires much of the verse:

> Beautiful Thing:
> — a dark flame,
> a wind, a flood — counter to all staleness.
> (p. 123)

> Let them explain you and you will be
> the heart of the explanation. Nameless,
> you will appear
>   Beautiful Thing
> the flame's lover —
>   (p. 148)

But it is also informed by what Williams calls "The riddle of a man and a woman":

> For what is there but love, that stares death
> in the eye, love, begetting marriage —
> not infamy, not death
>   (p. 130)

We thus begin to see that there are in fact *two* dreams of love: Myra's vision of her husband returned from the dead, and the dream of Thurber himself, at first abstract and highly idealistic, but finally foundering in the bed of Dotty Randall, who is no Helen of Troy.

Meanwhile, the promise of domestic love to the husband as well as the poet is given clarity by a further stanza from "Perpetuum Mobile" which Thurber and Myra both recite during their anxious scene together:

> *Doc:* All at once
>   in the east
>   rising!
>   All white
>   a northern flower!
>   (p. 191)
>
> *Myra:*   All white.
>   a locust cluster
>   a shad bush
>   blossoming
>   a wild
>   magnolia bud —
>   At night
>   it wakes
>   on the black
>   sky —
>   (p. 193)

The flower may well represent, as Whitaker proposes, a vision of "candid love in the east";[12] flowers are used over and over in Williams as symbols of the regenerative process. Yet Doc's fumbling explanations leave Myra unsatisfied, and amid this hurt she reveals, as Koch puts it, "a supremely damning lack of understanding,"[13] masochistically insisting on finding out the details of her husband's assignation in the New York hotel: "Where did you go before you took her to the room, my poor boy?" (p. 201). Doc retreats a bit, somewhat evasive, not wanting even in death to hurt the wife with whom he shares his love. He begins several long speeches, almost mesmerizing Myra, speaking of "sex, the monster!" (p. 203), and how it tormented him to distraction, pulling him first one way ("God, how I remember Delia! I almost pulled the breeches off her in the kitchen one night after supper," p. 204) and then the other ("And no women! No women! I didn't want women. Not much," p. 204).

But even without the actual presence of women there was always for Doc "the tormented thought of females" (p. 205), with all of the tension and ambivalence that this implies. "There's one thing about sex — you're never so happy as when you're rid of it," he grumbles in retrospect (p. 206). But Myra, emerging from her slumber, again brings the discussion back to specifics, complaining that "On the very day when your love for me should have been most alert, if any day is sacred to love, you walk out without a thought of me in your mind" (p. 207). It was, we have been told earlier, the anniversary of the day Doc had proposed to her; his infidelity is thus a kind of blasphemy, and he is labeled "perverted and disgusting." But it is at this point that Williams makes it emphatic why Doc has entered into the affair. It was, Doc explains in justification, "to renew our love, burn the old nest and emerge transcendent, aflame for you!" Yet Myra replies to this with an even greater asperity: "How can you talk like that?" (p. 207).

From Doc's point of view love is nothing if it is not recharged periodically, even if such revitalizing involves marital risk. Myra, who "thought our lives were just beginning to be reconciled each to the other" (p. 207), is alarmed. Thurber replies: "I was getting bored. I was afraid to be alone with you" (p. 208). There follows one of the most remarkable exchanges in all of Williams' plays, with Doc making it quite explicit why he turned to Dotty Randall:

> *Doc:* I knew that if we were to keep on loving each other something had to be done about it. This opportunity offered itself and I took it....
>
> Here's a beautiful woman who really needs me. I tell you she needed me — for private reasons I don't want to talk about. After all, it's none of your business. I needed her, too....
>
> Naturally, I did what had to be done.
>
> *Myra:* Had to be done!
>
> *Doc:* To keep love alive.

> *Myra:* To keep our love alive.
>
> *Doc:* It went all right. I loved you, as a consequence, more than I ever loved you in my life up to that time. It worked. I couldn't tell you—you couldn't have understood what I felt. It's impossible that you should have understood what I felt.
>
> (pp. 208-9)

Ultimately the blame is placed not on Doc's ego but on the confining institution of marriage itself, as it was in *Many Loves:* "There is/something in this man—as in/any man—not to be benefited by a marriage," Peter had observed (p. 101). (In a manuscript draft of the story "A Face of Stone," published in *Life along the Passaic River,* Williams had written of a married couple: "All I know is that no matter what we have dreamed or desired it slips away unless by a supreme effort we struggle to detain it.") But this is still not enough for Myra, who at the end of this vision is hurling epithets: "Oh come out of it, you dirty, lying, cheap guy!... God damn you!" (pp. 212-13). It is not until the very end of the play that there is the opening for forgiveness.

Dotty Randall

Dotty Randall first appears as one of those peculiarly vulnerable women so common in Williams' fiction and plays. Like Clara in *Many Loves,* Dotty is unhappy in her marriage, and she is made singularly unattractive by that unhappiness. Her husband Cliff, whom H. E. F. Donohue describes as "a small-time narrow gauge boor,"[14] is helpless and rather stupid. Thurber has averred that he loves Dotty—but exactly why?

In the first scene in which they appear together we see the psychological peripheries of that love. The two, who have apparently known each other for some three years, meet at the Randall home because Doc is ostensibly having Dotty type the manuscript of his new play. "A modern play," Doc explains. "I like that kind of stuff" (p. 131). Cliff asks, dully: "But I thought you were a poet." To which Doc replies curtly, "Anything there is—so long as it's writing. Fills up the time for me—when I got nothing else to do" (p. 132). (Again, Williams' self intrudes: the play veers toward becoming a personal statement about a doctor writing a play about writing a play.) When Cliff finally goes to the kitchen to fix drinks, Doc and Dotty display signs of their affection. But this is scarcely the kind of idealistic love intimated in his dream; it is all rather silly:

> [Doc goes toward her but she motions him off, puts her fingers to her lips and throws him a kiss. He is humorously in despair, pretending to tear his hair. She laughs. Impatient, he questions her feeling for him by gesture and his eyes. Smiling, she signifies,

A Dream of Love 115

"Yes!" He makes the exaggerated gesture of putting his fingers to his lips and throwing a kiss in the air....]

(p. 133)

After some conventional rites of flirtation, Doc leaves; tomorrow will be the big day in New York. If this is Doc's vision of how love can be renewed and refreshed, it appears to be almost entirely motivated by sex. But in the meantime Cliff begins to demand of Dotty his conjugal rights. It is marital discord on another level:

Cliff: Do you realize how long it is since we...

Dotty: Make it a year and I'll be happiest. Do you realize—*do you* know how long it is? Agh, you wouldn't understand. Don't touch me.

Cliff: Well, I'm still a man, by God.... Why don't you love me? I've done everything in this world a man can do to satisfy you but you treat me like a cur. Come here!

Dotty: Let go of me! [She frees herself.] Your idea of love is that every woman wants to be raped—by such as you. For God's sake get over it. You're disgusting. I hate you.

(pp. 141–42)

With that conversation in mind, it is interesting to note that in Act III, scene 3 (the hotel scene) the nature of the above two roles—male versus female—has scarcely changed. Dotty remains frigid, for the most part, blocked by a withering insecurity. Doc, allegedly out to renew his love for Myra, hoping to have an affair but wanting also to maintain the fantasy of what love might be, ironically changes places with Cliff. He himself becomes something of the crude male beast. Hence his dream at first seems destined to failure. The affair, filtered through Myra's nightmare, only sputters. It is a classic breakdown of communication, sexual or otherwise, reminiscent of *Paterson* and of so many of the stories in *The Farmers' Daughters*. "Doc goes to Dotty and tries to take her in his arms but she gently pushes him away," Williams instructs as the scene begins:

Doc: Let me undress you.

Dotty: Don't rush me. Order some drinks. Come on....

Doc: Why this slow torture? You are gloriously beautiful.

Dotty: Yes, I know. But give me time. So far I'm doing all right, for me. Don't you think so, pal?

(pp. 214–15)

So Doc, burning with desire and fired by his relentless drive for the new experience (the forbidden flesh), must cool his loins while Dotty plays her coquettish games. "I suppose you'd like me to rape you," Doc offers. "What good would that do either of us, big boy?" she rejoins (p. 215). In point of fact, Williams subtly directs the affair toward bitter bedroom farce, with Doc hopelessly trying to get Dotty's clothes off and Dotty adhering to a mindless standoffishness. Like so much of the fiction of F. Scott Fitzgerald, it appears there will be no happy consummation; the male will be deceived.

Dotty finally explains to her would-be lover that all she really wants him to do is talk. In Act I, she had extolled to Cliff the special virtues of his rival: "He's marvelous. I never knew a man who could talk the way he does—the way he can talk when he gets started" (p. 139). Again she is like Clara in *Many Loves* (and even like Doc's own Myra), mesmerized by the caress of his words. So Doc makes preliminary love to her by using the language. But in fact all the talk is really pointless—about the "bemused scholars" in the universities, the shameless expurgation of the classics, the sound of Greek verse, and the fatuousness of much of modern art. At the end of the harangue Doc says, "...doesn't it make you wanna puke?" Dotty's reply is hardly convincing: "No. It makes me want to love you, my darling, until I'm deaf and blind and..." (p. 222). Finally Doc gets what he has driven to New York for—sex. "You angel out of heaven," he cries out in all seriousness. Dotty's last line, as Koch has noticed,[15] seems to come directly from Joyce via Molly Bloom: "Yes. Now! Yes, yes, yes, yes!" (p. 222). It is, apparently, Doc's momentary dream of love, but there seems to be something ridiculous and even shabby about it. Yet despite the "wrong" inherent in the relationship—and there breaks through in Williams an occasional anxiety about the wages of sin—this love is, like that of Doc and Myra, hopeful in that it does at least temporarily assuage pain.

Thus over and above the hotel scene itself we begin to put the pieces together and see the importance of what might have been first sensed as a very trivialized "affair." It is most especially in an earlier encounter between Myra and Dotty (in Act II, scene 2) that we get a deeper understanding of the worth of Dotty. If in the seduction scene she behaves like a parody of a pampered movie idol ("Praise me! Flatter me!", p. 215), in this episode Williams shows that although she might be neurotic she is, compared to Myra, less suffocating in her love and less self-pitying in her loss. And she displays more courage as well. The confrontation takes place in the Thurber home a week after Doc's death, and is lengthy as well as violent. Myra is in mourning. Cliff is outside in the car waiting to take the Randalls away from "this dirty-mouthed little suburb" (p. 172). The scene is dramatically probably the best in the play. It is, of course, all talk and verbal dueling; one is oddly reminded in the reading of that later playwright of American marital desperation, Edward Albee.

The clash affords the audience extraordinary insights. Dotty, who for the first time in the play is presented sympathetically, arrives out of guilt to apologize: "Will you forgive me—please? Please!" (p. 166). But Myra is in no mood to make matters easy. "Why don't you get out of here—you're not wanted. There's nobody here wants you any more. Get out!" (p. 167). It is in the early part of the scene that the full extent of Myra's bitterness is uncovered, and we see here how dangerous and destructive were the risks involved in Doc's professed program for domestic renewal. Myra is literally at the end of her line. Her continued and nearly fatal passion is to punish herself with knowledge—to discover the most intimate details of her husband's affair, and to cling to them in hate:

> How many times—tell me! Tell me how many times you've been to bed with Doc.
> (pp. 167-168)
> What did he say to you while you were in bed with him? About me? What did he say?
> (p. 168)

But these gropings toward knowledge, Williams makes clear, are also attempts at rationalization. Remorselessly, Myra seeks both to indict the adulterers in her mind and absolve herself from blame. She does not want to consider the possibility of her own inadequacies. But what is worse is that she is as yet unable to imagine the affair from the point of view of her husband, to accept his infidelity as a tragic compulsion (which it is) rather than as a premeditated assault on her.

For want of a more suitable candidate, Dotty momentarily assumes the role of heroine. Brilliantly, Williams provides the audience with the necessary background to show the reasons for her actions. Her needs develop from an impoverished childhood: raised without a father, she grows up frightened of two things, loneliness and her body. In a relatively quiet interlude she tells Myra:

> I have always wanted something, someone who would listen to me—like a father. I dreaded to be alone. I have always dreaded to be alone—that's why I married. I remember once I was left alone in the house, I was just about sixteen. It was very hot and I was—I didn't want to dress so I was lying on the bed without clothes. I remember I got up for something. Suddenly I saw myself in a long mirror we had. I stared at it a long time and—I was frightened. I ran and got under the covers of my mother's bed and hid myself....I was ashamed of my own body—that it was evil. And I was right. I suppose I never really got over that, never really. That my own body was evil.
> (p. 170)

Thus for Dotty, Doc really becomes a father, not a lover. "I could talk to him," she says. "He understood me" (p. 171). Myra replies, wholly missing the point: "You picked him, I suppose, because he was a doctor. In case you needed an abortion. Did you get pregnant?" (p. 171).

At this point Williams has managed to hold in balance the terrible isolation of each of the three characters. Myra is too embittered to feel sympathy for either her dead husband or Dotty, and is on the verge of hysteria and insanity. Dotty's efforts to make her own behavior explicable are admirably but go for naught; even the maid Josephine loathes her. And the visage of Doc, seen through the memories of both wife and mistress, is a sad one, cursed by one and not understood by the other, leaving both unfulfilled. At least part of Doc's failure can be attributed to his work as artist, and the ego that accompanies it. Ultimately what matters most to Doc is his verse, and the women, like Alise in *Many Loves,* are unable to make the full sacrifice to that.

Dr. Thurber

It is as a poet that Dr. Thurber finds himself most at ease. Temporarily freed from the burdens of the household, the obligations of lover, the jangling responsibilities of pediatrician, he can escape to his private world and write. There is for Thurber something appealing about being alone, as indeed there was for Williams. In "Danse Russe" he had once written in exultation:

> "I am lonely, lonely.
> I was born to be lonely,
> I am best so!"
> (*Collected Earlier Poems,* p. 148)

Myra charges in Act I, scene 1: "You loved me, I think. But it's never been wholeheartedly me. It's always been as though you were trying to escape" (p. 123). The speech is said with resentment, but not entirely unsympathetically. Earlier in the scene she has said to her husband: "You know you're itching to get away. Please go. Write me a beautiful poem. Go out in your office and work" (p. 113). But he instead reads her some of his poems, which happen to be Williams' own lyrics. After "Love Song" she weeps, explaining:

> You don't understand. You can't. With all your interests—how can you? I don't expect it. Really, I don't expect it. I feel lonely, neglected. But I don't blame you. Ever. I love you.
> (p. 126)

> I'm not an accomplished person. I'm sorry. I think perhaps we should never have married. [She pauses.] But you're marvelous. You're a wonderful person. And a great poet.
> (p. 127)

But to be in love with a poet is one thing, to live with one is another; and as has been suggested earlier, this is where the trouble lies. The question is asked again, obviously with autobiographical implications: how should one apportion the allotted time of one's life?

It thus becomes evident that Doc's affair is arranged to help him in his writing as well as in marriage, to provide him with new material and a broader perspective. "The thrill of perpetual recovery from an illness" (p. 213), he foolishly explains of his philandering to Myra, a statement with implications for Williams' later play *The Cure*. In an earlier version at Buffalo he concludes that it is "the keenly acute perceptions renewed that come with convalescence—as of the lens of a microscope polished of accumulated dust...." To refine his verse and to recreate a more imaginative poetry are his stated goals; to accomplish these one has to break the rules, to be unconventional, to take chances, to be unfaithful to the past. Comparing the Greeks to the contemporary poets, Doc says:

> There is something in our day, common to them, that we can't talk about. "Figure it," as poor old mother used to say. We can't speak of it. We are too pure! Christ!
> (p. 219)

> ...we are bound by rule of procedure. Our imbecility cannot follow them—because of the ART of poetry. No less! A verse—multiplex, efflorescent, varied as the day in its forms—within the limits of their [the Greeks'] world, to be sure. But we, who inherit the ages, crawl from the light! Good God, what they would have done with what *we* have to do with! But we crawl off, night things—Joyce was right—monotonous in our voices as katydids....
> (pp. 220-21)

The only way to avoid monotony in both love and art, according to Doc (Williams?), is to seek or invent something new in order to revitalize the old. But if the dream of love remains "a little false"—after all, Doc says, sex is a "fake" (p. 203)—the vision of a new verse brings with it serious risks, too. This might be what Doc implies early in the play when he rather obliquely asks himself, "Is all poetry evil? I think so—since John Donne" (p. 127). That is, newness without commitment, direction, or skill does nothing but debase the art (one thinks of Carew's elegy on the death of Donne), just as purposeless promiscuity may corrupt. To cast aside the sonnet without replacing it with a form that is usable (the word is a favorite of Williams) accomplishes nothing. And to put aside one's wife or lover, even temporarily, without somehow repairing the loss, is likewise of little or no value.

The question of Doc's double career as poet and physician inevitably leads to the question of the autobiographical implications of *A Dream of Love*. B. J. Whiting, who directed the first production of the work in 1949, has written:

> The play is clearly autobiographical and Williams freely admitted it. As I recall, he discussed it primarily from that point of view. In retrospect, I think he must have written it to his wife to explain and justify himself to her.[16]

It would be misleading to compare, as Koch does, Williams' use of autobiographical detail with the method of such a dramatist as Ibsen in *The Master-Builder* or in *When We Dead Awaken*. Koch's qualifying statement, that "Williams has merely taken less trouble to maintain the fiction that all the characters are fictitious,"[17] is more to the point, but understates the complexity of identification.

On the one hand, Ibsen's characters are carefully externalized or fictional representations of his own experiences and fears. On the other, Doc is not a very profoundly imagined character. There is too little of art there, too much of the private William Carlos Williams. Williams had of course shown his hand on playwriting much earlier. "The drama is the identification of the character with the man himself," he had argued of Shakespeare (see Chapter 2). "When he speaks of fools he is one; when of kings he is one, doubly so in misfortune" (*Selected Essays,* pp. 62–74).

As Whitaker points out in his book, much of what is commendable in Williams' work is so because he closely "pays attention" to his relationship with the world and the experiences derived from that intimacy. And much of the experience, at least in the fiction (the poetry is quite another matter), is internalized and made personal with abstractions or imaginings only superficially worked in. (For example, many of the Flossie incidents in the Stecher trilogy are presented directly from the remembered experience of Florence Williams.) The lingering passion of *A Dream of Love* and the attendant guilt—the apparent moral failure of Dr. Thurber vis-à-vis Myra, for instance—are made excruciatingly painful. One might suggest that these have been "lived," and that this is what gives the play its hard reality. Is Doc anything but a mask for Williams?

The dangers in autobiographical fiction are obvious, and not unrecognized by Williams. He once cautioned in a letter: "remember, as Proust once wrote to Gide, you can say anything so long as you do not say 'I'. You write to reveal, then call it John Henry but surreptitiously reveal yourself" (*Selected Letters,* p. 274). But as Whitaker points out, such an explanation is not entirely satisfactory: "Proust was wrong: objectivity is not simply a matter of pronouns."[18] What is crucial, particularly in the drama (and in the theatre) is that what is revealed, by the very nature of the art, must be sufficiently objectified to communicate. Williams, who could objectify his feelings so successfully in his poetry (in *Paterson,* for example), found it more difficult in *A Dream of Love;* in a sense, as Whiting indicates, the play becomes an artifact to work out private problems. And it is this internalization, which takes for granted certain assumptions not necessarily known to the reader or viewer, that makes it difficult to obtain an unblurred view of Doc as a character. That is, Williams, already aware of Doc's motivation, at times forgets to clue us in.

Two examples come to mind. Why does Doc continue in his medical practice, hating it all the while? There is a "reason," apparently private, but we are not allowed to share in it. More serious for the play, however, is Williams' failure to make clear (at least in the 1961 version) why Myra finally forgives Doc. The hotel scene and Doc's "return," conjured up in her dream, precede the conclusion but only activate her hate. Then why the last-minute grace? Not to divulge the reason(s), I think, damages the integrity of the play by undermining the credibility of Myra.

Williams' failure as objective playwright is at least as obvious in the one wholly fictionalized scene, Act III, scene 1, which covers the conversation between Josephine the maid and Mrs. Harding, an older black woman. Jo is seeking advice about Myra, who has shut herself up in the kitchen following the death of her husband; the kitchen was the last place she had seen Doc alive, and she is afraid to move from it. "She's gone off her head and I don't know how to help her," Jo explains. "She stays in the one room all day and all night and I can't get her to leave it" (p. 183). Mrs. Harding is rendered as one of those stereotyped blacks so common in American folk literature, God-fearing, a mother figure with native common sense bordering on the supernatural. Mrs. Harding advises that Jo go home and pray for Myra:

> You say to the Lord: Lord, I want that woman to be free because she's a good woman and I love her. And I ask you, Lord, not to forsake her in her troubles.
>
> (p. 188)

But along with the prayer she gives to Jo "a piece of something that was give to me by my mother"; it is, apparently, a charm to aid in the process of recovery. The object is to be held in Jo's hand as she prays. "You do what I say, and, *if you believe,* when you go there tomorrow morning the woman will be cured!" (p. 188).

The episode ends with the two singing a hymn, "Now the Day is Over." There is no reason for its inclusion, despite the "pertinent" final stanza:

> When the morning wakens
> Then may I arise,
> Pure and fresh and sinless
> in Thy holy eyes.
>
> (p. 189)

But since *A Dream of Love* offers no religious resolution, even this is rather dubious; one can only suspect that Williams used the hymn because he admired it and thought it might "work." But the scene remains, on the whole, a failure. It does nothing to further the play. Koch is not looking very sharply when she argues that it "is well written, the idiom rich, colorful, and without quaintness, as it captures the cadences of Negro speech."[19] A simple reading will show that Williams' "colored woman," like so many of the nonwhites in his fiction, is generalized to the point of meaninglessness.

In another way, too, Williams avoids confronting the most critical problem of the play. Mrs. Harding serves as a kind of contrived *deus ex machina* to rescue Williams from the dilemma of writing Myra back into life. The lapse again reminds us of the nature (and dangers) of autobiographical fiction and drama: it succeeds well enough if the reader is keyed in sufficiently, if the writer does not take too much for granted. Again, Williams may have known why Myra is cured, but we are left in doubt. Josephine is a faithful woman, intensely loyal to her employer, but she is not the one to save her mistress from the terrible depression. In fact, Jo only figures passively in the play as a spectator from that scene on. She has not another line of dialogue. The episode is a dead end. The theatre group "We Present" was right in eliminating it from its production in 1949.

Much to Say of Suffering

Some years ago in *The Saturday Review* Richard Eberhart noted three "limitations" to the art of William Carlos Williams:

> One is the tragic. He neither writes tragedy nor has much to say about it. One is religion. He is not a religious writer, except in the broadest sense, and is opposed to Eliot in this regard. One I call suffering, as distinct from tragedy in a formal, Aristotelian sense. He does not speak for suffering, by and large, although he has seen probably more of it than many men. He elects to delete the connotations.[20]

It is a curious criticism, only partly true. Although Eberhart's remarks came in the course of a review on the *Selected Essays,* he was obviously speaking mostly of Williams' verse. It is necessary to be reminded that Williams was much more than a poet; to consider him only as that is to miss important aspects of the man. Let us admit at once that what Eberhart suggests about Williams and religion is, with some minor exceptions, true: Mrs. Harding and Jo are the only believers in *A Dream of Love,* and they are not important. In *Tituba's Children* formal religion is held up as insufficient and possibly harmful. In a more general way Williams, a casual Unitarian, only occasionally relates personal commitment to religious belief.

But of suffering and tragedy Williams has much to say. In Williams' fiction there is considerable suffering and anguish, although Williams has a way of working it through quietly and without the long catastrophe — working it through existentially in talk, for example. In *A Dream of Love* Myra is ultimately the one who suffers most, and it is also for her that the tragedy hits hardest. One is reminded of Chekhov's observation of *Hedda Gabler,* that Ibsen's play would have been a more honest tragedy if Hedda had lived, that suicide for her was the easy way out. In *A Dream of Love* Myra is forced to go on, rebuilding her life from sorrow; Doc, of course, is dead. Williams himself sees in this resolution elements of tragedy: "It is her tragedy which has to be evolved. It ends in her victory — over herself — and the rescue of the doctor. They are reunited in a love which they, and particularly she, bring to a triumphant — but losing — conclusion" (Thirlwall's *Notes,* p. 433).

Yet it is Myra at the end who has somehow arrived — Williams unfortunately does not show quite how or why — at the peace that comes after great pain. She has fought the final battle and has emerged from her struggle *alone,* chastened but stronger. From suffering she has somehow learned how to forgive ("What power has love but forgiveness?" asks the line from "Asphodel, That Greeny Flower"). From tragedy she has learned (and will continue to learn) how to live: it is the kind of knowledge essential for survival.

As usual in Williams, all of this is rendered through talk. Rarely is there what one might call "stage action," and this is why, according to some critics, two of the major productions of *A Dream of Love* were failures. Audiences do not like to listen very attentively. Yet Williams' prose may be the most important achievement of the play. To those who bother to really hear it, the dialogue moves; it carries the drama. The key to his prose, as Williams himself observed of *White Mule,* is that it presents "actual language," without poetic adornment.[21] Much earlier in his career he had made a distinction between his own "clear style" and "the 'plain' style" of such writers as Anderson, Hecht, and Bodenheim. The difference was in what was revealed:

> You've got to *know* — not as a journalist but as an understanding [?] The journalists see too much — see too much unrelated material. The understanding, sight, imagination creates the character and *sees* the material in relation to that — but sees it, not guesses — [22]

In prose dialogue the verbs are the most important syntactical unit: "It is not to place adjectives, it is to learn to employ the verbs in imitation of nature — so that the pieces move naturally — and watch, often breathlessly, what they *do*" (*Selected Essays,* p. 302). Although prose was "lower in the literary scale" than verse, "it throws jewels—which may be cleaned and grouped."[23]

One of the ways Williams purifies the language is through his use of the American idiom, which (except in the scene with Mrs. Harding) gives each character a particularly native authenticity. As in *Many Loves,* colloquialisms are strewn throughout short, abrupt sentences. Most of the dialogue is passed quickly from one character to another, but even in some of the longer speeches the drama pushes from the language itself. This is especially true in what might be termed Doc's dramatic monologues. The following one is addressed to Myra in Act III, scene 2:

> There is never a time, when young, that we are not tormented by our minds, those magnificent Stradiverii, presented to us intact by our beloved parents—tormented brats that we are and have not yet learned to play them. It traps us, we can't find a way out. We haven't the skills, we haven't the data. Yet the thing, the thing itself, is there and all our games, in consequence, are psychic assaults upon our masters, who suppress us. Sex comes in here. It did with me. How I ever got through the sixth grade for what the girl in the seat back of me used to say to me over my shoulder soon after breakfast every morning is more than I can understand. That was the second check. There I was, right up against it. I wasn't scared. Or was I? I was scared all right, but scared to lose something I instinctively wanted—if there was anything I wanted more than to bust out and forget myself in anything, which seldom happened....
>
> It was something else I wanted—wanted terribly—though I couldn't have named it to save my very life. I think that's where the fake of sex took its heaviest toll. I did nothing. As a consequence I never recovered! And this something else in my mind grew and grew, mushroomed up in me until I was a smalltime Emerson of ideas and determinations gone sour. Thus I conceived sex, the monster! Something somebody was trying to put over on me. Poor St. Lizzie saying, This is *it,* boy! Don't be a damned fool. Grab it. But I knew it wasn't it.
>
> (pp. 202-3)

The passage is typical of Williams. The progression of thought is broken down into sections: the romantic yearnings of the young, sensitive child; the terror of newly-discovered sex; and the conflict between the spirit and the flesh. The questioning is all internal (as it was with Washington in *The First President*); Doc is really addressing himself. "I wasn't scared. Or was I?"... "Bah! I couldn't take *this* because I wanted *that*. And what was that? Damned if I knew what it was."

It follows that the subject of communication itself becomes an important theme in *A Dream of Love*. Doc is known as a poet, a communicator, but the one thing that stands out is his inability to reach Myra. Williams had noted the importance of this alienation in an early fragment in the Buffalo papers:

> Blocked when she tries to find out WHAT was said. The rest she has taken for granted

and accepts it. But what is REVEALED, what actually took place—in his mind, to call it that. What is *real*.

And Doc's speech quoted above puts her to sleep. On the other hand, Myra is quite unable to say what she wants to her husband. There is the frustrating blockage so reminiscent of *Paterson:*

> Myra: I've been mortally afraid I'd lose you. That's the truth. It's so wonderful to see you again. Often. But that isn't what I want to say, either. What is it I want to say, dear, do you know?
>
> Doc: No, I don't know....
>
> Myra: I'm talking now—and I don't express myself well. But I've been so afraid to lose you when.... [She is bewildered but recollects herself quickly.] I'm sure I've offended you sometimes by the things I say and my refusals sometimes to do all the things you ask of me and which are beyond my power. But I can't tell you that. I, rather, let you alone.
>
> (pp. 196-97)
>
> Doc: I could have told you many things—had I dared.
>
> (p. 199)

As has been observed, Myra urgently wants Doc to tell her of his experience with Dotty in the hotel, but he refuses to comply; she must discover that information in the dream.

The most striking thing about this question of communication is that Doc is apparently able to relate to Dotty better than he is to Myra: "Here's a beautiful woman who really needs me. I tell you she's needed me—for private reasons I don't want to talk about. After all, it's none of your business. I needed her, too" (p. 208). The implication is again that sex with Dotty not only would recharge his married life but also unblock the language so that he could again write. In fact, blockage has been on Doc's mind through the play, from the irritation over his practice interfering with his writing to an angry denunciation of American censorship: "And we present the *Lysistrata* so befouled by omissions, so dirtied by reticences that even to have smelt of it Aristophanes would have thought himself a whoremaster" (p. 219). And yet Doc even has trouble with Dotty (in the hotel room). The more intimate are his relationships, the less satisfying they become, and one is reminded of the lines from "Sappho, Be Comforted":

> I, we'll say, love a woman
> but truth to tell
> I love myself more.

Meanwhile, the problem of having someone with whom one could make satisfactory connections is underscored by the relationship between

126   A Dream of Love

Dotty and Cliff Randall. Here is marriage on the rocks, with the sea crashing round unabated. Dotty's lament is familiar: "I've got to talk with someone. I have no one I can go to who would understand" (p. 170). But upon meeting Doc she says: "I could talk to him. He understood me" (p. 171). The estrangement between Dotty and Cliff appears almost complete; as Williams had Cliff say in his verse prologue:

> When a man's wife
> stops loving him and I mean won't even let
> him in her bed, he's in a bad way.

Their *talk* goes right past each other; there is no communication. It is odd that Williams allows Dotty, after coming to apologize to Myra for the last time, to leave town with her husband. Their life together, if following the pattern of the past, has absolutely no future. But perhaps this is Williams' ironic way of making Myra's triumph complete.

5
Tituba's Children

Witch Hunts Old and New

Tituba's Children[1] was completed in 1950, two years after the appearance of *A Dream of Love*. The play, originally intended to be the libretto for an opera, was for Williams both a return to past concerns and a sharp change of direction. His old interest in the history of the early colonies had returned once again, this time specifically to the Salem witchcraft trials of 1692. He had considered aspects of the same subject more than 40 years earlier in the playlet *Betty Putnam* (see Chapter 1). Later in *In the American Grain* (1925) he had quoted generously from Cotton Mather's book *Wonders of the Invisible World,* a pointed study of the witchcraft phenomenon by one who was a witness to and partisan of it.

Yet in *Tituba's Children* Williams is revealing a disillusionment as strong as the Whitman of *Democratic Vistas*. The difference in Williams is that he had grown somewhat politicized during the intervening years, and especially so following the emergence of Senator Joseph R. McCarthy and the concomitant anti-Communist hysteria. "Bill got so incensed at what was going on [in the late 1940's] that he went about writing the play," Mrs. Williams remembered.[2] The libretto thus joined together two traumatic episodes of American witch-hunting, separated by over 250 years but related by what Williams as a liberal so thoroughly abhorred: the recurrent and tragic inability of his country to tolerate actions or ideas which diverged, however innocently, from the accepted national consciousness. The American grain, Williams had discovered, was rigidly conformist. One was either in it or outside; and if one were even suspected of being outside there was danger.

If *Tituba's Children* was actually brought to boil by contemporary political events, it had been simmering in Williams' mind for some time. In Williams' *Autobiography* and in J. C. Thirlwall's notes one is given the impression that the play was written for Bill and Harriet Gratwick, Williams' close friends from Linwood, New York, who in the late '40's needed an original libretto for their amateur opera company; and one is also led to believe that the subject grew directly in response to the sweeping accusations of McCarthy and the subsequent hearings. Williams recollects: "Looking for a theme, I hit on the witch-hunt trials now or at that time prevalent in Washington and saw, naturally, the analogy between those and the others that had such a tragic end in Salem, Massachusetts, in 1696" (*Autobiography,* p. 328; Williams means 1692). Mrs. Gratwick has confirmed that statement in a letter: "It was the time of McCarthy & the hounding of liberals, so there was a definite parallel."[3] This is of course true. But what is not mentioned is that as far back as *In the American Grain* Williams had begun to draft the outline for a play which he called *Juba's Children,* "a fantasy in 2 acts."[4] It was clearly the forerunner of *Tituba's Children.* Juba was a surrogate for Tituba, and like the latter she was "an old African slave, a woman from the West Indies." To Williams' Juba (and later to his Tituba) goes the credit, affirmed by most historians, of unwittingly setting off the spark leading to the witchcraft mania of 1692. Extant notes on this play are dated as early as October 1930, but Mrs. Williams recalled that actual work had begun while research was being completed for his book on American history.

Typically for Williams, *Juba's Children* went through many transformations before it would finally emerge as *Tituba's Children.* Originally he had not intended to underscore the Salem witch trials with a modern-day witch hunt. It appears rather that the purpose of the play was simply to recount, in straightforward fashion, first the origin of witchcraft in New England, next the ensuing panic, and then the trials. As Williams viewed it, the "delusion" begins with Juba, who "tells them [the neighborhood girls] vivid stories of her past and the past of her race, African details that whip up their imagination." But much later, in the fall of 1949, with Williams turning once again to the material, the Washington, D.C. sections of the play began to take form. Unfortunately, this new material was inferior to what had preceded it. The poorly defined character of Mac McDee was the first to be introduced. Mac was "a rising young attache of the State Dep't"; he was under suspicion for some unspecified conspiracy with the head waitress of a Washington nightclub (later she is named Stella Rajaputsky, hostess of the National Club). The charge is soon made more specific by a detective: "He was a member of the Communist Party in 1935." Not surprisingly, the legislators who meet in the club are xenophobic, reflecting the jingoism and racism which darken the play throughout. One senator babbles, "We should have 100% Americans."

Still Williams attempted further experiments and additional rewritings. At one point there were to be three scenes instead of the present four, and for some inexplicable reason Juba was to be made a child. Williams had apparently also wanted to move the Salem half of the play back in time to 1669; but that is surely a mistake, perhaps a typing error in the manuscript, since the real witchcraft story comes more than two decades later. In the meantime, Williams had alternately retitled the libretto *Juba & The Fairies* and *The Waitress & the Fairy*, "An opera in 3 acts or so — varied as it may be." Most of the dialogue was in verse. The first completed draft on record at Yale is dated November 17, 1949, and the title was *Tituba's Children*, "A Fantasy (for music) in 2 acts." There is no explanation for the sudden replacement of Juba by Tituba, the slave. Since the second half of the play is concerned with contemporary politics, fragmentary notes dated June 20, 1950 include scraps of dialogue for Mac's defense against the charge of being soft on communism:

"Ostracism helps the Communists, plays into their hands."

"Their duplicity should be exposed, trickery should be unmasked but democracy can win only in the open. Do not drive them underground. Expose, not suppress them."

Finally, a single typewritten page dated August 9, 1950 records a speech by a chorus which is to serve, according to Williams, as "the *conscience* (and history) of the people." Omitted from the final version of *Tituba's Children,* this address at the beginning of Act 1, scene 2 (apparently directed to the audience) makes the Salem/Washington, D.C. analogy explicit:

> You fill me with fear, we are terrified that this
> is the fate of our people. We tremble at it.
> That this is not the first time — and that what
> we believed had been cured by the fire of old Salem
> is being repeated.... what have we done that
> our minds are not expiated as we believed. Must we
> go through still greater tragedies — steaming with
> blood — to expiate
> our sins?

As Atkinson points out,[5] the libretto as it now stands "seems considerably less violent" than preliminary versions at Yale. I have tried to show in a previous chapter that Williams occasionally toned down material prior to publication, eliminating what might be considered scandalous or offensive. But the bitter criticisms of earlier drafts of *Tituba's Children* are still felt, and are still devastating; bigotry and narrow-mindedness are shown for what they are, and time and place scarcely make any difference. Williams' indignation was clearly triggered by the rise of McCarthyism, but this was by no means his first response to affairs of government and politics. Dotted throughout his writings are references to the organization, perquisites, and responsibilities of the state. There is, for example, a recognition of the Soviet political ideal, to him somewhat appealing in its immediate post-revolutionary ideology but later starkly disillusioning. In the manuscript of *The Descent of Winter* he had written: "The United States should be, in effect, a soviet state. It is a Soviet State decayed away in a misconception of richess [sic]. The states, counties, cities are anemic Soviets." But in his poem "Russia," published in 1948 in *The Clouds,* Williams had found flaws in the Soviet experiment:

> O Russia, Russia! must we begin to call
> You idiot of the world? When
> You were a dream the world lived in you
> inviolate—
> *(Collected Later Poems,* p. 94)

It was in *The Pink Church* (1949), however, that Williams spoke most forcefully about politics and the relationship of man to the state. It is an ambiguous poem, and full of outrageous, seemingly flippant, observations:

> Milton, the unrhymer,
>   singing among
>   the rest...
>
> Like a Communist.
> *(Collected Later Poems,* p. 162)

Both this book and Williams' known relationship with Ezra Pound came back to haunt him cruelly, as he explains in *I Wanted to Write a Poem:* (pp. 76-78):

> ...the contemporary associations with the word *pink* are prejudiced. No doubt it got me into trouble. I was never one to duck trouble if it came to me in a fair way, not a lying way. My conception of Christ as a socialistic figure, related to a generous feeling toward the poor, also confusing many. Like Dean Inge of the Church of England I am not at all convinced that communism in its original meaning is any more communistic than Christ's own doctrine. I am obviously not talking about today's meaning of communism and its associations. In the previous book of poems, *The Clouds,* I had included a poem called "Russia" which was also misunderstood.
>
> "Bill was excoriating the Russians," Mrs. Williams said, "but a woman in Washington openly accused him in the press of communistic sentiments."
>
> Yes, excoriating them for their inhuman ways, their brutal and blind ways toward the poor. A poet is used to being misread, but this kind of misreading hurt me deeply. It was just at this time that I received the appointment for the Chair of Poetry at the Library of Congress. I had had a stroke at the time, not a bad one, but crippling for a brief period. Floss wrote them, and they said to take my time. When I was well enough to take care of the duties in Washington—I was anxious to live up to the obligations of

this honor—they didn't want me. A release from *The New York Post* Home News of August 4, 1949, more or less tells the story:

> A congressional move to reorganize or abolish the fellows of the Library of Congress was revealed today in the continuing controversy over the award of a poetry prize to Ezra Pound.... Javits (Rep.) pointed out that the Ezra Pound clique among the library fellows has been strengthened by the appointment of William Carlos Williams as a member....
>
> "What the whole mess did was drive Bill into a serious mental depression," Mrs. Williams said. "I am convinced if Bill had gone down as he was able to, he would have been as he is now. Coming after the stroke, it was too much; it set him back tragically, kept him from poetry and communication with the world for years."
>
> It's all in the past now but I should like to say for the record that I have always hated today's version of communism.... I was approached years ago, before communism was known to have its current frightening connotations, and even then I said this is not for me.
>
> (pp. 76–78)

Williams' long association with Pound was also probably the reason why, in 1952, his appointment as Curator of Poetry in the Library of Congress was overturned. The incident confirmed for Williams what he had suggested in *Tituba's Children*—that American politics had become an ignorant and dirty game—and left him embittered. What was ironic about the rejection was that he had argued against and later repeatedly denounced Pound's pro-fascist sentiments. Regarding Pound's approval of Franco's violation of the Spanish Constitution and Mussolini's support of it, Williams had written to his friend in protest, complaining that he "was a hell of an American" (*Autobiography,* p. 316). On the Spanish question Williams elaborated (*Autobiography,* p. 318):

> A year after the war was over I received the letter I had written Ezra cursing him out over the Franco matter. I had been chairman of the local Committee for Medical Help to Loyalist Spain; the letter had been opened by the authorities. Pound at least never saw it. That is how, I suppose, my name had been identified with his from the beginning.

As Mrs. Williams remembers it in *The Paris Review,* McCarthyism and Williams' connection with Pound ultimately combined to rule out Williams' appointment. But she cites other factors as well: "There was a woman who was lobbying for a reform in poetry, who had no use for free verse. She had a little periodical, I've forgotten the name of it, and she wrote a letter saying what an outrage it was that a man like that...."[6] The truth of the entire matter, as Mrs. Williams later confirmed, is that Willilams was a lifelong liberal who was never very passionate about politics except as an occasional national outrage—the McCarthy tactics, for example—forced him to be.

Tituba's Children is, of course, not the first dramatization of the Salem tragedy. In fact, what is probably the first play to consider the incident, Cornelius Mathews' *Witchcraft; or The Martyrs of Salem,* goes back to 1846. But it is interesting to note that Williams' reexamination of the Salem experience was concluded three years before Arthur Miller's more famous play, *The Crucible* (1953). It should be quickly pointed out that the two works are in most ways quite unlike: the focus of *The Crucible* is John Proctor, not Tituba; and Miller's play is not "updated" by reference to modern characters even though the visage of Joseph McCarthy seems near at hand. Dramatically, Miller is much more successful at bringing the Salem narrative alive than Williams, and *The Crucible* has a sweep and suspense far outmatching that in *Tituba's Children*.[8] Temperamentally, I suppose, Williams' libretto is closer to Lyon Phelps' play on the subject, *The Gospel Witch,* which was written in verse for and produced by The Poets' Theatre in Cambridge, Massachusetts, in 1952. There is music and song in Phelps' charming dramatization, and although Tituba does not appear as a character her presence is felt throughout:

Martha Corey:

> Heathen Tituba
> torn from the Barbados, her familiar forest
> of tropics, of snakes, of yellow birds,
> and shipped, a slave, to our foreign forest
> which Mr. Parris would people with anglified
> witches where we have natural wonders
> to haunt us, real Indians to hunt us;
> Parris enslaved her, pitiful priestess.
> She must have had carriage in her own clime,
> but here, a heathen, they cry out against her,
> the godly children she was brought to nurse!
> Tituba did badly to fear, not God,
> but foreign girls. So she confessed—

Giles Corey:

> —yes—

Martha:

> —the voodoo she knew.[9]

Of the three plays, *The Gospel Witch* is the most artificial, shot through with set speeches to show off the poetry. On the other hand it is politically less self-conscious, with no attempt to make it a comment on the witch hunts of the early 1950's.

Katherine J. Worth is right when she suggests that *Tituba's Children* is more "historical" than the other two plays and less "personal."[10] When

Williams leaves Salem and history and goes to Washington and polemic he is much less successful; oddly, in the "modern" scenes, as we shall see, his writing fails the imagination. But in the Salem scenes his faithfulness to the sense of history brings its rewards, since it is in the real incidents themselves that the drama of this story lies. Williams' knowledge of the subject, while not exhaustive, was more than adequate. Thirlwall writes that Williams visited Salem in 1948 "and studied the records in the Museum archives there" (*Notes,* p. 435). Williams had read Marion L. Starkey's short but informative book, *The Devil in Massachusetts, A Modern Inquiry into the Salem Witch Trials,* which had just been published in 1949; and he knew Charles W. Upham's classic account in two volumes, *Salem Witchcraft,* which had first appeared in Boston in 1867. Throughout the text of the play as printed in *Many Loves* are commentaries taken from both of these books. Williams also had the help of his friend Kathleen Hoagland of Rutherford, who was (as she writes) "a student of satanism and witchcraft for many years."[11] It is not clear what Hoagland contributed to the substance of the written text, but in the Yale folders there remain her costume designs in watercolor for some of the characters. "These are authentic vestments worn at *Black Mass,*" is her notation to some drawings. Even Harriet Gratwick was involved in the research, as she explains rather humorously in her letter:

> ...at one point we went to the Court House in Salem to look up something for him— I forget what now. He came to know a great deal about the witch trials & he found that a relative of mine, alas, had been involved, though he did say that this relative left the court-room (or failed to show up) on the day of judgment, on the plea of a headache![12]

As for *The First President* Williams tried mightily to have music composed for his play, but as before all attempts were unsuccessful. Gratwick writes in her letter:

> W. C. W. wrote a poem for Rogation day, for our Linwood Music School Chorus to perform & it was set to music for Brass choir & chorus by [Thomas] Canning. The 2 men met at this performance & we then began to talk about an opera which they might collaborate on. The opera became "Tituba's Children," but it was never completed & no music was written. It became evident that the work was too difficult for an amateur group to perform.[13]

Thirlwall includes in his *Notes* (p. 425) a portion of a letter from Gratwick to James Laughlin:

> My husband and I had founded an amateur touring opera company named York Opera. We started performing Gilbert and Sullivan but we were also interested in doing a modern American work if we could find one that was up to our standard of comic

opera and within the range of amateur voices. A brief search proved unrewarding (operas were not being written in '48 as they are today), so we asked Bill Williams and Thomas Canning of the Eastman School of Music if they would collaborate on one. They were delighted and Bill set to work. We followed the development of Bill's libretto with great interest, hoping that it would fit our needs, and those of other amateur groups similar to ours. But gradually we realized that *Tituba's Children* was too difficult for our inexperienced company to produce well, so matters came to rest there. It had a savage bite that our American scene certainly deserved at that time...it did not have the gay kind of satire that we were after. Bill knew this too. It was too bad but perhaps not fatal now that you are going to publish it. Maybe somebody will pick it up and give it a good production...I hope so.[14]

In his *Autobiography* Williams writes that he showed his libretto to Ben Weber, another American composer, who "spoke enthusiastically of it" (p. 348). This was at Yaddo in 1950. But nothing came of that possibility, causing Williams to shrug, again in the *Autobiography:* "Weber... seized it eagerly, but it burned a hole through the floor in the end. No contemporary problem may be touched in that mode!" (p. 328). But Williams had also apparently agreed with others that the libretto was "About as suitable for singing...as Veblen's *The Theory of the Leisure Class*"; and the play in final form is something like *The First President,* with far less music or singing in it than first intended. The songs of the Salem scenes and the miscellaneous music of the Washington episodes are ultimately not very important to the play as a whole. In fact, some of these are entirely irrelevant, even silly. And yet on face value it would appear that the subject of the witchcraft trials could be perfectly adapted to music and the medium of the opera, and that Williams' initial intentions toward that end were reasonable. For the story is a noble one with a natural structure to it. There would be a variety of voices. There is tragedy. But Williams, discouraged, did not push the matter. It would be the last time he was to write anything with musical production in mind.

Uncertain Focus

The most curious thing about *Tituba's Children,* and probably the most damaging to the play as a whole, is the uncertain narrative focus and direction of the work. There are two acts in the play, each with two scenes, and a reader is led to believe from the beginning that Salem will take precedence over Washington—the play is, after all, about the children in Salem Village and Danvers, Massachusetts, and the terrible havoc wrought by them. Williams begins with this aspect in the forefront (Act I, scene 1), but the second scene is set in the Washington nightclub and runs longer than the first by about 10 pages. By the second scene of Act II the attention given to Salem is only minimal, with Williams directing our final concern to the plight of Mac McDee, now indicted for contempt and put under arrest. It is as though Williams found as he progressed that he was ultimately more interested in the contemporary witch hunts than in the Salem trials, and thus the initial focus of the play is inevitably changed. Each side of *Tituba's Children* is, of course, a reflection of (but by no means equal to) the other, but Williams gives us too little of Salem and too much of Washington, D.C.

Oddly, the Salem passages of *Tituba's Children* are still more successful as theatre, perhaps because Williams is restrained in his writing by historical fact. In a typewritten critique of the play (apparently as it was being completed), now in the Williams papers at Yale, an unnamed but astute reader (James Laughlin?) writes regarding this point:

> I wonder if you are aware of a fact about your imagination that has for some time been evident to me. You must be, but maybe not consciously. It is this: When you are creating a fiction, you reach the level of imagination most successfully when you have a physical base to start from: a real town, a plant, a person, an experience; when you create a character, or plot structure, out of something in your mind that you want to say, your imagination does not seem to be released. (There aren't many examples of this that I can think of—which is why I think you are aware of the quality of your imagination—*A Voyage to Pagany,* the love story part, is an example.)
> Which is preliminary to my first general reaction to *Tituba*. The Salem scenes are wonderfully well worth working over until they satisfy you in all details. I think they are really good drama. The scenes with Stella and Mac...well, being brutally honest, I think they are awful. In plot structure they fit your needs exactly: good plot. But the people in it—nowhere near the level of the other. (By golly the letter of Creeley you just brought in says it: FORM IS NEVER MORE THAN AN EXTENSION OF CONTENT. In the Stella-Mac parts your structure comes down from above the material, comes from what you wanted to do with it rather than from what it is.)

The criticism is just. *Tituba's Children* opens *in medias res,* so to speak, decisively and with dramatic power; it ends sluggishly, with little resolved and the McDee business more or less hanging fire. The fact that the Salem segments remain interesting is all the more remarkable when one realizes that Tituba, ostensibly the central character, is hardly an engaging dramatic figure. What makes these scenes moving as drama is thus neither complexity of characterization nor facility of the language (the usual case with Williams); it is rather in the stage action of the narrative, beautifully imagined but growing from the events of history. Compared to *The First President,* for example, the pace of *Tituba's Children* is extraordinarily swift, cutting across the proscenium like clouds announcing a storm. There is nothing dreamy or moody about it. Fear is the predominant note from the start, with Betty Parris, the Reverend Mr. Parris' nine-year-old daughter, and Abigail Williams, her cousin of 11, chattering of witches:

Betty: We shall be sent to Hell.

Abigail: Then, we cannot help it, and I'll pray only for its finest room. But maybe not. Yet I must know if there be witches preying here and if so who they be.

(p. 229)

Just as in the opening of *The Crucible* Arthur Miller concurrently plays off the innocence of Betty, the ignorance and cruelty of Parris, and the psychotic malice of Abigail, so does Williams hold these same forces in relative balance. It is really Abigail, however, who provokes the ensuing action by goading Tituba into baking a "witch's cake," by indiscriminately accusing Sarah Good of witchery, and by planting the seeds of doubt throughout the Parris household. A morbid interest in the devil and his spirits, an interest aroused by the Puritan church, had early taken hold of her active imagination. "It would be going too far to say that Abigail loved the devil," Starkey writes. "For all her bold spirit, she sometimes quailed before him and had bad dreams. Nevertheless she took a horrid fascination in hearing about him, and while Betty beside her twitched and swallowed her sobs, Abigail leaned forward to catch every word on this subject,"[15] One is reminded of what Williams said of the Puritans in *In the American Grain:* "Here souls perish miserably, or, escaping, are bent into grotesque designs of violence and despair" (p. 68).

Abigail's intimidation of poor Betty is complete. When the latter cries for her mother, Abigail threatens to "kill" Mrs. Parris if there is an intrusion, and even uses another ruse which will soon become the order of the day. "I'll say you are bewitched" (p. 229). Her song in the opening lines of scene 1 is playful but threatening:

> The pretty truth
> the devil's truth,
> plays upside down
> with the whole world.
> (p. 229)

There is something about the coltish young girl which terrorizes everyone—Betty, Sarah Good, Mercy Lewis, even Mr. and Mrs. Parris, and finally and most forebodingly, Tituba. With her dark skin she is a likely victim for Abby and the rest of the household (racists at heart), who buzz around her like gnats at a scrap of food:

You've got to tell us. We've got to know. Who is tormenting us?...

What's in there? The witches' cake? I think I smell it....

They say in the Bahamas, where you come from, that there are witches there and sorcerers. Tituba, are they real? What can they do?

(p. 235)

Although Williams never makes it clear, Tituba allegedly had at first encouraged this "teasing" by naively fooling with the children:

> Left alone with the children, Tituba had long ago learned to amuse herself in ways that would have got her a thrashing from Parris had he got wind of them in time.
>
> The sport may have started quite harmlessly, possibly even within the hearing of Mrs. Parris, with nothing more questionable than reminiscences of life in the Barbados imported within Tituba's lawful moments of leisure. But there were presently occasions when, in the absence of the elder Parrises, Tituba yielded to the temptation to show the children tricks and spells, fragments of something like voodoo remembered from the Barbados. Once she started, Abigail, thirsting for excitement, must have egged her on to further revelation, conspiring with her to find occasion for the sport, and Betty became a timid accomplice.[16]

According to Williams, Tituba, who was no weakling, is at first less frightened by Abigail than deceived:

Tituba: What do I know about witches?

Abigail: You do know. You know you do. Find them. I order you.

Tituba: I know what I know. What do I care about you witches?

Abigail: Again, I warn you!

Mercy: You're in league with the Devil.

Tituba: Let the Devil take care of his own. I'm in league with nobody. What they come for and snatch me away up here.

[For a moment no one speaks. Suddenly Betty slips from Tituba's arms and falls to the floor, where she lies writhing.]

Abigail: Look!

Several Voices: You bewitched her.

(pp. 236–37)

Inexorably, Abigail's stratagem works, and Tituba is implicated shortly thereafter. (Actually, as in *The Crucible,* time is conveniently condensed. Tituba's "sorceries" were not generally known in Salem for some weeks, and then only by accident when her "witch's cake" was discovered.) Parris, coming out of his study, cries: "If that black woman is to blame, I'll beat her till her bones stick through her flesh" (p. 238). Williams, remembering Parris' moral responsibilities to Tituba, who was brought with him as servant to Salem Village in 1689, excuses neither his superstition nor his ingratitude. But at the end of scene 1 Abigail is fully the victor: Tituba is defamed, Sarah Good implicated, and the demons let loose.

The second scene shifts to Washington, D.C., and the modern witch-hunt. The relationship is obvious. But Williams attempts to connect the two events further by having the club entertainers stage a little review for the Washington political elite called "The Trial of Sarah Good." It is a clumsy and artificial device which really serves not to shed light on the victims and accusers of the Salem catastrophe, but rather to spotlight the immediate official concern in the capitol — the Red menace. But leaving that aside for the moment and moving to Act II, scene 1, it is interesting to see how Williams, returning strictly to the Salem material, has staged "the examination of the witches." This examination, a kind of preliminary hearing, is recorded as having occurred on March 1, 1692 in the Salem meetinghouse. Williams has captured perfectly the drama of the courtroom, with stern advocates of colonial inviolability (Parris, Hathorne) bearing down hard on the helpless and tainted accused (Sarah Good, Tituba). What Williams shows, like Miller, is the terrible inadequacy of good intentions. Samuel Parris is the arch-embodiment of that special Puritan self-righteousness which, in the name of a "cause" (religious or otherwise), served not to preserve but at the very least to pervert, and at the worst to destroy. There is a fulsome piety about him which Williams captures in Parris' speech as the hearing is gaveled to order:

> Omnipotent and ever-present God...On this spot, here in our own meetinghouse, the most momentous crisis in the world's history has on this day come to pass. A crime in comparison with which all other crimes sink out of notice is being notoriously and defiantly committed in our midst. The great enemy of God and man, Beelzebub, has been let loose among us. What has filled the minds and the hearts of mankind for ages, the world over, with dread apprehension has come to pass — and in this village the great battle, on whose issue the preservation of the kingdom of the Lord on the earth is suspended, has begun. Indeed no language, no imagery, no conception of ours can adequately express the feeling of awful and terrible solemnity which overwhelms us all.
> (p. 263)

So Parris launches the attack and Hathorne, for whom his descendant Nathaniel Hawthorne would apologize a century-and-a-half later, systematically follows it up:

> Sarah Good, you understand whereof you are charged: viz, to be guilty of sundry acts of witchcraft. What say you to it? Speak the truth — and inasmuch as you are afflicted, you must speak the truth, as you will answer for it before God another day.
> (p. 264)

There is a vindictiveness about the accusers which is scarcely masked by the affected politeness: "The court, in all kindness, must now ask you..." (p. 266). As defendants, Sarah Good and Tituba are badgered and abused. On Ann Putnam's evidence Sarah is brusquely removed from the court to await trial, while Tituba's examination is continued relentlessly. Dramatically, this is by far the most successfully conceived scene in the play, with Tituba losing both her good common sense and the strength to defend herself from the chimerical charges. Prodded by Hathorne, she begins to tell wild lies:

> *Hathorne:* What else have you seen with Osburne?
>
> *Tituba:* Another thing, all over hairy—all the face hairy—and a long nose, and I don't know how to tell how the face looked. It is about two or three feet high, and goeth upright like a man. And, last night it stood before the fire in Mr. Parris's hall.
>
> *Hathorne:* Did you not see Sarah Good upon Elizabeth Hubbard last Saturday?
>
> *Tituba:* I did see her set a wolf upon her to afflict her.
>
> *A Salem Woman:* We were with her, and she did indeed complain of a wolf and at another time she did complain of a cat with Good.
>
> *Hathorne:* What clothes doth the man go in?
>
> *Tituba:* He goes in black clothes—a tall man, with white hair, I think.
>
> *Hathorne:* How doth the woman go?
>
> *Tituba:* A black silk hood, and a white silk hood under it, with top knots.
> (pp. 274-75)

It is instructive to note the tone of the scene as compared with an analogous one in *The Crucible*. Williams conveys a pointed but dispassionate picture of the deception and malevolence of the interrogators, while at the same time making clear the anguish of the victims (especially Tituba). Miller's scene (near the end of Act I), while effective in its way, is far more emotional, striking a shrill and almost hysterical note. It is as though everything is out of control. The result is spectacular theatrics but not very credible psychology. In any event, near the end of Williams' scene Parris ruthlessly prepares the way for the horrible punishments that will follow; the denouement comes much more quickly here than in Miller. "They must be tried and then hung, all of them, by due process of the law— to rid our world of evil," Parris cries (p. 279). He then presents a peculiar case of intolerance—a case which will be made over and over again, though with less at stake, by the lawmakers in Washington, D.C.:

> The men who have sought this far-off nook and corner of the world, crossing the tempestuous and dangerous ocean and landing on the shores of a wilderness, leaving everything however dear and valuable behind, came to this country for themselves alone to serve God's holy will. Their resolve was inexorable not to suffer dissent or discord to get foothold among them. And they meant to make and keep this country after their own pattern. Let us go forward with the work.
> (p. 279)

One of the serious internal problems of *Tituba's Children* comes in the very next scene, the final one of the play. It is the famous trial of June 29, 1692. Nicholas Noyes, "fat and plethoric," the clergyman Williams had pilloried in *Betty Putnam,* is back leading the prosecution. His judgment is swift and merciless:

> *Rev. Noyes:* The court is ready to pronounce sentence. Sarah Good.
>
> *Sarah Good:* You lie—I am wronged.
>
> *Rev. Noyes:* You are a witch and you know you are a witch.
>
> *Sarah Good:* You are a liar. I am no more a witch than you are a wizard. And if you take away my life, God will give you blood to drink.
>
> [The constables finish binding her and take her out....]
>
> (p. 280)

Giles Cory is next, and then Elizabeth and John Proctor. Oddly, Tituba is not brought in at all. We know from history that she was not executed but later released, serving out her life as an indentured servant. But Williams has by now turned elsewhere. Only a few pages into the scene he appears to grow weary of Salem, writing stage directions rather than dialogue, leaving the details vague, and giving the director most of the real responsibility:

> [The delirium and absurdity of the trials have to be got into this scene—the courageous devoutness of some, the aged dignity of others, the masculine power of Proctor, the mob anger, the mad children. Somehow it all has to be worked into a whole—in the manner in which only a musical fantasy can be broken up. Flashes of color, with the iron wills on both sides caught and dazzled by the "wonder" of the whole. As Rev. George Burroughs, one of the victims who was hanged, said in amazement at his own part in it, he a minister of the gospel—"I do not understand but I am overcome by the providence of it."
>
> The director must break the action up, getting away from rigidity. He must make it show the mass of absurdity—the lack of real evidence, the unfairness of the legal procedures. The music can help to build the picture—a great swirling congeries of themes built upon the Giles Cory ballad.]
>
> (p. 283)

In all of this muddle, however, there is no sense of control and absolutely no dramatic climax, and as a result there is really no resolution. Now for Williams, who spent his life writing poetry that was essentially nondramatic, this flatness is very often a virtue. There is much to be said for the poem that states rather than concludes. But in his plays—especially in *Tituba's Children* and *The Cure*—such detachment seems to arise from indecision. It betrays an inability on the part of the playwright to pursue a critical problem to a close, or even to go beyond a one-dimensional characterization. Thus the trial scene, instead of holding to the questions raised in the hearing, drifts and then simply wastes away. Williams' John Proctor is abbreviated beyond significance. Abigail and Ann Putnam, two of

"Tituba's children," become shallow caricatures. The ballad of Giles Cory seems ludicrous:

> Giles Cory was a wizard strong,
> A stubborn wretch was he,
> And fit was he to hang on high
> Upon ye locust tree.
> (p. 287)

With the focus now turned around, the final half of the scene is given over to the growing predicament of Mac McDee. There is no break at all between the actions in Salem and Washington. Williams stretches hard to create a kind of continuum:

> [As the singing progresses, a transformation is taking place on the bench and among the persons of the trial. Elizabeth and John Proctor have become Stella and Mac. Governor Stoughton changes into Senator Pipeline, Hathorne into Senator Yokell, etc. This process continues—quite openly and in full view of the audience, the actors shedding their Puritan clothes to reveal the modern dress beneath—until we have all the principal figures of the Washington nightclub scene restored. About half of the on-stage audience, however, are still Puritans.]

As we shall see, *Tituba's Children* finishes more as polemic than as play. And thematically it is blurred. To have a single subplot is one thing, but to have two half-plots, with neither standing above the other, is another. Williams, by the final scene of the play, has lost control.

Striving Toward Currency

"The persistence of Salem bigotry is pointed by the repetition of the old grievances in a new idiom," writes Katherine J. Worth,[17] hinting at the dark underside of the American experience both now and in the past. That, of course, is the intended point of the play for Williams. The Chorus in Act II, scene 2 sings its reaffirmation:

> *Strophe*
> Must this terror be repeated? Is this
> the horror of Giles Cory's doom
> come to destroy us? The old fate which
> we thought to have lived down seems
> to have roused again.
> We are fearful of the outcome.
>
> *Antistrophe*
> It is late. We thought that crime
> had been expiated, that the devil days

> would not come again. "Progress," we
> said hopefully. But we have been
> corrupt, we have fouled our own beds—
> a list of our corrupt mayors and
> even justices would fill a large book.
>
> (p. 289)

> I dread what is to ensue.
> Now it approaches, the
> three-hundred-year-old scourge of
> our country. Oh I fear, I fear.
> Intolerance and the whispering
> of scandal.
>
> (p. 292)

And yet as drama and modern-day "scourge" is presented so ineffectively that the entire play, message and all, is acutely diminished.

There are, I think, three reasons for the failure of the Washington sequences. First, the characters—Mac included—are simply not believable; Williams only lets us see them in brief flashes or as ideological mouthpieces—the harassed liberal, the right-wing politician, and so on. Second, the phenomenon of Senator McCarthy, while suggestive of the close-minded intolerance of the Salem witch trials, is by no means the same thing as the latter; and Williams never makes it clear what the distinctions are, and where the real 20th-century menace lies. Finally, the "idiom" of which Worth speaks seems contrived or artificial or both.

First, to the Washington characters. Mac, an under-secretary in the State Department, carries the principal role. Williams intends for us to consider him a deprived hero, a sort of Kafkaesque victim, but for the most part (at least initially) he seems to be simply a luckless fool. Mac is unfaithful to his wife, who is in the hospital giving birth to twins, with Stella Rajaputsky, the blond hostess at the club. He drinks too much. He is both boring and boorish:

> *Stella:* Mac, why don't you go home?
>
> *Mac:* I like it here. I like you. Nobody else I can talk to, Stella. Go home to your wife. She asks too many questions. You don't ask questions.
>
> (pp. 241-42)

Mac's trouble, we slowly find out, is that he is suspect and/or accused by Washington officialdom of having committed a vague crime. This is what is grieving him and making him anxious, Williams leads us to believe. After the frantically inept skit on "old Salem days," performed by Stella and the club entertainers, the charge becomes more insidious. An F.B.I. agent, smelling red, is the one who pins it down: "Party member in 1935—

almost sure" (p. 260). Such capricious speculation—a Communist, like a witch, might be behind anyone's door—grows into direct and fierce interrogation in Act II, scene 2, with Mac, like Sarah Good and Tituba, taking the full force of the assault. Both Senator Yokell, a modern-day legislator, and Nicholas Noyes, whom Williams allows to remain "in Puritan costume," take up the cudgels; they are apparently his stand-ins for Senator McCarthy and associates, who have of course their own predecessors in the Reverend Mr. Parris and Judge Hathorne.

So Mac suddenly becomes the guardian of the liberal American's freedom, the champion of liberty under the law, the persecuted intellectual, defender of man's right to inquire and to know. His interrogation seems to have been patterned directly after the McCarthy hearings:

> Mr. McDee, have you ever been a member of the Communist party?
>
> Are you *now* a member of the Communist Party? Answer yes or no.
>
> You realize, Mr. McDee, that you will be held for contempt if you do not reply to my question?
>
> (p. 288)
>
> Oh, McDee! Confess that you were in the pay of the Soviet Government, that you carried a card and that you obtained a passport to Moscow under false pretences.
>
> Confess, or the law must take its course. Why should you go to Russia more than to Hell, if you were honest?
>
> (p. 295)

The questioning continues. Mac grows in stature because of the barbaric intimidation, the odds against him. For in truth, he defends himself without much distinction. There is no evidence that he is either noble or eloquent, or even courageous. His responses seem uttered by rote, and one senses it is Williams putting words in his mouth:

> I am a liberal—a thing apparently anathema to you gentlemen. If the history were known, I'd say that I am one of those who would support Hugh Peters when he preached before Parliament in our early days: "Why," said he, "cannot Christians differ, and yet be friends? All children should be fed, though they have different faces and shapes—unity not uniformity is the Christian word."...
>
> Based upon liberal thought, there was a time when it looked as though democracy was about to sweep the world. Sun Yat Sen was dominant in China. Mexico had thrown off Diaz. Bryce had written his *Commonwealth of Nations*. And Russia was beginning to awaken from her long sleep. A man's mind could stand up. I deplore, indeed, the very need to speak of a liberal as either innocent or not innocent. He is neither. There should be no such confusion among them. There never was before the Communist revolution. A liberal was simply a liberal—it was quite enough to be.
>
> (pp. 297-98)

With a Chorus intruding banalities—"Where shall/I turn the brain's wheel to carry me/to the truth? Blood rain is/falling" (p. 298)—Mac delivers his final apologia:

> I am no Communist, nor am I a totalitarian in any sense. But I say we cannot save ourselves by being like them in our political thinking and practices, in brutally forcing compliance from any one whom we wish to force into line.

But when at the end McDee is placed under arrest for contempt one feels little sympathy. Mac is Williams' polemical instrument, but as a kind of noncharacter, without human dimensions, he is unequal to the task given him by the playwright. He is scarcely worth defending let alone prosecuting.

Mac is not human in dramatic terms because we never see him acting or interacting, and Williams fails in much the same way with the other characters in the Washington episodes. (One is reminded of the wooden automatons in *The First President*.) Stella is the most obvious second example, but even Tony Proposito, headwaiter at the club, is narrowly drawn. Stella is a vague descendant of the old shady sirens; while profligate, she discloses a heart of gold. Her language is held together by cliches: "Face it kid! Don't let me down." "I know their kind." "Have they got something on you?" In the final scene of the play, Stella is implicated by Senator Yokell because she has remained loyal to Mac. The questioning is at first absurd:

> *Sen. Yokell:* Have you ever read Karl Marx's *Das Kapital?*
> *Stella:* I am a good Catholic. No, sir.
>
> (p. 292)

The charge is finally that Stella lured Mac away from his wife while she was in labor. "You cannot deny," cries Yokell, "that this woman suffered grievously and that you were the instrument in denying her her husband's comfort, solace and support in her extremity" (p. 293). In all of this suffering Stella really understands little. She is neither knowledgeable nor combative, so Williams does with her what any playwright in trouble does. He has her conveniently faint. (The note is: "Stella faints and falls with a crash. The scene becomes confused," p. 294.)

Without characters for whom one can care, *Tituba's Children* lacks warmth. But a more serious failing in these Washington segments cuts to the very core of the play itself. Williams gives the impression—in fact, insists on it—that what is happening in Washington, D.C., circa 1950, is derived from exactly the same source as the Salem witch trials; and this produces (according to Williams) a duplicate evil. Over and over the chorus groans, "The past repeats itself." But the analogy, when looked at closely, is dangerously imprecise. Arthur Miller writes in the text of *The Crucible:* "The witch-hunt was a perverse manifestation of the panic which set in among all classes when the balance began to turn toward greater individual freedom."[18] This is true. But there is a difference between the witch-hunts of Washington and Salem. The former was *politically* motivated, for the most part; the latter was *religious* in kind. Witches threatened the established order of the church; Communists, the state. Williams delineates very well the intensity of and reaction to each threat, and it is true that these feelings are emotionally comparable. But he fails to nail down the crucial distinction between the threats. Clearly, the kind of persecution in Salem comes, historically, from a different psychology from that in Washington in 1950 (or indeed, that in Washington of 1971). It is different because the threatened order is different. Ostensibly, witches war against God, Communists against the government; one is a question of theology, another of political theory. To bring both together, playing on the apparent similarities without carefully showing how unlike the issues are, is really quite unfair. It shows how dangerous an artist's striving toward currency can turn out to be. For example, on the face of it Samuel Parris is a far more destructive man than Senator Yokell (or, for that matter, than Joseph McCarthy), even though, in the passion of the moment, the danger of threatened liberals might appear as great. Jeopardizing a man's reputation, as horrible as that may be, is not so final as hanging him. In *The Crucible* Miller subtly (and rightly, I think) implies that the sort of intolerance practiced by Senator McCarthy *may* lead to the evil which rocked Salem, but Williams silently equates them.

A word has already been said of the inappropriateness of the idiom in the Washington scenes. Aside from the stilted rhetoric of Mac and the pedestrian jargon of Stella, there are other failings. Tony, the headwaiter of the club, assumes the role of master of ceremonies in the skit. He speaks in a kind of bastardized italianese: "Ridi, Pagliaccio! Opera buffa. Molto good feeling. Poco ability" (p. 249). Williams attempts to use the role as another way to establish the play's "relevance," but both the connections and the humor are weak:

>You remember your history, gentlemens.
>I puritani! Very fine people —
>Ancestors of Mayor Curley —
>Bostonesi perfetti. Scusate, no speak
>very good English.
>Hard-working people, but
>have very bad luck.
>
>[He makes a motion as if being hung by a rope.]

> Twenty-two persone! Squick!
> One, they push him up with big stones.
> Agh! I tell you in Italiano—
> all educated people talk my lingo.
>
> (p. 250)

At one point Tony "sings a patter song of Italian musical terms," as Williams himself describes it; it appears rather mindless:

> Agitato. Lento. Vivace. Largo. Molto allegro.
> Lento assai. Andantino. Molto agitato.
> Largo. Alengretto molto. Vivace. Presto. Lento.
> Allegro. Steinway piano.
> You get it.
>
> (p. 251)

The responses of the congressmen are equally fatuous. "What you want," says Senator Wise, "is an aria from that famous classic 'The Longhorns of Poker Flat,' or a yodeler from the oleo lobby. [He yodels.] Oleo lobby! Oleo lobby!" (p. 251). The idiom makes of Tony the stock Italian ("Wop") buffoon; and thus his attempts to hold the Salem entertainment together fail completely. The senators are utterly offensive, as broadly and as superficially caricatured as something out of *L'il Abner* or *Finian's Rainbow*.

Too Many Directions

In 1960 Clinton Atkinson wrote to Williams to inquire about the possibility of staging *Tituba's Children* at Wesleyan.

> He replied in amazement that anyone had even heard of the script. This introduction led to a lengthy correspondence and I was sent a copy of the script, typing several copies for him as a favor for the loan of his original. I decided not to do the play because it was just too didactic for me.[19]

Atkinson was undoubtedly right in rejecting the play in favor of *A Dream of Love* (see Chapter 4). It is true that the didacticism of *Tituba's Children*—or more to the point, its blatant polemic—would make it a risk onstage. On the face of it, however, such criticism sounds strange, since a quick reading of the script makes it appear that it is potentially Williams' most *theatrical* play. There is music, and dance, and mime. There is the intimacy of the cabaret and the broad drama and tension of the court of law. There is violence. Sex is just around the corner. There are a host of theatrical tricks, some of them in the manner of Bertolt Brecht or Tom Stoppard: for example, actors sometimes assume different roles, and they shatter the dramatic illusion by revealing to the audience, as they change costumes on the stage, that they are only actors playing the parts of characters. Demons appear on stage, trailing glory from the old English interludes. Clever use is occasionally made of the Salem/Washington juxtaposition. When Stella tells Senator Yokell that she has not read *Das Kapital,* that she is "a good Catholic," a man "still in Puritan costume stands up and shouts: A papist! An idolator!" (pp. 292-93). The point is proved brilliantly: one culture's pride is another's poison.

Why, then, is it yet not likely that *Tituba's Children* would be a very satisfactory play on the stage? It is possible, I think, to forgive didacticism. After all, one forgives Shaw that, and even Shakespeare. But what is wrong with the play goes beyond Atkinson's objection, or even beyond the imbalance of the Washington episodes or the other criticisms leveled thus far, although it shares in these. The fact of the matter is, *Tituba's Children* suffers most because it has no center, no real axis upon which the one or two major issues and characters may firmly balance. There is simply too much going on—fragments of this, flashes of that, pieces of something else. Williams holds neither to Tituba nor Mac, nor even to a central problem; he seems always to be distracted by another possibility. One sees this most clearly, perhaps, at the end of the play. With McDee indicted and Tituba long discarded, Williams has a singer complete the ballad of Giles Cory, the old victim who was pressed to death in terrible fashion:

> They got them then a good wide board,
>   They layd it on his breast,
> They loaded it with heavy stones
>   And hard upon him prest.
>
> "More weight," now says the wretched man,
>   "More weight," again he cried,
> And he did not confession make
>   But wretchedly he dyed.
>
>   (p. 299)

This is all well and good, but Giles Cory is not the one who has received the major share of the dramatist's earlier attention. So why bring him to center stage as the curtain falls? The question is the critical one in the drama: Williams is going in too many directions at once.

The fact that Williams was not content this time to deal with history as history, but felt it necessary to dress it up with a modern point of view, suggests that he was perfectly aware of one of the strange problems—lacks, really—in the American theatre. That is, in all of our drama there are very few distinguished plays which deal successfully with American history. Williams himself had failed in *The First President,* but he was not alone. Maxwell Anderson's histories, overpraised when they first appeared, have not withstood the test of the last several decades. Robert Sherwood's melodrama, *Abe Lincoln in Illinois* (1938), appears less and less palatable. *Sunrise at Campobello* (1958), by Dore Schary, is an interesting study of Franklin D. Roosevelt, but scarcely more than that. There has been a spate of synthetic histories like *The Caine Mutiny Court Martial* (1954), by Herman Wouk, but most of these are of not very far-reaching consequence. Of recent years our histories have been musicals—*1776,* for example. In any event the record, save for those few exceptions like *The Crucible,* is not very good. Williams' use of history in *Tituba's Children* is, for the most part, cogent and revealing, much more so than his use of it in the opera on George Washington. But because he was not content to stay with history, because he wished to do something more, he overburdened the play. One might have hoped that after the letter from Atkinson, Williams would have returned to the work with a sharper eye, perhaps to reshape it. But Williams was 77 years old, and his health was in decline. He chose instead to finish his final play, *The Cure.*

6
The Cure

Shaking Himself Free

In the winter of 1948, when Dr. Williams was 64 years old, he suffered what he called "a mild anginal attack" (*Autobiography*, p. 322). Nevertheless he remained active as a pediatrician until three years later when he had a stroke, the first in a series that would eventually lead to his death in the spring of 1963. Williams was forced to turn over his medical practice to his son William Eric Williams in 1951. But a year later, while visiting his friend Charles Abbott in upstate New York, Williams suffered a second stroke which, as J. C. Thirlwall writes, "paralyzed his right arm and left his eyes and brain in a damaged condition" (*Notes,* p. 436). "I tried to play it down," Williams remembered of the illness in *The Paris Review.* "I was conscious and rational; and I could joke about it. But I was in a strange house, and I needed to get home. I couldn't write—"[1]

It was while recovering from this cerebral hemorrhage that Williams came upon the idea which gradually was developed into *The Cure.*[2] In 1961 he told Thirlwall, reminiscing in the third person:

> When the man had his first serious stroke at about the age of seventy it was in August at the home of friends, where he and his wife had been spending their vacation. That was an embarrassing circumstance to all concerned. Let's not talk too much of that and of the weeks immediately following until he could be transported home on the "Phoebe Snow" and begin his climb toward comparative good health again.
>
> This is the story of a play which occurred to that excited and damaged imagination while the man was lying there. It was taken down day after day in longhand by his wife. The man's right arm was paralyzed from the first and he never recovered the full use of it. But as the days progressed he had a skillful local nurse who became very important to him and to his imaginings. This woman, as he recovered from his first blindness, began more and more to make herself a part of the life that he was now living. She had in her active days been a fully trained and registered nurse; the doctor (for the patient was a doctor) began to draw up her history as he had been trained to do and in doing that the play took form. How the title of the play, *The Cure*, came he will never know, but from the first that was the title that fastened itself upon his imagination.

150   The Cure

> This was to be a contemporary three-act play—about young people, at least young enough, who lived in the upper New York State country. The plot formed around an automobile accident in which one man was killed and another was so badly injured that the young couple were forced to keep him—an opportunity for the trained nurse to care for him during the duration of the play. Thus immobilized, the characters found an opportunity to work out their story.
>
> One of the incidents which puzzled the author was how to bring in during the third act a relief element which seemed to be necessary. It's not considered good play writing to introduce a new character during the third act. But the playwright, calling on his resources, had no choice but to force things a little and succeeded in bringing it off when the play had been stalled for over three years. Finally when James Laughlin took the play in hand in 1960 and showed a disposition to publish it, all seemed to grow clear. The playwright was inspired and got to work finishing the play, using his left hand for his typing and finishing his chore at a time when he thought the task was to be too much for him.
>
> (pp. 436–37)

The statement is only revealing to a point. That Williams was recuperating from a serious illness had a good deal to do with the fact that the play is about a man in the process of recovery. But according to Mrs. Williams,[3] credit for the basic story idea must go to the attending nurse. "She told Bill the story of a young man who was in an automobile accident," Mrs. Williams recalled. "She said she would have loved to have taken care of him. I remember that Bill decided she was in love with the man. The nurse was really sweet and charming. She was also married." Thus when Williams rather vaguely says "to draw up her history," he means he was imagining from that situation the narrative which would comprise the drama. The composition, as Williams suggests, was long and arduous. Bedridden, groping for words, he at first dictated to Flossie. Then when James Laughlin of New Directions approached him eight years later in 1961 with the notion of publishing his collected plays, Williams, slowed but not incapacitated, put *The Cure* in final form. Actually, there is at Yale University a typewritten draft of the play dated July 13, 1959; it is very close to the version which appears in *Many Loves and Other Plays,* and leads to the conclusion that the work had been substantially completed sometime after the mid-1950's. It has never been produced on the stage.

Laughlin has speculated that writing *The Cure* was "therapy" for Williams.[4] He is right, of course. Like the word "dream," "cure" has a special meaning for Williams, and is used over and over throughout his work. To be cured means variously to be once again physically robust, to be psychologically strong—but most of all, to be again ready to write. "For when I cannot write I'm a sick man/and want to die," Williams lamented in his short poem "The Cure" (*Collected Later Poems,* p. 23). In this latter sense cure can be conveniently set in opposition to that most threatening of all words in Williams, "blocked." The poet in *Paterson II,* for example, is blocked (*Paterson,* p. 78); it is a kind of drying up, a death. Later in *Paterson III* Williams can ask the question, "How to begin to find a shape— to begin to begin again" (p. 167). In Book V he finds in art a therapeutic lift:

> the cure began, perhaps
>   with the abstraction
>   of Arabic art
>
> Dürer
>   with his *Melancholy*
>   was aware of it—
> the shattered masonry.
>   (p. 259)

Art (specifically verse) provides a comfort and cure in "The Yellow Flower," from *The Desert Music and Other Poems* (1954):

> What shall I say, because talk I must?
>   That I have found a cure
>   for the sick?
> I have found no cure
>   for the sick
>   but this crooked flower
> which only to look upon
>   all men
>   are cured. This
> is that flower
>   for which all men
>   sing secretly their hymns
> of praise. This
>   is that sacred flower!
>   (p. 89)

So there is in the process of creating, even if the result of that effort is but a "crooked flower," a positive sign, a forward thrust. Art is both a touchstone of health and life and a means to both. One may take what Williams says in "The Basis of Faith in Art" as exactly this: "But I insist, yes, that the purpose of art IS to be useful. Why does a poet write as he does? It may be defiance but it is defiance because he sees something worth having. He must shake himself free, he himself as one man, from the destroying horror of an oppressive existence...." (*Selected Essays,* pp. 179-80). In *I Wanted to Write a Poem* Williams goes beyond that, arguing for the triumph of art over the body, almost sounding like the Yeats of "Sailing to Byzantium": "When you're through with sex, with ambition, what can an old man create? Art, of course, a piece of art that will go beyond him into the lives of young people, the people who haven't had time to create" (p. 22). Of course later, in the last months of his life, Williams suffered a great deal, and it appears then that he felt the only real cure available to him was death. David Ignatow writes, "His depression had turned into a kind of triumphant bitterness in which he looked forward to death as an event."[5]

Leanest and Toughest

The Cure uses as its *modus operandi* what might be called the dramatic interruption, or the unexpected visitation. The device, common enough in the literature of the theatre, is the sort of plot trick one finds in Kaufman and Hart's *The Man Who Came to Dinner*. A more striking use of a similar technique is seen in Friedrich Dürrenmatt's melodrama *The Visit;* more recently Edward Albee's *A Delicate Balance* and Harold Pinter's *The Homecoming* follow a comparable line. The plan in all of these works is simple and really quite obvious: into a relatively settled environment there is introduced a surprise guest (or intruder) who proceeds to shock or disturb the host population by the very ambiguity of his presence. The dramatist then studies the nature of the conflict which inevitably follows.

In *The Cure*, which runs through three short acts, the protagonist is a young man named Prospero, a troublemaker if ever there was one. His entry into the world of Williams' play appears to be wholly fortuitous. On "a stormy May night in 1952" (p. 361) in upstate New York, Prospero has been thrown from the back seat of a speeding motorcycle into an "old Dutch-type farmhouse," which turns out to be the home of George Mitchell and his wife Connie. Prospero is in his early 20's, the Mitchells are in their late 20's. The accident has occurred just before the play begins, and the curtain opens on general clamor and consternation. The driver of the motorcycle is pronounced dead. It is only after the firemen and other officials have departed that the Mitchells discover Prospero, who had been miraculously deposited alive in the cellar. George speculates:

> When the car came around the curve—the motorcycle I mean—it must have skidded and hit the corner of the house at top speed, killing the driver out-right—with a broken neck. But this guy on the back seat was catapulted over his friend's head and through the opening the motorcycle had made in the wall—saving his life—and right on through our "trap" which must have been left open last night—for some reason—and then the catch must have been jarred loose and the door slammed closed over him.
> (p. 382)

Thus Prospero makes his improbable entrance, with Williams working his own special *deus ex machina*. As in *The Homecoming,* the visitation sets into motion currents of tension which continue unabated to the end. As a matter of fact, the play as a whole reminds one of Pinter. *The Cure* is the leanest and toughest of Williams' works for the stage, and like *The Homecoming* it is held taut by the barely concealed violence of sex. There is strain everywhere. The prose is clipped, abrupt, occasionally even savage. It is interesting that Williams, who in much of his later poetry seems to mellow into a kind of forgiveness ("Asphodel, That Greeny Flower," for example), here seems to cling stubbornly to some of the bleaker themes touched earlier in *Many Loves* and *A Dream of Love*. Williams' view of love is that misunderstanding, inadequacy, and betrayal are the order of the day; to survive, one must keep one's defenses up. *The Cure* is also full of the uneasy silences and hesitations that are so characteristic of Pinter's plays. In Act I, for example, Connie and George discuss whether or not to keep Prospero:

[Connie and George come up out of the cellar.]

Connie [rubbing her back]: My back!

[George is completely noncommunicative.]

George: When do I go for the police?

Connie [after a pause]: Can't we keep him?

[There is another pause.]

George: You surprise me.

Connie [hanging her head]: I missed the operating room training when I realized I was giving it up probably forever—I was heartbroken. Do you think I'll soon have a baby? That will settle it.

George: Well...

(pp. 378-79)

It would be misleading to compare *The Cure* with *The Homecoming* and leave it at that, because they are ultimately not equals as art. Pinter knows full well how to make a scene dramatic, how to develop the rich complexity of his characters. Williams, although he proves able to do both, seems never quite sure how; when he succeeds it is almost by accident. In truth, the overall achievement of *The Cure* is rather slight. Whitaker is right when he says the play "is seriously weakened by thin motivation and by mechanical development."[6] The play exists as a kind of outline, with some possibilities and themes exploited and others only tentatively sketched. The result is that the reader or potential viewer never knows quite how to take the play. Williams suggests in Thirlwall's *Notes* that he wanted to lighten the last act by introducing "a relief element"—obviously the slatternly Rosy—but there are times earlier in the play when Williams is only barely avoiding comedy. Again, the point of view is not clear.

This difficulty is nowhere more evident in *The Cure* than in the relationship that develops between Prospero and Connie Mitchell. Each seeks to take something from the other, but it is not entirely clear who is the predator and who is the victim. The affair is complicated by the fact that Connie seems genuinely to love her husband, to whom she has been married for only six months. "But you can't realize it, George—I love you, completely" (p. 379), she insists in Act I. Her adulation appears banal but sincere: "George, my darling, you're wonderful" (p. 381). For his part George, who works in one of the local salt mines, is not the traditional inept husband. He is far stronger than Cliff Randall of *A Dream of Love*. He helps his wife, is at once solicitous but firm, and possesses a hardheaded common sense. He suggests, for example, that Prospero is in trouble with the law, and warns that to give him shelter is to admit danger. And he is in fact right: we discover later from Prospero's father that the son is wanted for a serious crime.

But prior to Prospero's arrival Connie has been unhappy, frustrated, torn by longings and desires and the need to have something to occupy her days. It is the classic case in Williams of the unfulfilled woman, a type with whom he had been acquainted in real life for 40 or so years, treating the sometimes imaginary ills of the suburban New Jersey housewife. There is more than a shade of likeness between Connie Mitchell and Clara (of *Many Loves*) and Myra Thurber and Dotty Randall (of *A Dream of Love*), although Connie seems less neurotic than the others and a bit more appealing as a character. But there is something selfish, even rapacious about her compulsion to treat Prospero's broken leg. She is as yet childless, and is not even pregnant—a lack which she deeply regrets if not resents. Before her marriage she had been a trained nurse—"I've had wonderful orthopedic training in the wards of the old hospital" (p. 379)—and she sees a chance to put that skill into practice once again, to become useful. But as she gives to Prospero, she withholds herself in a way that reminds one of that niggling characteristic in women which Williams had written about in *In the American Grain*. It was, he claimed, their "spiritual barrenness" that was so shocking, that defeated their men. He had also said:

> Women—givers (but they have been as reservoirs, empty) perhaps they are being filled now.... They are our cattle, cattle of the spirit—not yet come in. None yet has raised benevolence to distinction....

Then, pointedly, with reference to a hypothetical example:

> It so clear: A man without a woman finds one. She immediately starts to torture him.

It's all they can do. "Take it out of the son of a bitch" — he's put himself in a compromising position and deserves to be castrated.

(p. 181)

So, like Gurlie in the Stecher trilogy, Connie gives, but only at a price. On the one hand her giving keeps George more or less dependent, although, as mentioned earlier, he is no lapdog. On the other, her gift of curing Prospero is offered with the tacit understanding that he will allow her to love him. And it is here that there occurs one of the most interesting examinations of the ambiguity between love and sex in all of Williams' plays. Connie appears to be drawn to Prospero both as lover and mother, with the latter feeling ultimately holding sway. But to Prospero it becomes both bewildering and maddening that Connie does not follow through sexually, does not give herself physically to him. His final address to her in Act III is alive with despair and a kind of violent denunciation, for he had by this time learned (Williams suggests) to love *her:*

> But you didn't have the nerve. You were yellow, through and through and through. I could tell you about some married women I've known — you'd be surprised. Right around you, wherever you come from — good girls with kids in the grades, good-looking, the best. It's nothing against them — just the opposite — that they enjoy a little free screwing once in a while. Women are mostly unlike men in that respect — they get tired of it and want to go back to their knitting and contract after a while, unless they have a real hot buddy. But I thought you were wise to all that. Was I mistaken. You're a hick, a real hick.

(p. 424)

The unflinching toughness of the language is, for its time, rather unusual in American drama.

It all begins innocently enough. In the first act Connie casually tells George that caring for Prospero "will give me something interesting to do while I'm waiting" (p. 379). But this is more than an interlude, more than a pause between more consequential events. By the end of the act she has set Prospero's leg and it is clear that he will be staying. George has already begun referring to him, somewhat nervously, as his wife's "boyfriend" (p. 380). But it is in Act II that the relationship is fleshed out in more complete detail. It is morning, a week-and-a-half after the accident. Prospero is bedded down on a cot in the main room of the small house. George leaves for work, with Connie reassuring him that, "So far he's been a perfect angel" (p. 386). But by the end of this middle act we know just how black Prospero's history is. We also see him in action, clumsily attempting to seduce the wife. Like a malign presence, he "watches" Connie from his makeshift bed. She at first thrives on it; it invigorates her, gives her a purpose. She gives him a sponge bath, gets his breakfast, makes conversation.

156   The Cure

And when a suspicious state trooper returns to inquire about the stranger, she lies for him even though she is as yet uncertain about Prospero's exact status with the law.

The interruption in the middle of the act finally turns out to be Prospero's father, a cardboard villain:

> *Connie:* Who are you?
>
> *Visitor:* I'm his father. [to Prospero] We thought you were dead. No such luck. Your mother has had me covering the roads of three states on crazy tips from your gang trying to catch up with you. A waste of time. And now I found you. I ought to turn you over to the police, you crook.
>
> (p. 389)

The father's real function is to give us the sorry story of Prospero's life, but his very presence makes the reader aware of perhaps the major reason why the son is that way. We discover that Prospero was (1) christened Peter Prospero James; (2) expelled from Princeton in his senior year; (3) a "natural-born liar"; (4) fleeing from a girl he has gotten pregnant; (5) on the run after failing in an attempt to rob a bank; and (6) overloved by his mother, whom he guiltily scorned and abused. The final point is the one picked up by Williams, and there is even a warning from the father to Connie: "You're a woman and women are this sort of man's special bait" (p. 399). When the visitor abruptly departs Connie turns to Prospero, helplessly falling into a peculiar kind of love. Williams establishes the tone:

> *Connie:* ...You are my patient. And what I say to you is the law. I'm not giving you up. That's final—so relax and make the best of it. [With that decision, a great weight seems to have dropped from her shoulders; she becomes on the instant a different person. For her, and for Prospero also, though they are not fully aware of it, the whole atmosphere has changed.] I'm not giving you up. [She reaches in her pocket for the nurse's cap which she had discarded and places it, cockeyed, on her hair. She goes to the mirror and laughs at what she sees there.]
>
> [Prospero does not at first understand what is taking place within Connie's head but he quickly begins to catch on—she is divesting herself of the pretense of reverting to being a nurse. Now she takes off her nurse's cap and, with a wry smile, tosses it onto the table. Then she removes her nurse's apron, throwing it over the back of a chair. Now she is dressed more or less as any young housewife might be. She has been withdrawn into herself, not looking at Prospero. Now she turns back to him.]
>
> *Connie:* May I get you some lunch?
>
> *Prospero:* Sure, I'm hungry.
>
> (pp. 400-1)

Connie's feelings oscillate from the barely concealed sexual to the maternal. She plays on Prospero's remembered sympathy for his mother, using it to wedge herself into his thoughts, becoming both flirt and protectress. "Now really tell me about your mother," she commands. "You loved her, didn't you?" (p. 404). Near the end of Act II Prospero responds by trying to kiss her; but she refuses, then coyly inquires: "What are we going to do with ourselves while we're waiting for that bone to heal?" (p. 405)." Prospero, who knows his literature, prepares another advance by asking Connie if she is acquainted with the *Decameron,* or Rabelais, "Or a play by Tennessee Williams" (p. 405). Then he bluntly asks: "Take off your clothes and come here on the bed with me" (p. 405). But Connie, like Dotty Randall in the hotel scene in *A Dream of Love,* again refuses:

Connie: Old stuff. Every student nurse has to get used to that from her male patients.

Prospero: Come on.

Connie: I might hurt your leg.

Prospero: I'll take care of that.

Connie: You must think I'm awful simple.

Prospero: Just slip off your dress and lie down beside me.

Connie: Nothing could be simpler.

Prospero: So you refuse. Quit stalling. You know you want it as much as I do.

Connie: Poor dear. I think I'd better put on my cap again to remind you—have you forgotten that I am your nurse?

Prospero: You bitch.

(p. 406)

But the act ends with Connie throwing him a kiss on her way to the kitchen. Prospero vows: "I'll get you yet" (p. 407). The treacherous game continues.

Williams maintains the shadow-boxing in the final act, which occurs in time two weeks later, but he remains annoyingly inconclusive. There are fragments of vaguely suggestive dialogue like the following exchange, which reveal the growing intimacy, if not harmony, of the two:

Connie: Lean back on the pillow while I put away the breakfast things. [He does what she bids him do, and she puts a pillow behind his head.]

Prospero: You certainly are sweet to me.

Connie: I mean to be.

Prospero: Forget George.

Connie: There you go again.

(p. 411)

The same eagerness in Connie to love and a reluctance to give are shown shortly after when Prospero, nearly healed, takes a few halting steps out of bed. Williams chooses to describe the action rather than to have his characters work out their business in words:

> [Trying to use them, he finds the legs much stronger. He gimps lamely about the room. More to steady himself than anything else, he catches Connie about the waist and takes a few dance steps. She enjoys it and lets herself go. In the excitement of the movement she allows him to kiss her on the mouth but springs back immediately from the embrace, hands to her mouth as he, deprived of her support, collapses across the bed out of breath.]

But when Prospero cries "Give me another kiss!" (p. 412), Connie, "shaking her head," denies him roughly:

Prospero: Come on!

Connie: No.

Prospero: What do you mean, no?

Connie: Sooner or later we got to face it. I'm not going to bed with you.

Prospero: Quitter.

Connie: I'm not a quitter.

Prospero: Quitter.

Connie: Lie down on the bed again. You need it.

Prospero: I don't need it for what ails me now. Quitter.

Connie: Have it your own way — but don't think you can get anywhere by these methods.

Prospero: I'll rape you.

Connie: Don't try it. Be a nice little boy, and bury the hatchet.

Prospero: You bitch. I've said it before and I'll say it again. You cheap bitch! You know what you want. You know what you want to pay for it — nuthin'.

Connie: Speak for yourself, my dear.

Prospero: You've led me on.

(pp. 412-13)

Apparently, Connie has now been thoroughly frightened, and retreats to her husband's arms when he returns home. From a distance the affair had seemed glamorous and romantic; near at hand, it is a threat, something which only reflects one's own inadequacies. Thus with the entrance of Rosy the duel is jaggedly broken off, and Prospero, who had appeared to hold real (if undisciplined) affection for Connie, realizes his betrayal at last:

You cheapskate, you thought you could play both ends against the middle, didn't you? [Connie does not answer him.] From the very beginning I spotted you. No nerve. No guts. Just wanted to play like any other jerk. I really thought, after I came to and saw what had been going on, that you had something. Oh, I have to thank you for what you did for me. I acknowledge it. But I didn't realize how far you were over your head, wallowing around in the water. All that trained-nurse bunk! What does a trained nurse know that any tart from Eighth Street or the Bronx couldn't teach her, or Vassar College couldn't teach her — with the aid of contraceptives?

(p. 424)

It is a hard speech, and ruthless. Connie explodes, striking him in the face. Prospero, springing into action, returns a blow and knocks her into momentary unconsciousness; then he limps outside and into a car which is waiting to speed him away. (It is another contrived ending.) But by this time the play has gotten completely away from Williams. Connie gets up just in time to see Prospero blow her a kiss as the car pulls off. The braggadoccio of the act offends the reader but not the wife, who moans: "He's going away. There he goes. Forever" (p. 426). Then, as Williams describes it, "she breaks down and, in a violent fit of hysteria, begins pounding the bed with her fist and weeping" (p. 426).

What is one to make of all this? I think Williams' characterization of Connie Mitchell is less confusing than that of Prospero, but as in *Tituba's Children* very little is explicitly resolved. One is thus forced to make judgments based on what one feels were the intentions, rather than the performance, of the playwright. At the end of *The Cure* there is a little doubt that Connie will remain with George, nor is there much question that the marriage will continue. But on what basis? Marriage for Connie means security and probably love; but for her these are not sufficient. She needs to feel the master. Not satisfied as nurse, she will be the doctor — the one who heals and cures. Involved in that choice, which is to Williams' women an inevitable though unconscious one, is a dangerous meddling. First, Connie inspires in George a natural jealousy, and drives the marriage toward a perilous ground. More important to this play, her actions carelessly play on the heart of the other man, Prospero. Although Connie technically cures him, she bewilders him and finally appears to destroy his capacity for love of any sort. Thus there is truth to his charge that, "With a little assistance from you I could have made good.... but you ran out on me" (p. 424).

But it is the protagonist, Prospero, who seems to lose most. I say seems because it is never very clear what the full range of his possibilities are, what he has in front of him, what he needs to learn in order to grow. Here it is helpful to keep in mind Williams' fiction. In the short stories of

The Farmers' Daughters, especially, we are presented brief flashes of a man's (or woman's) life without much regard as to what has shaped him or where he will go. Prospero's father has given us some background, but that history is all bad and undigested. We can never be sure, for example, whether Prospero is married or not; he once declares he is, but he cannot be trusted to tell the truth. In any event, Prospero himself tends to exaggerate his faults, deliberately striking a swaggering pose. But despite his undeniable meanness, he is not irredeemable. He has the brightest mind of the lot. At Princeton he was named "the Brain." Prospero at one point calls himself John Keats, a name not wholly inappropriate, for there is something of the poet about him. He says exactly what he feels, sometimes with a kind of elegant bluntness. Williams forces us to consider the significance of the name Prospero, but the relationship between Shakespeare's magician and the young hellion of *The Cure* is tentative at best, perhaps lying only in the power each exerts over others.

At the end of the play, however, Prospero quickly departs, thus losing his control. Ostensibly, of course, his departure wounds Connie. But he is the one most defeated. Scarred by his father, misunderstood by his mother, a failure in his early experiences in sex and love, finally drawn to Connie, he is left rejected and disillusioned, and sets off for a life that would appear to offer little. It is instructive in this regard to see how Williams brings George back into the center of the play at the end, presumably to assume the strong male lead once again. He will be the stabilizing force, carrying along perhaps an increasingly captious wife. But even quiet desperation seems better than the bleak horror which Prospero will have to bear.

Familiar Limitations

The Cure throws into clear relief some of the familiar limitations of William Carlos Williams as playwright. For one, he continues to be unable to maintain a consistent point of control. The most obvious example of this is the use of Rosy, the neighbor who flirts with Prospero in the middle of Act III. Williams' notes to Thirlwall on the subject show that he was uneasy about the role. ("It's not considered good play writing to introduce a new character during the third act," he acknowledged, p. 437.) But that is really the wrong reason for uneasiness. A dramatist may introduce a new character into a play anytime he needs to make use of one. Indeed, there are plays where one anticipates the late entrance of a character; and such an introduction may often preserve the integrity of the work. (One need only think of the Roman comedies.) But in *The Cure* Rosy is not only quite unnecessary, she is a dramatic nuisance, and diverts our attention from the confrontation between the major antagonists. As comedy she is grotesque; as a sex object she is absurd.

There is another point here to be considered. Because there is no real dramatic climax or resolution, *The Cure* loses power as an artifact for the theatre. Williams squanders a subject that is in itself potentially *dramatic* by refusing to move it toward a suitably revealing close. This is not to suggest that the play ultimately fails because it discloses too little. *The Homecoming* yields few answers. Yet on the stage Pinter's play is charged with the drama of the human situation, its characters flailing in the dark, with the playwright persuading audiences through skillful revelation and tact to follow the struggle to the end. In *The Cure*, to be sure, there are several wonderful moments of theatre: the discovery of Prospero in the cellar in Act I, the wild seduction attempt in the beginning of Act III, and the ironic conclusion of the play, with the obnoxious state trooper nodding slyly and saying, "These hot days" (p. 427). But there is little drama in between. There is almost no suspense. Details are presented obliquely, often leading nowhere. *The Cure* deals with one of the major recurring issues of Williams' important work, the marital struggle, but only occasionally communicates with the persuasion and intensity of *Many Loves* and *A Dream of Love*. Like so many of the short one-act plays and like *The First President* and *Tituba's Children*, *The Cure* tells us some valuable things about Williams as an artist, but not very much about the world of the theatre or even the world at large.

Appendix A

The Living Theatre's *Many Loves*

When *Many Loves* opened in New York on Tuesday, January 13, 1959, in the Living Theatre's new quarters at 530 Avenue of the Americas at Fourteenth Street, Dr. Williams was 75 years old. Although he missed opening night (his health was not good, and Flossie attended in his place), he went to a performance on the following Sunday, and two days later (January 20, 1959) wrote to the Becks:

Dear Julian Beck & Judith Malina:
   That was a "tonic" experience, as Brooks Atkinson said and a particularly pleasant one for me to have seen your production of my play last Sunday afternoon. Really, I was thrilled. You two have made the thing come alive. From now on you have generated a confidence in me that would be hard to kill—it reminds me of the early plays of the Irish players, they had Sara Algood, who was hard to beat, but Malina is not far back of her and the rest of the company is recruited from the same sort of material and they have done an enviable job, sometimes they were brilliant, all that remains for you is to find the plays. I'm afraid that that will not be an easy matter. You can't go on producing the same play indefinitely or even a play with that quality of thought in the lines—but you'll have to look about for playrights [sic] that are interested in the same quality of thinking and encourage them to write for you. In other words you'll have to establish a school....
   But this isn't the letter that I wanted to write you. Someone has the inspiration for it, together you make a beautiful team. One or the other of you two selected that play for production years ago. The persistence of your effort in spite of disappointment was phenomenal—and you put it over triumphantly—to the least member of the cast, they worked together to produce not perhaps a finished performance but a performance in which you were all interested and showed your interest in the intelligent reading of the lines.
   There must be plays that have not got a performance on Broadway by many writers who are fed up with bucking the commercial theatre. Look around for them, they may be just the thing for you.
   I'd like to talk to the cast individually, that young red headed girl [Ann, played by Eileen Fulton] was a knockout but no better than Peter [Ronald Durling] and the Doc [Robert Berger] of the cast and the asthmatic old man [Rudd Lowry] of the cast. Very well done. Hubert [George Miller] was excellent, he put over his lines with conviction, piling them up against Peter's opposition to the very end with increasing emphasis until the big final speech which was convincing and led to the play's climax—and the resentment of the final resentment by the ladies of the press which you reported to me. I don't blame them. It was all due to the lines which Peter put over so excellently. My hat is off

to the two elderly ladies who with their mere presence held that scene on the farm together giving it the authenticity required. It was a good show and I enjoyed every minute of it....

Sincerely yours
W C W

The play, billed as "a comedy in verse," was directed by Beck with his wife Judith Malina playing the Alise-Serafina-Agnes Breen-Clara roles. The reviews were mixed, but it caught on and was to enjoy an initial run, first alone (eight performances a week) and then in the Living Theatre repertory schedule (with Jack Gelber's sensational *The Connection,* for one) of 216 performances. As Williams' letter indicates, Brooks Atkinson's review in *The New York Times*[1] was favorable. (It was a pivotal notice, since then as now the *Times* reviewer could literally make or close a show.) The play was, Atkinson wrote, "original in form, exhilarating in content and alive with knowledge about human beings," although he confessed that "This column takes the liberty of not thoroughly understanding the overall scheme." Emory Lewis in *Cue* applauded the play's "earthy, robust humor,"[2] and the reviewer in *Women's Wear Daily* compared it to Chekhov and termed it "a brillant play."[3] *The Village Voice* gave the play an unqualified rave, exclaiming that "nothing about 'Many Loves' is dull, all of it stimulates your finest attention."[4] Later and more importantly Beck would write to Williams: "Alfred Kreymborg was in to see the play last night and was very pleased. Did I ever tell you that Edward Dahlberg had been to see the play and that he had sent us a very enthusiastic letter?" (March 26, 1959).

Others were less enthusiastic. Donald Malcolm in *The New Yorker* was generally appreciative, but with important qualifications: "As an exercise in entertainment, 'Many Loves' succeeds; as an exercise in dramaturgy, it does not."[5] Henry Hewes in *The Saturday Review* was perplexed:

> Is there, as the earnest young playwright occasionally suggests an attempt here to use theatre in a new way, to draw life as it recognizably is, messy and vulgar, but to avoid the theatrical convention of over-simplification so that each member of the audience will be provoked to build his own play out of it? Or is Mr. Williams simply out to make fun of love with a random approach? One suspects that a less facetious approach to the performance might engross us more deeply in the play's events, and then perhaps "Many Loves" would seem less bizarre.[6]

The *Times Literary Supplement* admired the performances of the cast of the Living Theatre, but complained of "the whole smothered in a Pirandello dressing."[7]

Some reviewers were not at all complimentary. Judith Crist wrote in the old *New York Herald Tribune* that *Many Loves* was "disappointing if only in its glibness, its failure to settle for an implication or permit an inference, its insistence on its hidden subtleties."[8] Harold Clurman all but dismissed the play, arguing that writers who venture into theatre from other art forms are on perilous ground. Thus Arnold Bennett "wrote better novels than plays," Henry James "never could write a play worth a hoot," and so on.[9] The reviewer for *Variety* said the play was "meandering and without much point—a trio of unconnected novelties within a skimpy framework."[10] And Charles L. Mee, Jr., reflecting some time later in the *Tulane Drama Review,* offers this devastating though informative account:

> ...*Many Loves* is set in the framework of a dress rehearsal, and it is probably this that made it appealing to the Becks. The play's structure lets them throw lines to the audience

and even have some of the actors sit with the audience, delivering their speeches from the auditorium. It is a poor man's Pirandello.

I walked into the theatre at about 8:20, sat down, and watched actors milling around the stage, presumably rehearsing bits of business, movement, lines, and light cues. At 8:45 all the lights in the theatre suddenly blacked out, someone called that a fuse had blown, and when the lights came back on I think the play started. I say "I think" because there was another ten or fifteen minutes of author, director, and actors arguing about little matters. Finally, though, a scene began and it developed that the play was a fairly standard collection of three scenes, each attempting to explore a different sort of love: homosexuality, lesbianism, several other perversions, and a few ordinary relationships. Dr. Williams analyzes love with the same tender care and unflinching compassion he must lavish on a urine specimen. His play resembles Plato's *Symposium*, though it has considerably less action and precious little justification for its metaphysical pap.[11]

In any event, the play was continued in repertory through November 17, 1959. Julian Beck wrote Williams shortly before the closing (November 14, 1959):

> It will be a regretful and sentimental occasion for us all. We have been so in love with the play and so grateful to it and to you for the success it has brought us, for the job and pleasure we have gotten out of playing it, out of bringing it to audiences.
>
> It was the very perfect play for opening our theatre, really a play which set a high standard and which represents so much what we want to achieve in the theatre and which points the way in which we hope other poet-playwrights will travel....
>
> I hope this is not the end of our relationship to plays by William Carlos Williams. I hope we can do another of yours again, perhaps A DREAM OF LOVE, perhaps a revival of MANY LOVES, who knows....

There was, in fact, a revival of *Many Loves* in the spring of 1961. With Beck himself now in the role of Peter, and Martin Sheen (who later was such a favorite in Frank Gilroy's *The Subject Was Roses*) taking over for Allan Rosset as Horace, the play was introduced once again into the repertory on Monday, May 25. Joseph Chaikin, who was later to found the Open Theatre (which produced Jean-Claude van Itallie's *America Hurrah*), played Serafina's boyfriend and the real estate agent. Beck wrote to Williams (May 25): "The play opened with great success and those who saw the original production all said without exception, that the new production surpasses the old one." It played four times in repertory with two works by Gelber, *The Connection* and *The Apple,* and Brecht's *In the Jungle of Cities.* In the meantime, the Living Theatre had been invited to appear in the summer of 1961 at the Théâtre des Nations festival in Paris, and was to perform *Many Loves, The Connection,* and *In the Jungle of Cities* in competition with other experimental works by international playwrights. It was an honor; the Becks were ecstatic. ("To make this trip would be something of a consummation," Julian Beck had written to Williams on March 24, 1961.) But the United States government, through the State Department, balked at the idea of providing the necessary financial support. One official reportedly told the Becks: "You ask me to help you get to Europe with one play about fairies, another about junkies, and a third written by a Commie. Do you think I'm nuts?"[12] The United States instead sponsored another entry, a production of Thornton Wilder's *The Skin of Our Teeth* starring Helen Hayes. Nevertheless, through extraordinary perseverance, aided by artists of all kinds and Howard Taubman of *The New York Times,* the Living Theatre raised enough cash, and, with its 26-member company, went to Europe for five weeks. In Paris in July, the troupe won the International Young Critics Circle prize for experimental theatre in the Théâtre des Nations competition.

Performances of all three plays were also given in Rome, Turin, Milan, Berlin, and Frankfurt; audiences were generally receptive.[13] Beck has since reported:

> many loves was liked on that tour, but so much of the strength of the play resides in its language that could not come thru to italian/french/german audiences, they seemed more impressed by judith's performance.[14]

Back in the United States, the Living Theatre opened its 1961-1962 season, which would include such works as Brecht's *Man is Man*. *Many Loves* remained in the repertory, but was only performed occasionally (15 times, apparently) through Sunday, April 15, 1962. But the Becks, who seemed to do everything on a shoestring, were by this time threatened more than ever by financial catastrophe. Even during the earlier run of *Many Loves*, Williams, who was supposed to be paid five percent of the weekly gross at the box office, had some trouble getting his money.[15] In any event, after the European tour and the 1962 season, there were many difficult days, much struggling with creditors and considerable bitterness; the end came finally in 1964 when the doors of the Living Theatre were closed by Internal Revenue agents. The charge was that the Becks had failed to pay taxes.

The "new" Living Theatre, which emerged after gestation in Europe several years later, emancipated even further with touring productions of *Frankenstein, Paradise Now, Antigone,* and *Mysteries and Smaller Pieces,* is another story, with something of a caricature about it.[16] It is doubtful that Williams would have approved of productions that were visually dramatic (occasionally) but so careless about the scripts, the language. For that was what the "old" Living Theatre was about. The early Living Theatre might well be compared to the original Provincetown Playhouse — it consisted of a group of people who wanted to stage imaginative works in a new theatre, preferably plays with a high literary quality, and whenever possible plays in verse. As Judith Malina wrote in 1946, developing the idea for what would be eventually the Becks' theatre:

> We can only expect that our audience understand and enjoy our purpose, which is that of encouraging the modern poet to write for the theatre, and of bringing interest and stimulation to an art medium which tends to become repetitive in its form rather than creative.[17]

The unpublished exchange of letters between Beck and Williams is a fascinating account of the development of a relationship and the process by which a play finds a production. In 1948 Julian Beck and Judith Malina, married that year, wrote to a number of artists — Paul Goodman, Merce Cunningham, Robert Edmond Jones, Kenneth Rexroth, and Williams, to name a few — and boldly proposed the idea for their new theatre. To Williams, Beck wrote, in part (May 21, 1948):

> We are about to set into motion a theatre group (non-professional), the purpose of which will be to present plays which in concept and spirit and method will correspond to the enormous advances made during this century by the other arts: painting, literature, music, the dance.
>
> Since we first began formulation of our plans, it has been our intention to write to you. We have delayed only because we first wished to be absolutely certain of a theatre-building. Now that this is certain we write to you, hoping that we might be able to see you, discuss our plans with you, and arrange, if it is agreeable to you, for production of one of your plays.

Williams replied less than a week later (May 26):

> You've got me shaking in my shoes! Nothing in and perhaps out of this world could possibly give me more satisfaction than a performance on an actual stage of a suitable play by me. And that's putting it mildly.

Williams said he had two plays (they were *Trial Horse No. 1* or *Many Loves,* and *A Dream of Love*) that were promising, but "unsuitable" for Broadway. He writes of the first, clearly *Many Loves:*

> The doubts rise like a fog creeping over the sun. Is my first play, the one that appeared in the issue of New Directions, *witty* enough to carry the dialogue. I had hoped that it was so and perhaps the ability of the actors may be able to add just that edge that would make the lines successful—but I am scared! scared to think that what should sound light may sound heavy—to the unwilling. In other words, it's a battle I see before me, a battle to sell myself to you and a possible audience. With help I might do it. I deeply appreciate your wish to give me the opportunity to put up a fight.

By September of that same year it was determined that *Many Loves* would be the play the Becks would first perform. But it was not until March 1951, that Beck asked Williams for permission to stage it, and a production planned for the following year never materialized. In 1951, meanwhile, the Living Theatre had performed *Doctor Faustus Lights the Lights* (see Chapter 1), and in the following year a remarkably ambitious program—including Alfred Jarry's *Ubu roi*—was presented. After an interval of two years (the Fire Department had closed the theatre in Greenwich Village), the Becks were back in business in a loft at Broadway and 100th Street; a rendering of W. H. Auden's *The Age of Anxiety* opened the 1954 season, with novelist James Agee playing the radio announcer. Dramas by Strindberg, (*The Ghost Sonata*), Cocteau (*Orpheus*), Pirandello (*Tonight We Improvise*), and Racine (*Phaedra*) were produced, all with varying success. There was also a reading of *Many Loves,* but unless there were two readings (which seems unlikely), the exact date is uncertain. In his letter to me, Beck remembers the reading as occurring in 1954 in the loft, which is very probable. But he oddly did not write Williams with the information until February 6, 1956:

> The play had a remarkable effect. By the time the evening was over, one felt that somehow every aspect of love had been touched upon. It was exhausting, in a real kind of Aristotelian sense. The form of the play stood up wonderfully; all of the calculated effects seemed to come off with a genuine aplomb. The actors enjoyed acting it (always a sign of a good play), and the response was truly exciting. The language rang so clean that it seemed as if the play was written in an altogether new tongue. One listened for every word; and yet there was the constant feeling that what was being said was a factual duplication of everyday speech. It sounded as if this was the first time that a writer had succeeded in reproducing the rhythms and vocabulary of actual speech on the stage. The characters too, in the traditional sense, were full of variety and less like the single projections of a single mind that one finds in so many contemporary plays. Surely it must please you to know that this play, which you wrote perhaps 15 years ago sounds more contemporary on the stage than anything else that we know of that is around today. It really sees and feels straight thru to the core of things.

By 1956, meantime, sponsors of the Living Theatre included, along with Williams, such luminaries as Tennessee Williams, Shelley Winters, Allen Ginsberg, and Lionel Abel.

There was another theatre closing in November of 1956, this time by New York's Department of Buildings, but the Becks moved into a new theatre—actually an old department store—on the Avenue of Americas in June 1957. At the same time, encouraged by the response to the reading (two years earlier?), the Becks scheduled *Many Loves* to open their new season on September 9, 1957. But there was constant trouble with the building and costly renovations, all causing delays and all carefully chronicled in the letters.[18] Finally the play was ready for production and opened. "The comedy was played as comedy, straight as straight, etc.—," wrote Karl Bissinger, a member of the company. "The response was very often good, and with a small majority it became a *cult* play."[19] (Donald Malcolm had written: "Beards and chino trousers were much in evidence at the premiere....")[20] The set, designed by Beck, consisted of platforms and slats tacked together at odd angles; the effect was like that of an erector set. For the Living Theatre script at Yale Williams had written:

> The audience comes into the theatre as though it were a semi-literate friend of the assistant stage manager's. They have no business here since it is about a week or so before dress rehearsal...."

For the published *Many Loves* Williams says the audience "finds itself in a darkening, menaced space, included in what is going on up there on the stage" (p. 4). Williams had come to no rehearsals but, as Beck writes, he had done some slight rewriting: "serafina became a puerto-rican instead of a swede because it seemed more relative to time/place and also to adjust to judith's physical 'type'."[21] (Actually, in 1942 she was called a "Lithuanian.")

In the traditional accompanying piece in the Sunday *New York Times*,[22] Beck tried to emphasize some of the things he felt were most important about the play—the language, the verse, the form (from Pirandello, Cocteau, and others). The Living Theatre, he wrote, was "taking a stand against the prose drama of today and against contemporary poetic drama that imitates Elizabethan verse...." (Williams had written to Beck less than a month after the play had opened on February 4, 1959: "The 'American Idiom' in the dialogue is at last coming into its own as I have always said that it would.") Beck continued:

> If we want to revolutionize the theatre it is because we have faith in a modest mystical awareness we have of things that could happen in the theatre, things no one has yet imagined, things that could happen in the theatre and in life as well. It is like a dream of things to come, a dream we have all dreamed but cannot quite remember.

Through the spring of 1970 there were at least five other productions of *Many Loves*. The Society Hill Playhouse of Philadelphia presented the play during the fall of its 1961-1962 season. "It was an 'artistic' although not 'financial' success," writes Mrs. Deen Kogan of the production. She continues:

> The director and producer were fortunate enough to visit Dr. Williams at his home to discuss the play. It seemed to be one of his favorites. He had no particular guidelines about production. The characters in the play were real people of his experience, specifically real as well as being abstracted for the universals which meant so much to Dr. Williams. He did not see the production as he was up in years and not traveling at the time.[23]

In 1962 there was a production by the now-defunct Pasadena Playhouse in California. Instead of combining the Alise-Serafina-Agnes Breen-Clara roles into one, the director apparently used three actresses. According to Mrs. Williams, it was not a successful production.[24] In 1963 a group called the Abelard Players staged the play in a Unitarian Church in Toronto. St. John's College, Santa Fe, New Mexico, sponsored a production in 1967, and the Art Institute of Chicago gave performances during its 1969-1970 season.

Appendix B

Productions of *A Dream of Love*

There have been a number of stage productions of *A Dream of Love*. The first and most important occured in late July of 1949, a year after the play had been completed and published in New Directions 6. The young troupe which did the premier staging called itself "We Present." Performances were held in the tiny Hudson Guild Playhouse, a reconverted community center at 436 West 27th Street in Greenwich Village. As J. C. Thirlwall points out in his notes (p. 433), the production suffered the misfortune of opening "in the middle of one of New York's worst heat waves," and since the theatre had no air conditioning, the play was unable to attract much of an audience. In addition, the critical reception was something less than enthusiastic. Richard Watts, Jr. wrote in the *New York Post* with particular hostility:

> Since Dr. Williams is a veteran in years and authorship, the odd thing about his "A Dream of Love" is that it gives every evidence of being the work of a young, naive and inexperienced writer. Its excursions into both sex and dramaturgy are ponderous and terribly serious-minded in the manner of an eager and youthful neophyte whose innocent conviction it is that he has just come upon something wonderfully important and original, when actually all he has done is grow breathless about the melancholy facts of life and love.
> I am afraid that, in the process, he has become pretentious, humorless and just a little silly.[1]

Williams and Flossie, who attended opening night, were themselves rather unhappy with the production. In *I Wanted to Write a Poem* (pp. 75-75) Edith Heal quotes Mrs. Williams as complaining: "They emasculated it. It was not the play Bill wrote." Williams added: "It didn't run very long—a few nights. All my fellow workers from the Passaic General Hospital brought their wives to see it, said they liked it—one never knows." On August 24, 1949, about a month after the play closed, Williams wrote to the Becks, who had at that time begun to express an interest in producing *Trial Horse No. 1* (*Many Loves*):

> I'd be happy, very happy, to have you produce my play "Trial Horse No. 1" but my consent to have you do so, due to a recent experience, would be contingent to some minimal extent at least upon my having a say in the selection of actors for the parts. There is no surer way to kill a production than to have the parts poorly cast. I am not unreasonable but upon this point I must insist.

One point of consolation about the "We Present" run, however, is that despite the difficult circumstances of mounting the play—the staging area was actually "a beastly hot basement room," as Mrs. Williams recalled[2] — *A Dream of Love* did attract some favorable attention. Margo Jones admired it, for one, and so did William Saroyan. The director, Barbara J. (B. J.) Whiting, then just a shade over 20 years old, reminisced some years later:

> Under the circumstances, we decided to close on Saturday night. The weather remained an uncertain question, additional advertising would cost money, and we wanted to husband our small remaining funds (believe it or not, we had some, along with what came in at the box office — some people were braving the heat, albeit few) in order to do another production. So, we closed on Saturday night and found out too late that if we had held on and dug in, we would have become a hit. On July 31, 1949, the Sunday after we closed, the front page of the drama section of the New York Harald Tribune ran a long piece on off-Broadway written by William Saroyan. Saroyan devoted a good portion of the piece to A DREAM OF LOVE, lavishing praise upon it. (He said I ought to be remembered forever). It was the kind of testament that writers and theatre people dream of papering their walls with. But it was too late. All day Monday our phone rang with calls from eager ticket seekers. But it was too late. The set had been struck, the cast disbanded, and everyone connected released from the commitments necessary to run a production.[3]

Saroyan and Williams, who knew and apparently admired each other's work, did in fact meet at the play; Mrs. Williams says that on the way out Saroyan had stopped and told her husband, "That's a swell play, Bill."[4] As Thirlwall says, Saroyan's review was "rave" (p. 434). After praising Whiting and "We Present' and wrongly saluting *A Dream of Love* as "the first produced play by William Carlos Williams,"[5] Saroyan wrote:

> I would like to appropriate to myself the honor of being among the first to say that this is a great play: a brand-new kind of play with a brand-new kind of tragedy revealed in it; a lean play written in lean common language; a play without any lapse from the interest to tell the truth....

The last point especially pleased Williams, since he had been often disappointed in Broadway's willingness to make the easy and profitable compromise. One is again reminded of the letter to Norman Holmes Pearson, written at this time: "I don't think our world is interested in accuracies. It hurts too much to hear discussion of 'real' situations, and people just don't go to the theatre to have themselves shown up, that is, to be caused pain" (Thirlwall's *Notes,* p. 434).

Even before *A Dream of Love* was published Williams had been hoping for a possible production. On July 6, 1948 he had sent a copy of the script to Julian Beck, writing:

> Dear Beck:
> The enclosed play will be published in August but I had them pin together a few copies in order to send you one. Look the thing over and let me hear from you one way or another, then we can get together for our talk.
> Many or several people rather high in theatre circles saw the play in manuscript. All liked it and a few, like Margo Jones, were enthusiastic. You would be interested in one of her letters. But all thought it would be difficult to produce. I imagine the cost and the risk, considering the cash someone would have to put up, was too much for them.
> To me it seems that some sort of schematic compromise on the sets could be made. Certainly if we go in for full realistic portrayal of each separate scene the cost would be

exhorbitant [sic]. But if the basic scene were set, the one with the multiple entrances etc everything else could easily be managed from above—except perhaps what Audrey Wood called "the cabin scene," the scene with the two colored women. But given the slanting ceiling, not difficult to arrange, even that could be managed.

In the hotel scene light would play a great part, lights and a bed.

Anyhow, here we are. And where do we go from here? Shakespeare did pretty well with his conventional set-up. Not that I want to stress that. I put my trust in your genius because, as Margo Jones said, there's a play there if one can only find a way to produce it.

Sincerely,

Williams

But when the Becks decided in the late '40's that *Many Loves* was better adapted for the repertory of their new Living Theatre, *A Dream of Love* became available. According to Williams (in a letter to Julian Beck, June 27, 1948), several nonprofessional groups had been discussing possible production rights; such sudden interest astonished him. At the same time, the play also had become known at the Yale Drama School where Clinton Atkinson first read it. But Whiting, who twice visited Williams at Rutherford, convinced him that the play was suitable for "We Present." Williams had always supported new ventures (and new adventures) and gave her his permission.

"We Present" was founded by and composed of seven young men and women: Whiting, Susan Frank, Lester Feingold, Martin Silk, Marcus St. John, Alfred Gussman, and Erica Feydn. All were acquaintances from common work at the Dramatic Workshop of New York's New School for Social Research. They were just beginning their careers. All were under 30 years of age, many just past 20. "Our group was in the vanguard of the movement that burgeoned into today's off-Broadway," Whiting wrote in her letter. "Young people trying to do the same thing today are the present off-off-B'way groups."[6] Then as now money was a problem, but each member contributed $100 to the kitty for *A Dream of Love,* which had been scheduled as the opening production. The total capital outlay was thus $700, which by today's standards on off-Broadway is inconceivably small. Although Williams' health had begun to fail by this time, making it impossible for him to go back and forth to rehearsals, he did some work on the script with Whiting and willingly undertook some changes. She writes:

> The first time I went to see him I discussed changes and cuts with him. I remember there was a scene between two black women that was totally extraneous to the play and somewhat offensive in its primitiveness. The first thing I told Dr. Williams was that I would like to remove it. He agreed. He told me that Margo Jones had read the play and urged him to take it out, referring to it as "the hovel scene."... I clearly remember that conversation with Williams as he shook his head and said, "So, you don't like it either."

Thus, when Mrs. Williams talks about the emasculation of the play, as though to suggest that the revisions were inserted without her husband's knowledge or approval, she is not really correct. Whiting continues:

> He gave me a completely free hand in cutting and rearranging it.... When he spoke to me, it was always as a writer rather than a dramatist. He thought like a poet and indicated little sense of dramaturgy. He was delighted to get the play on and evidently willing to see what these young people would do with it. I did, of course, solicit his

174   *Productions of* A Dream of Love

approval on all changes — and I always got it. I cannot remember any situation in which I fought for anything.[7]

In considering her task as director, Whiting started with the idea that the work was "an examination of love from the point of view of a woman trying to come to terms with the death of a man she had loved but never understood." That explanation became the controlling motivation for the production, and to make the emphasis clear Whiting began the play with Act II, scene 2 — the beginning of the dream with Doc already dead. It was a shrewd rearrangement. The action in the living room of the Thurber house before the death was picked up later through simple flashbacks. Hence the dream became more important both structurally and thematically:

> In terms of concept, I felt the play was truly a dream of love and not to be projected literally. Hence, the flash back technique to give it a frame. I also attempted to heighten the dream sequence by adding music and choreography. I seem to recall having three female dancers to intensify Myra's concern and confusion about Doc and women. I have no idea anymore whether that worked, but it seemed like a good idea at the time (and it may have been. I no longer recall.).[8]

Again, one might agree that Whiting's instincts were right. There was one further change. The first scene of Act III (with Jo and Mrs. Harding), which seemed awkward in the reading, was eliminated — not, as Thirlwall suggests, so that there would be no need for a second set, but simply because it was dramatically intrusive. For his part Williams had imagined a conventional stage design: the play would be staged on the traditional box set so common in the proscenium theatre. It was to be mostly realistic. In the manner of O'Neill, Williams had provided elaborate stage directions:

> The living room of the Thurber's home, a rather old-fashioned house, built probably in the early 1900's, in a suburb near New York. It is evening — just after dark — in the early fall. The time is a few years previous to the Second World War. The fittings of the room are somewhat somber, with an appearance of settled home surroundings. In the middle of the room, at the back, is a large davenport couch with pillows at both ends; on the wall above this couch is a large modernist painting done in bold colors and with a white frame — the only object of the sort in the room.
>
> (p. 108)

The dream sequences were to be evoked only by variations in the lighting.

On the other hand, the set used by "We Present" was, as Whiting writes, "highly suggestive, non literal"; for its imaginative expressionism it won the Obie award for the best off-Broadway set of the season. Whiting writes:

> Obviously, we had very little money to allot to it. I didn't want a box set in any case. Because I felt it would work conceptually and we knew where to get wood for nothing, we decided on a framework set.... It was Les Feingold, professionally Lester Robin who suggested that we do not merely the walls but everything framework. I remember his suggesting that we make a framework of a refrigerator and put a wire coil in to suggest the motor.[9]

The choice was a wise one, because if the crucial actions of the play were to take place in Myra's mind, a realistic set might not facilitate but rather interfere with the movement. Jo

Productions of A Dream of Love 175

Mielziner's set for *Death of A Salesman* is a perfect case in point: the kitchen table and refrigerator and walls needed only to suggest the scene. The real drama was to be in the head of Willy Loman, drawn back into his confused imaginings.

Thus "We Present" opened *A Dream of Love* in the final week of July, with Lester Feingold (Robin) playing Doc, Gerien Kelsey playing Myra, and Erica Yohn (Feydn) in the role of Dotty. "Dr. Williams was, of course, in the audience," Whiting recalls. "He got a cry of 'author' and took a bow."[10] That the production ultimately failed was perhaps due more to forces outside the play itself — especially the heat and the cramped facilities — than Williams' script. The meager budget and relative inexperience of the producing group also took its toll. Whiting reflects: "Our technical facilities were hopelessly inadequate (particularly lighting) and I could not get on the stage what I saw in my head. Also, I made some mistakes that I was aware of at the time." But as she also recalls of the short run, "there was good in it, too."[11] some of which did not go unnoticed by the critical spectator. Mrs. Williams remembers that when Margo Jones organized her theatre in Dallas *A Dream of Love* was a possible choice for production, mostly on the strength of what she saw at the Hudson Guild Playhouse.[12] But Jones died before that could be realized.

It was 11 years before *A Dream of Love* was again presented before an audience, this time by Clinton Atkinson in the spring of 1960 at Wesleyan University. Atkinson was a young and able director who has since left Wesleyan to make his way in the theatre in New York, but he remembers the experience of *A Dream of Love* with particular warmth. In 1970 he wrote:

> The whole production started when I was looking for something special and unproduced (you know how college theatre departments are these days — do it NEW, do it DIFFERENT, and maybe TDR [*Tulane Drama Review*] will acknowledge your existence. Well, back in 1960 I was no different). I wrote to Dr. Williams inquiring about his play, TITUBA'S CHILDREN. He replied in amazement that anyone had ever heard of the script. This introduction led to a lengthy correspondence and I was sent a copy of the script, typing several copies for him as a favor for the loan of his original. I decided not to do the play because it was just too didactic for me.[13]

After next considering *Many Loves,* Atkinson turned finally to *A Dream of Love,* "which I had admired since I first purchased a copy while I was at the Yale School of Drama in 1949." Under the auspices of the '92 Theatre at Wesleyan, the play ran one night, May 14, 1960. Accompanying it was the short fragment *Under the Stars* (see Chapter 1). Atkinson himself took the role of Cliff Randall and of course handled the direction. Robert Lucid played Doc, Virginia Tenzer was Myra, and Geri Roberts acted Dotty.

The work was performed intact as it appeared in New Directions 6, including the Mrs. Harding scene (Act III, scene I) which had been excised by "We Present". Atkinson discusses the production:

> I produced it as a semi-staged reading, with all actors present on stage in a seated group throughout the evening. Two or three of the scenes were actually performed — without book — although all the play was blocked. I had better clarify? No one memorized lines for the entire play but the whole play was staged. Several scenes were memorized — the battle between the ladies and the sequences with the maid. I used colored slides — photography of buildings, etc. — projected on to the plaster cyclorama to set locales. I had some help in setting tone from Wyman Parker, librarian at Wesleyan.... The production was sparsely attended but lovingly received. The cast was student, faculty, faculty wives and townspeople.

After the production I wrote Dr. Williams a long letter trying to explain what I had attempted and he replied: "Your letter gives me just the feeling that I most want to communicate about married love which tells something about its failure heretofore to succeed on the New York stage." I thought the play was very successfully done (within our collegebound limitations).[14]

There was a third production of *A Dream of Love* less than a year later, this time by a group of professional actors on a sort of busman's holiday. The actors belonged to the Mannahatta Theatre Club, and performed the play at New York City's National Arts Club in February of 1961. The National Arts Club in Gramercy Park then maintained a private membership for persons interested in and willing to support the arts. The Mannahatta Theatre Club itself no longer exists, but for some time it had given private readings of plays and other material, including works by Robert Lowell and Conrad Aiken, as well as by Williams. Two semi-staged readings of *A Dream of Love* were presented, with direction by the veteran actor Fred Stewart. E. G. Marshall as Doc Thurber and Nan Martin as Myra led the cast. According to Stewart, the production made no use of sets or props; actors mostly read their lines.[15] Stewart had consulted with Williams in Rutherford regarding interpretation. "Dr. Williams liked my approach," Stewart recalled. There was no rewriting; the reading scrupulously followed the text as it had been written. Williams and Flossie both attended one of the performances, held in the Club's gallery. They were, according to Mrs. Williams, delighted with it.[16] Stewart recalls the audience reaction was "excellent."

In 1964 there was a second reading of the play in New York, this one at Yeshiva University, and in 1965 there was a third at the Gramercy Arts Theatre in New York. I was unable to uncover any specific information on either of these readings. Apparently they were, more or less, private events.

There was one other major production of *A Dream of Love* on the stage. Philadelphia's Theatre of the Living Arts, a professional company with a growing reputation, performed the play in the fall of 1966 as the opening production of its third season. It was, according to Samuel A. Rulon, the resident playwright, "a Disaster."[17] Most of the Philadelphia critics concurred. Jerry Gaghan of the *Philadelphia Daily News* (September 14, 1966) called it a "pallid (by today's standards) study of extra-curricular sex." Michael Segal in the *Jewish Exponent* wrote that, "in the interest of good theatre, the Theatre of the Living Arts might well scrap this production and we can all pretend it never happened."

What went wrong? Rulon cited certain "weaknesses inherent in the script," then adds, with hindsight: "Had I been the Director I would have cut and chopped and tightened and pointed the work...."[18] Now Whiting had shown how the work could be reshaped internally to provide a sharper focus, but both of the successful readings about which we have information are proof that cutting and reorganizing the material are not really necessary if there is proper and intelligent direction. Such was not the case, apparently, at the Theatre of the Living Arts. All phases of the production—acting, directing, scenery—were poorly defined and/or heavy-handed. As Rulon describes it, for example, the set was exactly the wrong kind of design:

> The scenery was no help at all. Eugene Lee had sliding platforms which didn't (thanks to inadequate winches on a stage that was not equipped for this sort of mechanics). The walls were skeletal lumber with store-bought window units. The stage was sharply raked. The up-the-stairs stairway visibly went nowhere. The details of the set-dressing (which the script calls for in such detail) were omitted in favor of a constructivist approach that looked great on a lay-out, but was very off-putting when built. (There was also a 900 pound folding ceiling unit, which changed shape for different scenes; but had to be

scrapped at dress rehearsal when the actors refused to walk under it.) Generally, the physical production did not serve the play.[19]

Segal wrote in his uncomplimentary review: "There was a great deal of suspense at the opening night of the Theatre of the Living Arts third season Tuesday. Two sections of the sliding stage failed to meet and the audience sat on the edge of their seats lest the actors fall into the pit as they leaped the two-foot gap." Gaghan pointedly added: "Eugene Lee's scenery appears to have been picked up from the pre-fab section of the Sunday paper's classified ads."

The acting, so crucial in the back-and-forth exchanges between Myra and Doc, was apparently inferior. Rulon writes:

> It was unfortunate that our lead [George Bartenieff as Doc Thurber], excellent actor that he is, was physically wrong for the role of a small-town Don Juan with whom all his lady-patients immediately rhapsodized. (Maybe this is not what Williams intended, maybe he thought of it all in the mind of the Doctor Thurber... but a 5' 8" skinny actor who was positively brilliant in Poor Bitos is somehow not the physical type to make the Thurber role believable.)[20]

Gaghan speaks of Lois Smith's "Ophelia-style twisted mouth takeoffs into lunacy, when she learns her spouse has suffered a heart attack." This is precisely the sort of exaggerated overplay that would turn the play into a melodrama, which it of course is not.

Although Rulon applauded the directorial intentions of Lawrence Kornfeld (he "directed with total respect for the Williams work"), it is clear from the reviews that Kornfeld succumbed to the temptation to make things "relevant." Such anachronisms as a Vietnamese radio broadcast and a current *Time* magazine set in the midst of period furniture were unnecessary, artificial, and harmful to the *real* play. Thus Ernest Schier in the *Philadelphia Bulletin* commends Williams' wit and "spareness with words," then argues that neither came through in Kornfeld's muddled version. It was on all levels a missed opportunity.

Notes

Chapter 1

1. *The William Carlos Williams Reader* (New York, 1965), p. ix.
2. Interview with Mrs. Florence Williams by David A. Fedo at 9 Ridge Road in Rutherford, New Jersey, August 19, 1970.
3. Notes to *Many Loves and Other Plays* (New York, 1961), p. 429.
4. WCW, *I Wanted to Write a Poem,* ed. Edith Heal (Boston, 1958), p. 2. All quotations from and references to this work will be from this edition.
5. *The Autobiography of William Carlos Williams* (New York, 1951), p. 15. All quotations from and references to this work will be from this edition.
6. WCW, *Yes, Mrs. Williams* (New York, 1951), p. 15. All quotations from and references to this work will be from this edition.
7. "William Carlos Williams: The Art of Poetry VI," interview by Stanley Koehler, *The Paris Review,* xxxii (Summer-Fall 1964), p. 121.
8. Interview with Mrs. Williams, op cit.
9. An important recent source of information about Williams' life is found in Paul Mariani's biography, *William Carlos Williams: A New World Naked* (New York, 1981).
10. Emily Mitchell Wallace calls attention to the picture in *A Bibliography of William Carlos Williams* (Middletown, Conn., 1968), p. xii.
11. Both plays exist in typescript in the American Literature Collection at Yale University. All quotations from and references to these works will be from these manuscripts. A third short play, *Plums,* discussed briefly by Vivienne Koch in *William Carlos Williams* (1950), was apparently from this early period. It dealt with the Revolutionary War from the royalist point of view. I could not find the manuscript in any of the Williams collections.
12. "The big fight came at the beginning when I was making up my mind what to do with my incipient life.

    "The preliminary skirmish concerned itself with which art I was to practice. Music was out: I had tried it and didn't qualify. Besides, I wanted something more articulate. Painting—fine, but messy, cumbersome. Sculpture? I once looked at a stone and preferred it the way it was. I couldn't see myself cutting stone, too much spring in my legs to stand still that long. To dance? Nothing doing, legs too crooked.

"Words offered themselves and I jumped at them. To write, like Shakespeare!..." (*Autobiography*, p. 48)

13. *William Carlos Williams* (Norfolk, Conn., 1950), pp. 146-47.
14. Koch, p. 147. The Yale manuscript, however, bears the address of Williams' Rutherford home at 9 Ridge Road, which suggests that he may have written much of it some years later, or at least after his marriage in 1912.
15. Koch, p. 147.
16. Koch, pp. 147-48.
17. Interview in *The Paris Review*, op. cit., p. 139.
18. Mrs. Williams could not recall what part Dr. Williams played. In a letter to the author dated March 27, 1970, Mrs. Williams writes that her husband "acted in his plays whenever he could." She adds: "He was a *very* good actor."
19. Interview in *The Paris Review*, op. cit., p. 139.
20. *Sauerkraut to the Cultured,* Yale University Library, American Literature Collection. All quotations from and references to this work will be from this typescript.
21. Unpublished WCW letter to Julian and Judith Beck, September 13, 1948, from correspondence in the University of Texas Library, Austin.
22. Interview with Mrs. Williams, op. cit. Mrs. Williams was unable to remember the event for which the play was performed. Williams directed, and perhaps played one of the roles himself. It is possible that *Sauerkraut to the Cultured* was written in deference to the Dutch populace in Rutherford and the New Jersey environs, since the area was first settled by Dutch and called New Netherlands; there is a considerable Dutch population still in the area.
23. Koch, p. 151.
24. Koch, p. 151.
25. *The Build-Up* (New York, 1952), p. 166. This novel is the third volume of the so-called Stecher trilogy. It was preceded by *White Mule* (1937) and *In the Money* (1940).
26. This essay has been reprinted in *Selected Essays* (New York, 1954), pp. 196-218. This piece is subtitled "A Study of the Artist." Other playwrights cited included Lorca, Shakespeare, and Sophocles.
27. This essay appeared in *The Little Review,* V (June 1918), pp. 5-10. All quotations from and references to this work will be from this publication.
28. Williams does not specify the date, only indicating in a preceding paragraph that he is speaking about the 10 years from 1912 to 1922. But since *Fanny's First Play* was published in 1914, *Frances for Freedom* was obviously written after that date. It has apparently not survived, its subject remaining undisclosed.
29. "A Serious Play" (1918), reprinted in *Pound/Joyce Letters and Essays,* edited with commentary by Forrest Read (New York, 1967), p. 51.
30. Interview with Mrs. Williams, op. cit.

31. "Prologue to *Kora in Hell*," reprinted in *Selected Essays,* p. 21.
32. *Lima Beans* (New York, 1925).
33. Alfred Kreymborg, *Troubadour, An Autobiography* (New York, 1925), p. 309.
34. *The Provincetown, A Story of the Theatre* (New York, 1931), p. 6.
35. *O'Neill, Son and Playwright* (Boston, 1968), p. 376.
36. Interview with Mrs. Williams, op. cit. As a theatre-goer, Williams probably saw more plays by O'Neill than by any other American. He was fascinated by *Desire Under the Elms* and *The Emperor Jones*. In the late 1940's, the '50's and the '60's, when such writers as Arthur Miller, Tennessee Williams, William Inge, and Edward Albee dominated Broadway (and Off-Broadway), Williams was not able, due to illness and age, to attend the theatre as regularly as he once had. But he had an affection for some of Tennessee Williams, and admired Robert Anderson's *Abe Lincoln in Illinois*.
37. Kathleen Hoagland letter to David A. Fedo, July 5, 1970.
38. Interview with Mrs. Williams, op. cit.
39. Robert McAlmon, *Being Geniuses Together,* revised and with supplementary chapters by Kay Boyle (New York, 1968), p. 191.
40. "Author's Note" to theatre program for Wesleyan University '92 Theatre production of *Under the Stars* and *A Dream of Love,* May 14, 1960.
41. *The Comic Life of Elia Brobitza, Others,* V (April-May 1919), pp. 1-17. All quotations from and references to this work will be from this publication.
42. McAlmon, p. 158.
43. *The Art of William Carlos Williams, A Discovery and Possession of America* (Urbana, Illinois, 1968), pp. 206-7.
44. "Portrait of a Woman in Bed," *The Collected Earlier Poems of William Carlos Williams* (New York, 1951), pp. 150-51. All quotations from and references to this work will be from this edition.
45. See note in Guimond, p. 206.
46. The title of the would-be play was *No Love or What Use to Grow Old*. See the Williams collection in the American Literature Collection at Yale University.
47. Guimond, p. 206.
48. Guimond, p. 207.
49. "Prose about Love," p. 8.
50. "Writer's Prologue to a Play in Verse," *The Collected Later Poems of William Carlos Williams* (New York, revised edition 1963), pp. 12-15.
51. *Under the Stars* exists in manuscript in both the Buffalo and Yale collections. They are almost identical, but for convenience all quotations from and references to this work will be from the Yale typescript.
52. "Author's Note" to Wesleyan program, op. cit.
53. Kathleen Hoagland letter, op. cit. Hoagland, friend of Williams, is a writer in her own

right—playwright, novelist, Rutherford town historian, and anthologizer of Irish poetry.

54. Quoted in a letter from Atkinson to David A. Fedo, July 2, 1970.
55. Koch, p. 153.
56. Atkinson letter, op. cit.
57. *The Battle of Brooklyn* exists in manuscript at the SUNY Buffalo Library. It is not dated. All quotations from and references to this work will be from this text.
58. Koch, p. 153.
59. McAlmon, p. 218.
60. See the *Autobiography,* pp. 59, 224-25. *Dr. Knock* is about a small-town quack who dupes the populace. In the *Autobiography,* Williams wrongly calls Cocteau's play *Juliet and Romeo.* This production was held at the Cigalle, with Yvonne George playing the nurse.
61. Interview with Mrs. Williams, op. cit.
62. George J. Firmage, introduction to E. E. Cummings, *Three Plays and A Ballet* (New York, 1967), vii.
63. Notes for "Sweet Land of Prurience" in *The Descent of Winter,* Buffalo Library.
64. "Office Play," Yale Library collection.
65. In the Yale Library collection.
66. "The Play," dated October 11, 1947, Yale Library collection.
67. Yale Library collection.
68. Yale Library collection.
69. Each of the five major plays will be discussed at length in separate chapters in this book.
70. Clinton J. Atkinson, "In Search of Theatre," *The Massachusetts Review,* III (Winter 1962), p. 331.
71. Arthur Pollock, "Poet's 'Dream of Love' Naughty, but Not Nice," *The Daily Compass* (New York, 1949), p. 18.
72. James Laughlin letter to David A. Fedo, August 28, 1970.

Chapter 2

1. *The First President* was originally published as "The First President, Libretto for an Opera (And Ballet) in Three Acts," in *The New Caravan,* edited by Alfred Kreymborg, Lewis Mumford, and Paul Rosenfeld (New York, 1936), pp. 563-602. It has since been collected, with Williams' Introduction, in *Many Loves and Other Plays,* pp. 301-58. Unless otherwise indicated, all quotations from and references to the play in this chapter will be from the text in *Many Loves.*
2. This performance (in concert form) took place in the "Spring and All" Festival at Kean College of New Jersey, May 12, 1979. For a discussion of this production see Elizabeth Huberman, "The First *First President,*" *William Carlos Williams Review,* VI (Spring 1980), pp. 23-26.

3. WCW, *In the American Grain* (New York: New Directions Paperbook, No. 53, 1956), pp. 140–43.

4. Interview with Mrs. Williams, op. cit.

5. Williams has titled this introductory essay "Introduction for the Composer: An Occasion for Music."

6. Marvin Kitman is the latest to take aim at Washington in *George Washington's Expense Account* (New York, 1970), a satirical evaluation of the man who was "the undoubted Father of Expense Account Living." Kitman explains how General Washington, who refused a salary as commander of the continental army, padded his expense account shamelessly during his term of service. His wife Martha's visit to Valley Forge, for example, cost the taxpayers $27,665.30.

7. Quoted in introduction by George Freedley to *Three Plays by Maxwell Anderson* (New York, 1962), p. viii.

8. McAlmon, p. 218.

9. There is a folder with notes on and manuscript copies of *The First President* in the Yale Library collection. Some of the early dialogue is handwritten on paper from Williams' prescription pads.

10. WCW to Marianne Moore, *The Selected Letters of William Carlos Williams* (New York, 1957), p. 148. Unless otherwise indicated, all quotations from and references to the Williams letters will be from this edition. The major exception is the Williams/Julian and Judith Beck correspondence in the University of Texas Library.

11. Tibor Serly letter to David A. Fedo, July 4, 1970.

12. From *Selected Essays,* p. 162. The essay was originally written in 1935.

13. Virgil Thomson letter to David A. Fedo, September 8, 1970.

14. Regrettably, I could not contact Mr. Harris, and consequently can say nothing of his score. In his letter to me of August 28, 1970 James Laughlin writes: "I never saw Ted Harris' score, but there was a lot of correspondence with him at one point about his efforts to get it produced or published." Elizabeth Huberman notes: "Unfortunately . . . he [Williams] left the composer altogether too much to do, and too little to go on." See "The First *First President*," op. cit., p. 24.

15. Yale Library notes on *The First President,* op. cit.

16. W. H. Auden, "A Public Art," reprinted in *Aspects of the Drama,* eds. Sylvan Barnet, Morton Berman, William Burto (Boston, 1962), pp. 129–30.

17. Koch, p. 155.

18. *William Carlos Williams* (New York, 1968), p. 111.

19. Unpublished draft of *The First President,* in the Williams collection of SUNY at Buffalo.

20. "In Search of Theatre," op. cit. p. 332.

21. Koch, p. 158.

22. Koch, p. 156.

23. Whitaker, p. 112.

24. *William Carlos Williams* (Minneapolis, 1963), pp. 32-33.
25. Guimond, p. 102.
26. Whitaker, p. 27.
27. Benjamin Spencer, "Dr. Williams' American Grain," *Tennessee Studies in Literature,* VIII (1963), pp. 6-7.
28. *Paterson* (New York, 1963), pp. 95, 101. All quotations from and references to this work will be from this edition.

Chapter 3

1. *Many Loves* was originally published as *Trial Horse No. 1 (Many Loves)* in the New Directions anthology 7 (1942), edited by James Laughlin. It was revised and retitled *Many Loves* for the Living Theatre production in 1959, and published in *Many Loves and Other Plays* (1961), pp. 1-104. In this version (with slight alterations) it was printed in *Theatre Arts,* XLVI, 2 (February 1962), pp. 25-56. Unless otherwise indicated, all quotations from and references to this play in this chapter will be from the text in *Many Loves and Other Plays.*
2. Koch, p. 160.
3. "In Search of Theatre," op. cit., p. 333.
4. Hoagland letter, op. cit. In October and November of 1982, "To Fall Asleep" was performed as part of a special homage to Williams called "Williams' Rutherford," a staging of Williams' poetry and prose. This special production was adapted by Mark St. Germain and performed by professional actors at the Marcus Recital Hall in Rutherford. I am grateful to Terrence Markovich, one of the performers, for calling this event to my attention.
5. Hoagland letter, op. cit.
6. Quoted in Koch, p. 160.
7. *Tonight at 8:30* (New York, 1935).
8. Koch, p. 159.
9. "A Serious Play" (1918), in *Pound/Joyce Letters and Essays,* op. cit., pp. 141-42.
10. Unpublished WCW letter to the Becks, January 20, 1959.
11. Notes for *The Comedy of Love* in the library of SUNY at Buffalo, op. cit.
12. From notes in the Williams collection at the Yale University Library.
13. "Why Vanguard," *The New York Times,* Sunday, March 22, 1959, section II, p. 1.
14. The poem, originally published in Williams' book *The Wedge* (1944), has been reprinted in *The Collected Later Poems,* pp. 12-15. The Buffalo version from which I am quoting is much longer.
15. To judge precisely the extent of the European influence on American theatre and its dramatists is a very difficult business. James Rosenberg suggests that our theatre has, for the most part, cut itself off from the continental moderns: "To what extent has America 'bought' Ibsen, Strindberg, Chekhov, Shaw, Pirandello, Lorca, Brecht, etc.? A

quick glance at the annals of Broadway—still, and probably forever, the only real home of American professional theatre—is enough to tell the story. It would be only a very slight exaggeration at best to say that none of the foregoing playwrights has ever had a success on Broadway. Some, like Lorca, have never even been attempted there." ("European Influences," *American Theatre,* London, 1967, p. 61)

But Francis Fergusson notes the special influence of the European dramatists, especially the French, on other writers, including those in the United States: "The most considerable effort in our times to make a poetry of the theatre comparable to that of the masterpieces of the tradition, centered in Paris during the 'twenties and early 'thirties. In that brief period, in the center of Western Europe, the theatre lived 'at the height of its times': it was contemporary with the thought of Bergson, Valery, and Maritain, the 'metopoetic' labors of Joyce, the painting of Picasso, the music of Stravinsky and Milhaud. It enjoyed the resources of the Russian and Swedish ballets of the never-quite-broken French theatrical tradition, and of the patient labors of M. Jacques Copeau of the Théâtre du Vieux Colombier. This theatrical activity was centered in Paris but it was shared by many artists from other countries, some of whom did not even live and work there. Eliot, Lorca, and the later Yeats all belong in one way or another to this movement—this quest for a contemporary poetry of the theatre. In our country the Gertrude Stein-Virgil Thomson operas, E. E. Cummings' *him,* many ballets, and the plays of Thornton Wilder, different though they are from each other, all take their start and get their clue from elements in this Parisian theatre." (*The Idea of A Theater,* New York, Anchor Books, 1953, pp. 206-7)

Obviously Williams would have been alerted to such influences. And in recent years, of course, the various plays of Beckett, Genet, Giraudoux, Ionesco, and certainly Brecht have all enjoyed good runs in New York.

16. Conversation with Thirlwall in New York, August 18, 1970.

17. *Pirandello and the French Theater* (New York, 1960), p. 42.

18. *Le Théâtre et son double,* translated as *The Theatre and its Double* by Mary Caroline Richards (New York, 1958), p. 31.

19. *Modern French Theatre from Giraudoux to Genet* (New Haven, 1967), p. 287.

20. Hoagland letter, op. cit.

21. *The Idea of A Theater* (New York, Anchor Books, 1953; originally published in 1949), p. 209.

22. See Appendix A.

23. Most of the notes and draft manuscripts for *Trial Horse No. 1* and/or *Many Loves* are in the Williams collection at SUNY at Buffalo. A major portion of these drafts is on microfilm #24 in this collection.

24. Julian Beck letter to David A. Fedo, July 5, 1970. The absence of capitalization in the writing is Beck's style.

25. Koch, p. 161.

26. Raymond Kennedy, " 'Let's to Music, Hubert!': An Impertinent Piece," *The Massachusetts Review,* III (Winter 1962), p. 336.

27. Whitaker, p. 112.

28. On matters of sex, especially, Williams offers evidence of naïvete as a young man on the one hand and experience on the other. In the *Autobiography* (p. 78) he writes: "How old was I? Twenty-three or -four before I became fully aware of what had been a mystery theretofore called 'love.' No wonder I thought to myself when I remembered Doc Martin's lecture on the subject, 'Everyone in this class has committed masturbation including your present instructor—don't let's be overimpressed by its importance.' I hadn't known what he meant." But in an interview by Walter Sutton in *The Minnesota Review,* I (1961), p. 323, Williams says: "I was very sexually successful as a young man, but I did not believe in going so far that I lost my head. I wanted always to be conscious. I didn't want to indulge in sex so much that I lost my head."

29. Guimond, p. 147.

30. Quoted in *The New York Times,* June 16, 1961, p. 29.

31. Homosexuality—both male and female—is presented or alluded to often in Williams' writings, usually without overt condemnation but clearly as an unnatural phenomenon, representing a breakdown in the normal love relationship. The *Autobiography* reports many examples of gay sex, beginning with a frightening experience for Williams when he was a boy in Switzerland in 1898 (pp. 33-34). In the poetry (the Corydon and Phyllis episodes in Book 4 in *Paterson*) and in the fiction (several stories in *The Knife of the Times*) he treats the subject quite explicitly. In his unpublished discussion (microfilm #24) of Gore Vidal's novel *The City and the Pillar* (1948) he seems to approve of those writers who deal with the subject honestly, who clear away false prejudice. "For homosexuality has always, dealing with the survival of the race, been a major subject in the world." And yet he later seemed to grow weary of it, accusing the "Beat" poets of the '50's with a tiresome emphasis. "And they [these poets] tend toward homosexuality," he said in the interview in *The Minnesota Review,* op. cit., p. 324. "For God's sake, what's homosexuality. A variant of sexuality. The same thing. There's nothing new about that. It's been done before. And no enlightenment...."

32. Review in *The Nation,* clxxxviii, 6 (February 7, 1959), p. 125.

33. One is reminded of Leslie Fiedler's assertion in *Love and Death in the American Novel* that American literature has plenty of sex but little mature domesticity. The males "light out for the territory" instead.

34. *The Minnesota Review,* op. cit., p. 323.

35. *The Poetic World of William Carlos Williams* (Carbondale, Illinois, 1966), pp. 76-77.

36. Guimond, p. 149.

37. This passage was printed in the program for "The Living Theatre, Repertory 1959." There are copies in the Living Theatre collection of the Lincoln Center Library for the Performing Arts, New York.

38. WCW, Introduction to "Some Flower Studies," printed in *This is My Best,* edited by Whit Burnett (Cleveland, 1942), p. 641.

39. Brinnin, p. 14.

40. Guimond, pp. 150-52.

41. "The Turns of Art," review of WCW, *Imaginations* (1970), *Time,* September 21, 1970, p. 104.

42. *American Drama Since World War II* (New York, 1962), p. 196.

43. Koch, p. 166.
44. Weales, p. 196.
45. Wallace, pp. xiv–xv.
46. See interview in *The Paris Review,* op. cit., pp. 122–24.
47. Koch, p. 166.

Chapter 4

1. *A Dream of Love* was first published in the New Directions anthology 6 in 1948. It was reprinted with revisions in 1961 in *Many Loves and Other Plays,* pp. 105–223. Unless otherwise indicated, all quotations from and references to this play in this chapter will be from the text in *Many Loves.*
2. "Williams Collected," review of *The Farmers' Daughters* and *Many Loves and Other Plays, Yale Review,* LI, 2 (December 1961), p. 329.
3. "In Search of Theatre," p. 335.
4. Interview with Mrs. Williams, op. cit.
5. Koch, p. 168.
6. Most of the material regarding *A Dream of Love* is in folders in the Buffalo collection, although Yale holds some notes as well.
7. Interview with Mrs. Williams, op. cit.
8. From the collection in the Yale University Library, op. cit. The page is not dated.
9. Koch, p. 183.
10. Whitaker, p. 43.
11. On this point Kurt Heinzelman writes: "The creative process is the subject of *A Dream of Love.* The object to be created is, quite simply, love." See "Staging the Poem: William Carlos Williams' *A Dream of Love,*" *Contemporary Literature,* 18 (Autumn 1977), p. 49.
12. Whitaker, p. 114.
13. Koch, p. 179.
14. "An Occasion for Tremendous Music," *The Massachusetts Review,* op. cit., p. 341.
15. Koch, p. 182.
16. B. J. Whiting letter to David A. Fedo, June 1, 1970. For more on Whiting's production see Appendix B.
17. Koch, p. 182.
18. Whitaker, p. 116.
19. Koch, p. 177.
20. "Prose, Poetry, and the Love of Life," *The Saturday Review,* xxxvii (November 20, 1954), p. 20.
21. " 'White Mule' Versus Poetry," *The Writer,* 1 (August 1937), p. 245. For a fuller discus-

sion of Williams' prose see Linda Welshimer Wagner's *The Prose of William Carlos Williams* (Middletown, Conn., 1970).

22. Manuscript copy of *Descent of Winter,* dated December 15, 1928, SUNY at Buffalo.
23. Kay Boyle and WCW, "A Note on the Status of Modern Poetry," unpublished manuscript in SUNY at Buffalo.

Chapter 5

1. *Tituba's Children,* published for the first time in *Many Loves and Other Plays,* op. cit., pp. 225-300. All quotations from and references to this play will be from this text.
2. Interview with Mrs. Williams, op. cit.
3. Mrs. Harriet L. Gratwick letter to David A. Fedo, July 1970.
4. All notes on *Juba's Children* and *Tituba's Children* referred to here are in the Williams collection at Yale University.
5. "In Search of Theatre," op. cit., p. 333.
6. Interview in *The Paris Review,* op. cit., p. 333.
7. Interview with Mrs. Williams, op. cit.
8. Eric Bentley is one critic who might disagree. Bentley dismisses *The Crucible* as "melodrama" and writes: "There is a terrible inertness about the play." See "The Innocence of Arthur Miller," in *The Dramatic Event, An American Chronicle* (New York, 1954), pp. 90-92.
9. *The Gospel Witch* (Cambridge, Mass., 1955), p. 21.
10. "The Poet in the American Theatre," *American Theatre* (London, 1967), p. 98.
11. Hoagland letter, op. cit.
12. Gratwick letter, op. cit.
13. Gratwick letter, op. cit.
14. Efforts to locate Thomas Canning have been unsuccessful. There is no longer a man by that name on the faculty of the Eastman School of Music (University of Rochester). A recent professional listing of faculty members at American colleges and universities turned up a Thomas S. Canning in the Department of Music at West Virginia in Morgantown; but I have received no response from an inquiry to him.
15. *The Devil in Massachusetts, A Modern Enquiry into the Salem Witch Trials* (Doubleday & Company, Dolphin Books edition, New York, 1961), p. 25.
16. Starkey, p. 30.
17. Worth, p. 98.
18. *The Crucible* (New York, Bantam Books paperback, 1959), p. 5.
19. Atkinson letter, op. cit.

Chapter 6

1. Interview in *The Paris Review,* op. cit., p. 142.

2. *The Cure,* published for the first time in *Many Loves and Other Plays,* op. cit., pp. 359–427. All quotations from and references to this play will be from this text.
3. Interview with Mrs. Williams, op. cit.
4. James Laughlin letter to David A. Fedo, August 28, 1970.
5. David Ignatow, "Introduction" to "William Carlos Williams, A Memorial Chapbook," *The Beloit Poetry Journal,* 14 (Fall 1963), p. 1.
6. Whitaker, op. cit., p. 111.

Appendix A

1. "Avant-Garde 'Many Loves,'" *The New York Times,* January 14, 1959, p. 28.
2. Review in *Cue,* January 24, 1959.
3. L. D. K., "Living Theatre Offers Sophisticated Drama," *Women's Wear Daily,* January 15, 1959, p. 56.
4. Jerry Tallmer, "Theatre: Many Loves," *The Village Voice,* January 21, 1959, p. 9.
5. Review in *The New Yorker,* January 24, 1959, pp. 68, 70. In the column "Goings On About Town," the magazine ran in its capsule summary during the weeks ahead nearly the same statement, and Julian Beck, reacting to it in a letter to Williams dated February 2, 1959, wrote: "Not so bad. Didn't know they were so bright over there."
6. Review in *The Saturday Review,* January 31, 1959, p. 24.
7. "The Off-Broadway Mixture," *The American Imagination* (New York, 1960), p. 95.
8. "'Many Loves', Verse Play by William Carlos Williams," *New York Herald Tribune,* January 14, 1959, p. 16.
9. Clurman, op. cit., p. 125. This review apparently annoyed Williams, for in a letter from Beck to Williams on February 9, 1959 Beck wrote: "I agree with you that Clurman's review is a pain in the ass but we are dealing here with a man who is trying to show off his 'literary' background and also with a man closely identified with the theatre of the 30s, Odets, et al, and all that kind of well made play stuff."
10. *Variety,* January 21, 1959, p. 84.
11. "The Becks' Living Theatre," *Tulane Drama Review,* vii, 2 (Winter, 1962), p. 197.
12. Quoted in Jack Poggi, *Theatre in America: The Impact of Economic Forces, 1870–1967* (Ithaca, New York, 1968), p. 179.
13. Rome's *Momento Sera* said, as reported by *The New York Times* (June 16, 1961, p. 29): "In *Many Loves* this avant-garde company reaches artistic perfection with the language of poetry, a language charged with symbolism and at the same time closest to our reality."
14. Beck letter, op. cit.
15. Money matters regarding *Many Loves* were a source of embarrassment for and some friction between Williams and Beck, as their letters attest. The apparent largest weekly gross for *Many Loves,* $2,628.95, was taken during the week ending February 1, 1959, the third week of performance. Williams received $131.44 as his share, and Beck admitted to him in a letter (February 2, 1959): "I, who have scorned the whole concept of

money during most of my more mature years, now find it has pleasurable aspects, regarded as a game." Still, by the middle of March, Beck asked Williams to take a cut in his percentage (to 2½ percent) whenever business slacked off; Williams agreed, and also consented to have deducted from his salary the tickets used by his friends to see the play. He averaged well under a $100-a-week royalty from that time on.

Beck, busy with putting new productions into the repertory, often was late getting checks in the mail, and even after the initial run was over Williams had to complain in order to set matters straight (February 14, 1960): "Isn't it time you made good on your promise made in your letter of Nov. 10th to send a check cleaning up your account with me? It's embarrassing to me as it must be to you to have to refer to this long overdue account, you must be in a much improved financial position by this time. Don't theatre people own to some sense of responsibility? I've given you plenty of time to make good, let me hear from you at an early date." Beck replied (March 1, 1960) that he would get the check (for $176.75) to him "during the next month" but said that the theatre was, for various reasons, $26,000 in debt.

16. Clive Barnes said of these new productions, answering Eric Bentley in *The New York Times,* October 27, 1968, that "At its best, the Living Theatre is virtually nonverbal...." Robert Brustein, who helped bring the group to Yale, writes in *The Third Theatre* (New York, 1969) that these productions "showed original techniques" but not one of the works fulfilled its promise "largely because a gifted playwright was lacking to shape it" (p. xiv). In January of 1970 there were, in effect, three *cells* of the Living Theatre—in Paris (where the Becks lived), in Berlin, and in London; it was also rumored there was a fourth cell in Borneo. It was all a kind of self-imposed exile. In May of that year a documentary film on the Living Theatre, by Sheldon Rochlin, was screened at Cannes.

17. Quoted in Mee, op. cit., p. 195.

18. Beck wrote on May 29, 1957: "There have been so many false alarms, so many starts that have never come to realization, that I wonder that you still have any faith in us. I hope you do. We are more anxious to make the play live by putting it on the stage."

On August 13, 1957: "Always an excuse but never a theatre."

On November 19, 1957: "We are optimistically setting February 15, 1958 as the opening date."

On July 24, 1958: "We have temporarily set September 30th as the opening date for *Many Loves,* but I do not promise that we shall actually open then. That is a working date. But it shouldn't be far from that date. A matter of weeks at the most. And we may make it on time."

On December 5, 1958: "Allen Ginsberg came in last night and said he had seen you and that you were not certain as to when the play would finally be done.... In any case the play is now scheduled to open Sunday evening Dec. 21. Looks like it really will too. The rehearsals are going marvellously well...."

19. Karl Bissinger letter to David A. Fedo, postmarked June 30, 1970.

20. *The New Yorker,* op. cit., p. 68.

21. Beck letter to David A. Fedo, op. cit.

22. "Why Vanguard," op. cit.

23. Mrs. Kogan letter to David A. Fedo, July 28, 1970.

24. Interview with Mrs. Williams, op. cit.

Appendix B

1. "A Peculiar Drama of Sex and Dreams," *New York Post* (July 27, 1949), p. 44.
2. Interview with Mrs. Williams, op. cit.
3. Whiting letter, op. cit.
4. Interview with Mrs. Williams, op. cit.
5. "Off Broadway Producers Show Way with Rare Plays," *New York Herald Tribune* (July 31, 1949), pp. 1-2, section 5.
6. Whiting letter, op. cit.
7. Whiting letter, op. cit.
8. Whiting letter, op. cit.
9. Whiting letter, op. cit.
10. Whiting letter, op. cit.
11. Whiting letter, op. cit.
12. Interview with Mrs. Williams, op. cit.
13. Atkinson letter, op. cit.
14. Atkinson letter, op. cit.
15. Fred Stewart letter to David A. Fedo, June 12, 1970.
16. Interview with Mrs. Williams, op. cit.
17. Samuel A. Rulon letter to David A. Fedo, July 10, 1970.
18. Rulon letter, op. cit.
19. Rulon letter, op. cit.
20. Rulon letter, op. cit.

Bibliography

Works by William Carlos Williams

"The Art of Poetry," interview with Stanley Koehler, *The Paris Review,* XXXII (Summer-Fall 1964), 110–51.
"Author's Note" to theatre program from Wesleyan University '92 Theatre production of *Under the Stars* and *A Dream of Love,* May 14, 1960.
The Autobiography of William Carlos Williams. New York: Random House, 1951.
Buffalo Collection of Williams' Papers, Notes, and Manuscripts, some of which are available on microfilm. Lockwood Memorial Library Poetry Collection, State University of New York at Buffalo, Buffalo, New York. (See Neil Baldwin Meyers, *The Manuscripts and Letters of William Carlos Williams in the Lockwood Memorial Library, State University of New York, Buffalo: A Descriptive Catalogue.* Boston, G. K. Hall, 1978.)
The Build-Up. New York: Random House, 1952.
The Collected Earlier Poems of William Carlos Williams. New York: New Directions, 1951.
The Collected Later Poems of William Carlos Williams. Revised edition. New York: New Directions, 1963.
The Comic Life of Elia Brobitza, in *Others,* V, 3 (April-May 1919), 1–16.
A Dream of Love. (Direction 6.) New York: New Directions, 1948.
The Farmers' Daughters. Introduction by Van Wyck Brooks. New York: New Directions, 1961.
The First President, in *The New Caravan,* ed. Alfred Kreymborg, Lewis Mumford and Paul Rosenfeld. New York: W. W. Norton & Company, Inc., 1936) 563–602.
"Galley and Page Proofs" of *Many Loves and Other Plays,* Houghton Library, Harvard University, Cambridge, Mass.
I Wanted to Write a Poem, ed. Edith Heal. Boston: Beacon Press, 1958.
In the American Grain. Introduction by Horace Gregory. Norfolk, Conn.: New Directions, 1956. Originally published by Albert and Charles Boni, New York, 1925.
In the Money. Norfolk, Conn.: New Directions, 1940.
Interviews with William Carlos Williams, ed. Linda Wagner. New York: New Directions, 1976.
Kora in Hell: Improvisations. San Francisco: City Light Books, 1956. Originally published by The Four Seas Co., Boston, 1920.
Many Loves, in *Theatre Arts,* XLVI, 2 (February 1962), 25–56.
Many Loves and Other Plays. New York: New Directions, 1961.
Paterson. New York: New Directions, 1963.

194 Bibliography

Pictures from Brueghel and Other Poems. New York: New Directions, 1962. This edition also includes *The Desert Music and Other Poems* and *Journey to Love,* which were originally published by Random House, New York, 1954, 1955.
"Prose About Love," *The Little Review,* V (June 1918), 5-10.
Selected Essays. New York: Random House, 1954.
The Selected Letters of William Carlos Williams, ed. John C. Thirlwall. New York: McDowell, Obolensky, 1957.
"Seventy Years Deep," *Holiday,* XVI (November 1954), 54-55, 78.
Introduction by Williams to "Some Flower Studies," *This Is My Best,* ed. Whit Burnett. Cleveland: World Publishing Co., 1954.
Spring and All. Dijon: Contact Publishing Company, 1923.
Texas Correspondence of Williams and Julian Beck. Unpublished Letters, Cards and other Material at the University of Texas Library, Austin, Texas.
Trial Horse No. 1 (Many Loves). (Direction 7.) New York: New Directions, 1942, 233-305.
"A Visit with William Carlos Williams," interview with Walter Sutton, *Minnesota Review,* I(1961), 309-24.
White Mule. Norfolk, Conn.: New Directions, 1937.
The William Carlos Williams Reader, ed. with introduction by M. L. Rosenthal. New York: New Directions, 1966.
Yale Collection of Williams' Papers, Notes, and Manuscripts. Collection of American Literature, Yale University Library, New Haven, Connecticut.
Yes, Mrs. Williams: A Personal Record of My Mother. New York: McDowell, Obolensky, 1959.

Other Works Consulted

Artaud, Antonin. *Le Théâtre et son double,* translated as *The Theatre and Its Double* by Mary Caroline Richards. New York: Grove Press, Inc., 1958.
Atkinson, Brooks. "Avant-Garde 'Many Loves,'" *The New York Times* (January 14, 1959), 28.
Atkinson, Clinton J. "In Search of Theatre," *The Massachusetts Review,* III (Winter 1962), 331-336.
―――. Letter to David A. Fedo, July 2, 1970.
Auden, W. H. "A Public Art," reprinted in *Aspects of the Drama,* eds. Sylvan Barnet, Morton Berman, William Burto. Boston: Little, Brown and Company, 1962.
Beck, Julian, Letter to David A. Fedo, July 5, 1970.
―――. "Why Vanguard," *The New York Times* (March 22, 1959), section II, p. 1.
Bentley, Eric. "The Innocence of Arthur Miller," in *The Dramatic Event, An American Chronicle.* New York: Horizon Press, 1954.
Bishop, Thomas. *Pirandello and the French Theatre.* New York: New York University Press, 1960.
Bissinger, Karl. Letter to David A. Fedo, June 30, 1970.
Blum, Daniel. *Theatre World, Season 1961-1962.* Philadelphia and New York: Chilton Company, 1962.
Breslin, James E. *William Carlos Williams, An American Artist.* New York: Oxford University Press, 1970.
Brinnin, John Malcolm. *William Carlos Williams.* Minneapolis: University of Minnesota Press, 1963.
Brown, Frederick. *An Impersonation of Angels, A Biography of Jean Cocteau.* New York: The Viking Press, 1968.

Brustein, Robert. *The Third Theatre.* New York: Alfred A. Knopf, 1969.
———. "Why American Plays Are Not Literature," in *American Drama and Its Critics,* ed. Alan S. Downer. Chicago: University of Chicago Press, 1965, 245-55.
Clurman, Harold. Review of *Many Loves* in *The Nation,* CLXXVIII, 6 (February 7, 1959), 125.
Coward, Noel. *Tonight at 8:30.* New York: The Sun Dial Press, 1935.
Cummings, E. E. *Him,* in *Three Plays and A Ballet,* ed. with introduction by George J. Firmage. New York: October House Inc., 1967.
Deutsch, Helen and Hannau, Stella. *The Provincetown, A Story of the Theatre.* New York: Farrar & Rinehart, Inc., 1931.
Dijkstra, Bram. *The Hieroglyphics of a New Speech: Cubism, Stieglitz, and the Early Poetry of William Carlos Williams.* Princeton: Princeton University Press, 1969.
Donohue, H. E. F., "An Occasion for Tremendous Music," *The Massachusetts Review,* III (Winter, 1962), 338-44.
Downer, Alan S., ed. *American Drama and Its Critics.* Chicago: University of Chicago Press, 1965.
Doyle, Charles, ed. *William Carlos Williams, The Critical Heritage.* London: Routledge & Kegan Paul Ltd., 1980.
Eberhart, Richard. "Prose, Poetry, and the Love of Life," *The Saturday Review,* XXXVII (November 20, 1954), 20.
Engels, John. *Checklist of William Carlos Williams.* Columbus, Ohio: Charles E. Merrill Publishing Company, 1969.
Fergusson, Francis. *The Idea of A Theatre.* New York: Anchor Books, 1953. Originally published in 1949.
Firmage, George J. Introduction to E. E. Cummings, *Three Plays and A Ballet.* New York: October House Inc., 1967.
Freedley, George, ed. *Three Plays by Maxwell Anderson.* New York: Washington Square Press, 1962.
Gallup, Donald. "T. S. Eliot and Ezra Pound: Collaborators in Letters," *The Atlantic,* CCXXV, 1 (January 1970), 48-62.
Gottfried, Martin. *A Theatre Divided, The Postwar American Stage.* Boston: Little, Brown and Company, 1967.
Gratwick, Mrs. Harriet L. Letter to David A. Fedo, July, 1970.
Guicharnaud, Jacques. *Modern French Theatre from Giraudoux to Genet.* New Haven: Yale University Press, 1967.
Guimond, James. *The Art of William Carlos Williams, A Discovery and Possession of America.* Urbana, Illinois: University of Illinois Press, 1968.
Heinzelman, Kurt. "Staging the Poem: William Carlos Williams' *A Dream of Love,*" *Contemporary Literature,* 18 (Autumn 1977), 491-508.
Hewes, Henry, ed. *The Best Plays of 1961-1962.* New York: Dodd, Mead & Company, 1959.
———. Review of *Many Loves* in *The Saturday Review* (January 31, 1959), 24.
Hoagland, Mrs. Kathleen. Letter to David A. Fedo, July 5, 1970.
Huberman, Elizabeth. "The First *First President,*" *William Carlos Williams Review,* VI (Spring 1980), 23-26.
Ignatow, David, ed. *William Carlos Williams: A Memorial Chapbook,* in *The Beloit Poetry Journal,* XIV, 1 (Fall 1963).
K., L. D. "Living Theatre Offers Sophisticated Drama," review of *Many Loves, Women's Wear Daily* (January 15, 1959), 56.
Kennedy, Raymond. " 'Let's to Music, Hubert!': An Impertinent Piece," *The Massachusetts Review,* III (Winter 1962), 336-38.

Kitman, Marvin. *George Washington's Expense Account.* New York: Simon and Schuster, 1970.
Knapp, Bettina. *Antonin Artaud, Man of Vision.* New York: David Lewis, 1969.
Koch, Vivienne. *William Carlos Williams.* Norfolk, Conn.: New Directions, 1950.
Kogan, Mrs. Deen. Letter to David A. Fedo, July 28, 1970.
Kreymborg, Alfred. *A History of American Poetry: Our Singing Strength.* New York: Tudor Publishing Company, 1934.
———. *Lima Beans.* New York: Samuel French, 1925.
———. ed. *Poetic Drama, An Anthology of Plays in Verse from the Ancient Greek to the Modern American.* New York: Modern Age Books, 1941.
———. *Troubadour: An Autobiography.* New York: Boni and Liverwright, 1925.
Kronenberger, Louis. *The Best Plays of 1958-1959.* New York: Dodd, Mead & Company, 1959.
Laughlin, James. Letter to David A. Fedo, July 1, 1970.
———. Letter to David A. Fedo, August 28, 1970.
Lewis, Allan. *American Plays and Playwrights of the Contemporary Theatre.* New York: Crown Publishers, Inc., 1965.
Lewis, Emory. Review of *Many Loves* in *Cue,* January 24, 1959.
———. *Stages, The Fifty-Year Childhood of the American Theatre.* Englewood Cliffs, N.J.: Prentice-Hall, Inc., 1969.
Lincoln Center Collection of Theatre Materials, including reviews of *Many Loves* and *A Dream of Love* and memorabilia of the Living Theatre. Library of the Lincoln Center for the Performing Arts, New York.
Malcolm, Donald. Review in *The New Yorker* (January 24, 1959), 68, 70.
Mariani, Paul. *William Carlos Williams: A New World Naked.* New York: McGraw-Hill Book Company, 1981.
———. *William Carlos Williams, The Poet and His Critics.* Chicago: American Library Association, 1975.
McAlmon, Robert. *Being Geniuses Together.* Revised and with supplementary chapters by Kay Boyle. Garden City, New York: Doubleday & Company, Inc., 1968.
Mee, Charles L., Jr. "The Becks' Living Theatre," *Tulane Drama Review,* VII 2 (Winter 1962), 194-205.
Miller, Arthur. *The Crucible.* New York: Bantam Books, 1959.
Miller, J. Hillis, ed. *William Carlos Williams: A Collection of Critical Essays.* Englewood Cliffs, N.J.: Prentice-Hall, 1966.
"The Off-Broadway Mixture," *The American Imagination.* New York: Atheneum Publishers, 1960.
Ostrum, Alan. *The Poetric World of William Carlos Williams.* Carbondale, Illinois: Southern Illinois Press, 1961.
Paul, Sherman. *The Music of Survival: The Biography of A Poem by William Carlos Williams.* Urbana, Illinois: University of Illinois Press, 1968.
Peacock, Ronald. *The Poet in the Theatre.* New York: Harcourt, Brace and Company, 1946.
Pearson, Norman Holmes. "Williams Collected," review of *The Farmers' Daughters* and *Many Loves* in *Yale Review,* LI, 2 (December 1961), 329-32.
Phelps, Lyon. *The Gospel Witch.* Cambridge, Mass.: Harvard University Press, 1955.
Poggi, Jack. *Theater in America, The Impact of Economic Forces, 1870-1967.* Ithaca, New York: Cornell University Press, 1968.
Pollock, Arthur. "Poet's 'Dream of Love' Naughty, but Not Nice," *The Daily Compass.* New York, 1949, 18.
Pound, Ezra. "Dr. Williams' Position," in *Literary Essays,* ed. T. S. Eliot. Norfolk, Conn.: New Directions, 1954, 389-98.

———. "A Serious Play," in *Joyce/Pound Letters and Essays,* ed. with commentary by Forrest Read. New York: New Directions, 1967.

Rigdon, Walter. *The Biographical Encyclopedia and Who's Who of the American Theatre.* New York: J. H. Heineman, 1966.

Rosenberg, James. "European Influences" in *American Theatre.* London: Stratford-upon-Avon Studies 10, 1967.

Rulon, Samuel A. Letter to David A. Fedo, July 10, 1970.

Serly, Tibor. Letter to David A. Fedo, July 4, 1970.

Sheaffer, Louis. *O'Neill, Son and Playwright.* Boston: Little Brown and Company, 1968.

Spencer, Benjamin. "Dr. Williams' *American Grain," Tennessee Studies in Literature,* VIII (1963), 1-16.

Starkey, Marion L. *The Devil in Massachusetts, A Modern Inquiry into the Salem Witch Trials.* New York: A. A. Knopf, 1949.

Stein, Gertrude. *Doctor Faustus Lights the Lights* in *Last Operas and Plays,* ed. with an introduction by Carl Van Vechten. New York: Rinehart & Company, Inc., 1949.

Stewart, Fred. Letter to David A. Fedo, June 12, 1970.

Tallmer, Jerry. "Theatre: Many Loves," *The Village Voice* (January 21, 1959), 9.

Tashjian, Dickran. *William Carlos Williams and the American Scene, 1920-1940.* New York: Whitney Museum of American Art, 1978.

Thomson, Virgil. Letter to David A. Fedo, September 8, 1970.

Thirlwall, John C. Conversation with David A. Fedo in New York, August 18, 1970.

———. "Notes on William Carlos Williams as Playwright" in *Many Loves and Other Plays.* New York: New Directions, 1961, 429-37.

———. "William Carlos Williams' 'Paterson': The Search for the Redeeming Language—A Personal Epic in Five Parts," *New Directions 17* (1961), 252-310.

"The Turns of Art," review of William Carlos Williams' *Imaginations* (1970), *Time* (September 21, 1970), 104-6.

Variety, January 21, 1959, 84.

Wagner, Linda W. *The Poems of William Carlos Williams.* Middletown, Conn.: Wesleyan University Press, 1964.

———. *The Prose of William Carlos Williams.* Middletown, Conn.: Wesleyan University Press, 1970.

Wallace, Emily Mitchell. *A Bibliography of William Carlos Williams.* Middletown, Conn.: Wesleyan University Press, 1968.

Watts, Richard, Jr. "A Peculiar Drama of Sex and Dreams," review of *A Dream of Love, New York Post* (July 27, 1949), 44.

Weales, Gerald. *American Drama Since World War II.* New York: Harcourt, Brace & World, Inc., 1962.

Weatherhead, A. Kingsley. *The Edge of the Image: Marianne Moore, William Carlos Williams, and Some Other Poets.* Seattle: University of Washington Press, 1967.

Whitaker, Thomas R. *William Carlos Williams.* New York: Twayne Publishers, Inc., 1968.

Whiting, Barbara J. Letter to David A. Fedo, July 1, 1970.

Whittemore, Reed. *William Carlos Williams: Poet from Jersey.* Boston, Houghton Mifflin Company, 1975.

Williams, Florence. Interview with David A. Fedo in Rutherford, N.J., August 19, 1970.

———. Letter to David A. Fedo, March 27, 1970.

Williams, Raymond. *Drama from Ibsen to Eliot.* New York: Oxford University Press, 1953.

Worth, Katharine J. "The Poet in the American Theatre," *American Theatre.* London: Stratford-upon-Avon Studies 10, 1967.

Index

Abbott, Charles, 149
Abel, Lionel, 167
Abelard Players, Toronto, 169
Aeschylus, *Agamemnon*, 107
Agee, James, 167
Aiken, Conrad, 176
Albee, Edward, 116, 181n.36; *A Delicate Balance*, 152
Anderson, Maxwell, 148; *Valley Forge*, 37
Anderson, Robert, *Abe Lincoln in Illinois*, 181n.36
Anderson, Sherwood, 123
Antheil, George, 15, 39-40
Aristophanes, 125
Arnold, Benedict, 47, 49-50
Art Institute, Chicago, 169
Artaud, Antonin, 62, 72, 75, 76, 92, 93; *Les Cenci, Le Théâtre et son double*, 76
Atkinson, Brooks, 163, 164
Atkinson, Clinton J., 25, 34, 54, 67, 101, 129, 146, 147, 173, 175-76
Auden, W.H., 78; *The Age of Anxiety*, 167

Bach, Johann Sebastian, 15
Barnes, Clive, 190n.16
Bartenieff, 177
Beard, Charles and Mary, 37
Beaumont, Francis, and Fletcher, John, *The Knight of the Burning Pestle*, 75
Beck, Judith Malina, 9, 17, 24, 32-34, 62, 72, 94, 163-68
Beck, Julian, 9, 17, 22, 24, 32-34, 62, 72, 74, 77, 80, 94, 163-68
Beckett, Samuel, 96, 185n.15
Beecher, Janet, 3
Beethoven, Ludwig van, 15
Bellow, Kyrle, 3
Bennett, Arnold, 164
Bentley, Eric, 188n.8, 190n.16
Bishop, Thomas, *Pirandello and the French Theater*, 76

Bissinger, Karl, 168
Bodenheim, Maxwell, 123
Boyce, Neith, *Two Sons*, 17
Boyle, Kay, 19
Bramhall Theatre, 19
Brecht, Bertolt, *In the Jungle of Cities*, 165; *Man is Man*, 166, 184-85n.15
Brinnin, John Malcolm, *William Carlos Williams*, 60, 94
Broadway, 181n.36
Browning, Robert, 2
Brustein, Robert, 190n.16
Burke, Kenneth, 16
Burr, Aaron, 36, 63
Butler, Samuel, *Hudibras*, 26
Byron, George Gordon, 110

Canning, Thomas, 134
The Canterbury Tales, 22
Carew, Thomas, 119
Chaikin, Joseph, 165
Chekhov, Anton, 123, 164, 184n.15
Clurman, Harold, 84, 164
Cocteau, Jean, 72, 75, 76-77, 91, 96, 168; *Beauty and the Beast*, 76; *Le Dieu bleu*, 77; *La Machine infernale*, 77; *Orpheus*, 167; *Romeo and Juliet*, 28, 76, 182n.60
Comedie Francaise, 15
Copeau, Jacques, 185n.15
Coward, Noel, 15, 69; *Tonight at 8:30*, 69, 70
Cowley, Malcolm, 16
Crist, Judith, 164
Cummings, E.E., *Him*, 17, 28, 185n.15
Cunningham, Merce, 166

Dahlberg, Edward, 164
Dekker, Thomas, 18
Deutsch, Helen, and Hanau, Stella, *The Provincetown, A Story of the Theatre*, 16
Donahue, H.E.F., 114
Donne, John, 119

Dürrenmatt, Friedrich, *The Visit,* 152

Earle, Charlotte, 69
Eberhart, Richard, 98, 122
Eliot, T.S., 122, 185n.15

Feingold (Robin), Lester, 173, 174, 175
Fergusson, Francis, 77, 185n.15
Feydn (Yohn), Erica, 173, 175
Fiedler, Leslie, *Love and Death in the American Novel,* 186n.33
Finian's Rainbow, 146
Firmage, George J., 28
Ford, John, *'Tis Pity She's a Whore,* 32, 76
Franco, Francisco, 131
Frank, Susan, 173
Freud, Sigmund, 49

Gaghan, Jerry, 176, 177
Gelber, Jack, *The Connection,* 164, 165
Genêt, Jean, 185n.15
Gide, André, 120
Gilbert, W.S., and Sullivan, Arthur, 15
Gilroy, Frank, *The Subject was Roses,* 165
Ginsberg, Allen, 167, 190n.18
Giraudoux, Jean, 185n.15
Goodman, Paul, 166
Gramercy Arts Theatre, 176
"Grantwood group," 16
Gratwick, Bill, 127-28
Gratwick, Harriet, 127-28, 133
Group Theatre, 18
Guicharnaud, Jacques, *Modern French Theatre from Giraudoux to Genêt,* 76
Guimond, James, *The Art of William Carlos Williams, A Discovery and Possession of America,* 20, 21, 22, 60, 81, 90, 96
Gussman, Alfred, 173

Harris, Theodore, 42
Hawthorne, Nathaniel, 138
Hayes, Helen, 165
Heal, Edith, *I Wanted to Write a Poem,* 69, 171
Hecht, Ben, 123
Heinzelman, Kurt, 187n.11
Hewes, Henry, 164
Hoagland, Clayton, 68
Hoagland, Kathleen, 17, 24, 68, 69-70, 76, 81, 133; *Mallows in the Moonlight,* 69
Huberman, Elizabeth, 182n.2, 183n.14
Huckleberry Finn, 86

Ibsen, Henrik, 14, 15, 120, 184n.15; *A Doll's House,* 14; *Ghosts,* 14; *Hedda Gabler,* 14, 123; *The Master-Builder,* 120; *When We Dead Awaken,* 120; *The Wild Duck,* 14
Ignatow, David, 152

Inge, William, 181n.36
Irving, Henry, 29
Itallie, Jean-Claude, *America Hurrah,* 165

James, Henry, 2, 164
Jarry, Alfred, *Ubu roi,* 75, 167
Jefferson, Thomas, 36, 37, 47, 65
Jones, Margo, 101, 172-73; 175
Jones, Robert Edmond, 166
Jonson, Ben, 12
Josephson, Mattie, 18
Joyce, James, 14, 116, 185n.15

Kafkaesque, 142
Kaufman, George S., and Hart, Moss, *The Man Who Came to Dinner,* 152
Kean College, New Jersey (production of *The First President*), 42, 182n.2
Keats, John, 4, 160
Kelsey, Gerien, 175
Kennedy, Raymond, 80
Kitman, Marvin, *George Washington's Expense Account,* 183n.6
Koch, Vivien, *William Carlos Williams,* 4, 6, 10, 11, 25, 27, 43, 59, 67, 70, 97, 101, 106, 113, 116
Kogan, Deen, 168
Kornfeld, Lawrence, 177
Kreymborg, Alfred, 16, 18-19, 164; *Lima Beans,* 16-17

Laughlin, James, 32, 34, 133-34, 135, 150, 183n.14, 184n.1
Lawrence, D.H., 3
Lawrence, Gertrude, 70
Lee, Eugene, 176-77
Lewis, Emory, 164
Li'l Abner, 146
Lincoln, Abraham, 40, 64
Little Theatre of Rutherford, New Jersey, 24, 32, 68-69, 77-78
Living Theatre, 9, 17-18, 32, 62, 76, 77-78, 79, 81, 84, 97, 163-68, 186n.37
Lorca, Federico García, 72, 180n.26, 184-85n.15
Lowell, Robert, 176
Loy, Mina, 16
Lucid, Robert, 175
Lysistrata, 63, 125

McAlmon, Robert, *Being Geniuses Together,* 28
McCarthy, Sen. Joseph R., 63, 127, 128, 129, 131, 132, 142, 143, 145
Maeterlinck, Maurice, 15
Malcolm, Donald, 164, 168
Mannahatta Theatre Club, 176

Mantle, Burns, 37
Mariani, Paul, *William Carlos Williams: A New World Naked,* 179n.9
Markovich, Terrence, 184n.4
Marshall, E.G., 176
Martin, Nan, 176
Marx, Harpo, 17
Marx, Karl, *Das Kapital,* 144, 147
Mather, Cotton, *Wonders of the Invisible World,* 132
Mathews, Cornelius, *Witchcraft; or The Martyrs of Salem,* 132
Matthison, Edith Wynne, 3
Mee, Charles L., Jr., 164
Mielziner, Jo, 174-75
Millay, Edna St. Vincent, 16, 19; *Aria da capo,* 19
Miller, Arthur, 7, 132, 181n.36; *The Crucible,* 7, 132, 136, 137, 138, 139, 145; *Death of a Salesman,* 175; *A View from the Bridge,* 83
Moore, Marianne, 16, 40
Mussolini, Benito, 131

The New Caravan, 41, 182n.1
New Masses, 105

Odets, Clifford, *Golden Boy,* 18
Oklahoma, 54
O'Neill, Eugene, 17, 72, 99, 174; *Before Breakfast,* 17; *Desire under the Elms,* 181n.36; *The Emperor Jones,* 181n.36; *Fog,* 17
O'Neill, James, 17
Open Theatre, 165
Ostrom, Alan, *The Poetic World of William Carlos Williams,* 89

Pailleron, Edouard, *Le Monde où l'on s'ennuie,* 15
Parker, Wyman, 175
Pasadena Playhouse, 168
Pearson, Norman Holmes, 72, 101, 172
Phelps, Lyon, *The Gospel Witch,* 132
Picasso, Pablo, 77
Pinter, Harold, *The Homecoming,* 152-53, 161
Pirandello, Luigi, 68, 72, 75-76, 77, 91, 96, 165, 168; *Six Characters in Search of an Author,* 75; *Tonight We Improvise,* 167
Poe, Edgar Allan, 63
The Poets' Theatre, 132
Pollock, Arthur, 34
Pound, Ezra, 14, 15, 32, 40, 72, 77, 131; *The Testament of Francois Villon,* 39
Proust, Marcel, 120
Provincetown Playhouse (Players), 16-18, 29

Rabelais, Francois, 157
Racine, Jean, *Phaedra,* 167

Ray, Man, 16
Rexroth, Kenneth, 166
Robbe-Grillet, Alain, 96
Roberts, Geri, 175
Rochlin, Sheldon, 190n.16
Romains, Jules, *Dr. Knock,* 28, 182n.60
Roosevelt, Franklin D., 148
Rosenberg, James, 184-85n.15
Rosenthal, M.L., *The William Carlos Williams Reader,* 1
Rulon, Samuel, 176-77

St. John, Marcus, 173
St. John's College, Santa Fe, New Mexico, 169
Saroyan, William, 172
Satie, Erik, 77
Schary, Dore, *Sunrise at Campobello,* 148
Schier, Ernest, 177
Schiller, Friedrich von, 14
Segal, Michael, 176-77
Serly, Tibor, 38, 40-41
1776, 148
Shakespeare, William, 2, 3, 28, 42, 58, 81, 99, 120, 160, 173, 180n.26
Shaw, George Bernard, 14-15; *Candida,* 14-15
Sheaffer, Louis, *O'Neill, Son and Playwright,* 17
Sheen, Martin, 165
Show Boat, 46
Silk, Martin, 173
Society Hill Playhouse, Philadelphia, 168
Sophocles, 180n.26
Smith, Lois, 177
Spence, Andrew, 28
Spencer, Benjamin, 63
Starkey, Marion L., *The Devil in Massachusetts,* 133, 136
Stein, Gertrude, 185n.15; *Doctor Faustus Lights the Lights,* 32-34, 72, 167; *Four Saints in Three Acts,* 41
Stevens, Wallace, *Three Travelers Watch a Sunrise,* 17
Stewart, Fred, 176
Stoppard, Tom, 96, 146
Strauss, Johann, *Electra,* 15
Strindberg, August, 62, 184n.15; *The Ghost Sonata,* 167
Sudermann, Hermann, 14
Sutton, Walter, 186n.28
Symonds, J.A., *The Greek Poets,* 107
Synge, John Millington, 6

Taubman, Howard, 165
Tenzer, Virginia, 175
Théâtre des Nations Festival, 165
Theatre Guild, 37
Theatre of the Living Arts, Philadelphia, 176-77

Thirlwall, John C., "Notes" to *Many Loves and Other Plays*, 2, 38-39, 68, 71, 75, 102, 123, 127, 133-34, 149-50, 153, 160, 171, 174
Thomson, Virgil, 15, 40-41, 59, 64, 185n.15
Thoreau, Henry David, 11

Upham, Charles W., *Salem Witchcraft*, 133

Veblen, Thorstein, *The Theory of the Leisure Class*, 134
Vidal, Gore, *The City and the Pillar*, 186n.31
Virgil, 11

Wagner, Linda Welshimer, *The Prose of William Carlos Williams*, 187-88n.21
Wagner, Richard, 42; *Götterdämmerung, Parsifal, Tristan*, 15
Wallace, Emily Mitchell, 99, 179n.10
Wallace, Mike, 28
Washington, George, character in *The Battle of Brooklyn*, 26-27; *The First President*, 35-65; *A September Afternoon*, 5-6; *Under the Stars*, 24-26
Watts, Richard, Jr., 171
Weales, Gerald, 97, 98
Webb, Alan, 70
Weber, Ben, 134
Wellcome, Emily Dickenson, 2, 20
"We Present," 32, 122, 171-75
Wesleyan University production of *Under the Stars* and *A Dream of Love*, 24, 101, 175-76
Whalen, Grover, 41
Whitaker, Thomas R., *William Carlos Williams*, 45, 59, 80, 109, 112, 120
Whiting, Barbara J. (B.J.), 119-20, 172-75
Whitman, Walt, 62; *Democratic Vistas*, 127
Wilder, Thornton, 185n.15; *The Skin of Our Teeth*, 165
Williams, Edgar, 7, 38
Williams, Florence Herman, 1, 2, 6, 7, 13, 15, 17, 18, 28, 29, 36, 69, 81, 101, 102, 120, 127-28, 130-31, 150, 163, 169, 172, 173-74, 175, 176
Williams, Tennessee, 157, 167, 181n.36
Williams, William Carlos: works and plays; *The Battle of Brooklyn*, 26-27, 36, 53; *Betty Putnam*, 4, 6-9, 12, 13, 24, 127, 140; *The Comic Life of Elia Brobitza*, 19-23, 48; *The Cure*, 22, 32, 119, 140, 148, 149-61; *A Dream of Love*, 13, 22, 24, 31, 32, 34, 48, 62, 67, 85, 90, 101-25, 127, 146, 153, 154, 157, 161, 167, 171-77, 181n.40; *The Fifth Star or No Love*, 31; *The First President*, 5, 6, 15, 24, 25, 27, 28, 32, 35-65, 85, 93, 101, 124, 133, 134, 135, 144, 148, 161; *Frances for Freedom*, 14, 18; *Intimate Strangers*, 28; *Many Loves*, 4, 10, 13, 22, 24, 30, 32, 33, 34, 62, 65, 67-99, 101, 103, 105, 108, 114, 116, 118, 124, 153, 154, 161, 165-69, 171, 173; *Many Loves and Other Plays* (New Directions Collection), 1, 32, 34, 36, 77, 78, 80, 133, 150, 182n.1, 184n.1, 188n.1, 189n.2; *Never Bore a Woman*, 31; *No Love or What Use to Grow Old*, 31, 181n.46; *The Old Apple Tree*, 18-19; *Plums, ?; Sauerkraut to the Cultured*, 7, 9-13; *A September Afternoon*, 4-6, 7, 23, 25; *Tituba's Children*, 6, 7, 15, 32, 59, 62, 63, 64, 122, 127-48, 159, 161; *Under the Stars*, 24-26, 36, 47, 50, 175, 181n.40; *Women are Such Fools*, 31; other works; *Adam & Eve & the City*, 35, 59, 102; "Against the Weather," 60; *Al Que Quire!*, 18, 20, 109; "Asphodel, That Greeny Flower," 58, 107, 111, 123, 153; *The Autobiography*, 2-4, 6, 14-17, 18-19, 28, 41, 48, 59, 63, 64, 69, 71-72, 76, 91, 101-2, 127-28, 131, 134, 149, 186n.28, 186n.31; "The Basis of Faith in Art," 108, 151; *The Build-Up*, 108, 180n.25; *The Clouds*, 130; *The Collected Earlier Poems*, 20, 59, 97, 102-3, 118; *The Collected Later Poems*, 32, 130, 150, 181n.50, 184n.14; "Danse Russe," 118; *The Descent of Winter*, 48, 58-59, 78, 79-80, 130, 182n.63, 188n.22; *The Desert Music*, 32, 151; *The Farmer's Daughters*, 20, 115, 160; *The Great American Novel*, 18, 92; *I Wanted to Write a Poem*, 2, 4, 18-19, 69, 70, 130-31, 151-52, 171; *In the American Grain*, 1, 5, 24, 36, 38, 63, 64, 127, 128, 136, 154-55; *In the Money*, 99, 108, 180n.25; *Journey to Love*, 32; *The Knife of the Times*, 30, 186n.31; *Life along the Passaic River*, 69, 99, 114; "Love Song," 109, 118; "Notes in Diary Form," 58-59, 78, 79-80, 102; "A Pound Stein," 41; *The Paris Review* (Interview), 2, 131, 149, 187n.46; *Paterson*, 1, 22, 23, 28, 30, 32, 36, 53, 64, 76, 92, 94, 98, 101, 103, 111, 115, 120, 125, 151, 186n.31; "Perpetuum Mobile: The City," 102-3, 110, 112; *Pictures from Brueghel and Other Poems*, 58, 107, 111; *The Pink Church*, 32, 130; *Poems*, 4; "Portrait of a Woman in Bed," 20; "Prologue to *Kora in Hell*," 15; "Prose about Love," 15; "Russia," 130; *Selected Essays*, 36, 39, 58, 60, 78, 79-80, 102, 108, 120, 122, 123, 151, 180n.26, 183n.12; *Selected Letters*, 40, 81, 98, 120; *Sour Grapes*, 18; *Spring and All*, 18; "To Fall Asleep," 69; *A Voyage to Pagany*, 135; "The Wanderer," 59; *The Wedge*, 184n.14; *White Mule*, 98-99, 108, 123, 180n.25; "Writer's Prologue to a Play in Verse," 23, 74-75; *Yes, Mrs. Williams*, 2
Williams, William Eric, 149
Williams, William George, 2, 3

Winters, Shelley, 167
Wolfe, Thomas, 82
Worth, Katharine, J., 132, 142
Wouk, Herman, *The Caine Mutiny Court Martial,* 148

Yale Drama School, 173, 175
Yeats, William Butler, 72, 185n.15
Yeshiva University, 176

Zorach, Bill, 16-17